SHORT FICTION by HISPANIC WRITERS OF THE UNITED STATES

Edited by Nicolás Kanellos

Arte Público Press
Houston
Texas
1993

Short Fiction by Hispanic Writers of the United States

Edited by Nicolás Kanellos

Arte Público Press
Houston
Texas
1993

This book is made possible through a grant from the National Endowment for the Arts (a federal agency), the Lila Wallace-Reader's Digest Fund and the Andrew W. Mellon Foundation.

Arte Público Press
University of Houston
Houston, Texas 77204-2090

Cover design by Mark Piñón
Original painting by Alejandro Romero:
"Comediante," Copyright © 1990

Short fiction by Hispanic writers of the United States / edited by Nicolás Kanellos.

p. cm.

ISBN 1-55885-044-9: $15.00

1. American Fiction—Hispanic American authors. 2. Hispanic Americans—Fiction. 3. Short stories, American. I. Kanellos, Nicolás. II. Title.
PS647.H58S48 1992
813'.0108868–dc20 92-20826

CIP

The paper used in this publication meets the requirements of the American National Standard for Permanence of Paper for Printed Library Materials Z39.48-1984. ∞

Second Printing, 1994
Printed in the United States of America

Contents

Short Fiction by Hispanic Writers of the United States

Introduction

Hispanic literature in the United States develops out of both the Spanish- and the English-language literary traditions. In what has become the United States, Hispanic literature has roots that predate the landing of the *Mayflower* and go deeper than just the European layer of culture that was brought to the Americas by the Spaniards and the English. In Spanish America, in particular, a blending of European, African and Amerindian cultures produced one of the most broadly embracing literary and artistic traditions known to man. Through time, both an oral and a written literature have prospered and survived in the descendants of that encounter of peoples that began in the late fifteenth century. This literature has prevailed in what has become the United States for as long as it has in the rest of the Spanish-speaking hemisphere.

Primarily a working-class people to this day, Hispanics in the United States have produced a living corpus of oral lore that reflects their history, religion, language and, most importantly, their alternate or outsider status to "official" culture and society in the United States. Their ballads, songs, prayers, proverbs, legends, stories and personal experience narratives provide not only an ongoing narrative history and political perspective but also a school for storytelling, for communicating efficiently and eloquently through the spoken word. The immediacy, rhythms, formulas and reverence of working-class people as manifested through their oral expression characterize much of Hispanic narrative, even among the most stylized and academic of writers. Related to this reverence for orality as both a communicative and ideological strategy—because identifying with working-class roots is a conscious political choice among our writers—is the importance of the short story as a genre throughout the Spanish-speaking world. No matter how much their American education has fixed the models ranging from Hawthorne to Hemingway, Hispanic writers in the United States soon encounter and commune with Jorge Luis Borges, Julio Cortázar, Guillermo Cabrera Infante and, most importantly, Juan Rulfo and others who, through the short story, have identified with the indigenous and marginalized peoples of the Americas. This is without even mentioning the strong influence on both the oral and written traditions of Spanish medieval tales and fables, Cervantes's *Exemplary Novels* (which are really more akin to short stories than novels) and the whole picaresque narrative tradition, which itself has roots in medieval Arabic literature.

Through the evangelization of the American Indians, the colonization of Mexico, the Caribbean and the Southwest, and the importation of African slaves, this Judeo-Spanish-Arabic literature eventually merged with the dance-drama and the epics of both the Amerindians and the Africans (much of this is the subject of ongoing research today). The most powerful remnants of non-European contributions, of course, are to be found in the folk songs and folk tales, the syncretic religious practices and their own literature and the overall non-European—call it mestizo or creole or New World—sensibility. This sensibility is most manifest in the contestatory nature of the literature, its resistance to the establishment and to Eurocentrism, its tenaciously open and embracing definition of culture in the Americas (including the United States and Canada) as incorporating the European background as an important factor in a far more complex and encompassing equation. Included in that equation is bilingualism and biculturalism and a complete range of icons, experiences, lexicon and rhetoric that derive from the African and Amerindian cultures presumed to have been obliterated by melting-pot theorists—and targeted for extinction by nativists and the English-only movement.

More than ninety percent of creative writing by Hispanics in the United States has been produced in Spanish. Up to World War II, most of the short stories, local-color chronicles (*crónicas*) and poetry were published in Spanish-language newspapers. Longer, more substantial works were issued by publishing houses which flourished in the major Hispanic population centers of Los Angeles, San Antonio and New York. San Antonio alone served as a home to fifteen or sixteen publishing houses during the 1920's. The Great Depression and the forced repatriation of Mexicans dealt a death blow to much of that industry. After the war, Hispanic communities turned their attention to becoming "legitimate Americans" and began to demand their civil rights on a large, organized scale. The returning veterans struggled to obtain the rights that they had protected by spilling their blood on foreign soil—even while their younger siblings were being assaulted as un-American by the yellow press and rowdy servicemen during the Zoot Suit Riots of Los Angeles. After the war, the conversion to a peace-time economy and meeting the demands of mass production required a larger and more educated work force. Greater access to schooling resulted for Hispanics in the United States. By the 1960's, there was a critical mass of Hispanic students in college, and they pressed for the next wave of open education and civil rights gains. Along with the greater access to education and the greater representation of Hispanics—if not their culture—in mainstream institutions, came greater use of the English language and greater acceptance and identification with the Anglo-Saxon American tradition and its literature.

Resistance to languages other than English goes back to the nineteenth century in the United States, but it became more intense and aggressive during the McCarthy era and the Cold War, a period when it was a common practice in such states as Texas to punish and fine little children for speaking Spanish on school grounds. To this date, nativists are attempting to outlaw Spanish in government institutions and functions, including elections. The publishing industry in the United States is still predominantly monoliterate, even to the extent of being inaccessible through translation for many of the world's most important writers. And, of the major European-origin languages, Spanish still remains the least translated in the book industry.

Needless to say, there were few options for Hispanics in a literary world that only published, reviewed, distributed and awarded prizes for books in English. (There is no need to review here all the barriers that still exist for racial minorities in the publishing and the teaching of literature in the United States.) Hispanic authors either had to try to write and get their works published in English or they had to publish abroad. During the 1960's, two other options surfaced: Spanish-language and bilingual newspapers began to reappear, and small, alternative Hispanic literary magazines and publishing houses were born. Both participated in a civil rights and education movement that gave strength to the resurgence of Hispanic writing in the United States. At the same time, from the post-war period to the present, Hispanic culture in the United States has been renewed and reinforced by an unending wave of Hispanic immigration that has continued to expand the need for print and electronic media in the Spanish language. Although we are still living in an age where to be well published and widely distributed in the United States, one has to write in English, the day is not far off when a novel written in Spanish in New York can be published in Houston and distributed from Alaska to Tierra del Fuego. Today, it is not difficult to foresee the editing and composition of a Spanish-language magazine in Miami to be downlinked from satellite to printing plants—or even home computers—in Buenos Aires, Lima and Mexico City.

Many Hispanic writers of the United States are not only bilingual, but they are biliterate and write in both English and Spanish, despite the frustrating reality that their works in Spanish may not get published or distributed. This has been the reality for such writers as Lucha Corpi, Roberta Fernández, Roberto Fernández, Rolando Hinojosa, Alejandro Morales, Elías Miguel Muñoz and Tomás Rivera. These writers are among the most familiar to Hispanic communities in the United States, but they are virtually unknown to the mainstream. And, they are probably the writers most representative of the larger Hispanic writing culture that exists today in the United States. There are too many bilingual authors to count, and there are just as many writing only in Spanish as there are those writing only in English. That the names of those who write in English have become better known than those of the Spanish-language authors is attributable to the inability of small or large presses to distribute and sell their works, given that the reviewing media and distributors in this country uniformly deal only with books written in English and that Spanish-language bookstores and distributors only serve as importers, because of the profits to be made through the high mark-ups given books published in Mexico or Argentina. Quite often, librarians and critics have said that U.S. Hispanics no longer speak or write in Spanish. This simply is not true; it is that their works in Spanish do not have access to the publishing, distributing and reviewing networks.

The present anthology, therefore, has the limitation of presenting only a partial segment of the community of Hispanic short fiction writers—those who write in English. And although it is a sampling of writers published over the last decade in a small press, Arte Público Press, it is a segment that is representative of the breadth and depth of Hispanic writing emerging from Cuban American, Mexican American and Puerto Rican communities in the United States. In these pages the reader will not find the picturesque and touristy rendition of our culture that may prevail in more mainstream publications. Rather, here are writers committed to a clear and incisive vision of themselves and their community, knowing full well that they will not be regaled with wealth and celebrity for their commitment to literature, truth and the authenticity of representation that has often eluded a community maligned by stereotypic representation in all of the media.

Whether in Max Martínez's outrageous challenge of prevalent racial and sexist social structures in rural Texas, or Roberta Fernández's construction of literary models from women's handicrafts, or Victor Villaseñor's veneration of his family's personal experience tales, or Rolando Hinojosa's and Roberto Fernández's linguistic code-switching and literary inversion of Hispanic/Anglo tropes and styles, U.S. Hispanic authors are engaged in an esthetic and epistemological experiment that is preparing the United States for the multicultural, hemispheric reality of the next century. In every respect, Hispanic culture in the United States will and must serve as a bridge to the creation of an hemispheric identity that has been five centuries in the making. The scope of their literary experimentation has implications far beyond the small, independent presses that are struggling to impress upon the national conscience the important role that Hispanics—as well as other racial and cultural minorities—play in redefining our nation's culture and the role our nation has to play in the newly reconceived and ever-evolving cultural makeup of the world.

That this literature—no matter how humble and reduced the scope of a particular story—can have such weighty implications may be beyond the understanding or even concern of the casual reader. It is the very intercultural nature of these works that breaks down barriers of race, language, nationality—the great themes of these last two decades. But these stories can and should be appreciated in a more direct and less self-conscious manner. They are inventive, ingenious, entertaining; they open windows upon scenes rarely represented in most media today.

It is my wish that this somewhat professorial exposition not get in the way of the pure enjoyment of what these writers have to offer the reader. Perhaps I should have placed this paragraph at the beginning of the introduction with instructions for skipping it in order to get to what is really valuable about this book: American writing at its best.

Nicolás Kanellos
University of Houston

Denise Chávez

Denise Chávez is a novelist, playwright and poet who, through her writings, has brought to life entire populations of memorable characters of the Southwest, both Mexican American and Anglo-American. Born on August 15, 1948, in Las Cruces, New Mexico, Chávez was raised principally by her mother, Delfina, a teacher, because her father had abandoned the family while she was still young. After attending schools and colleges in Las Cruces, Chávez obtained a master's degree in theater arts from Trinity University in San Antonio, Texas, in 1974, and a master's degree in Creative Writing from the University of New Mexico in Albuquerque in 1984. During her career she has taught and been a writer-in-residence at numerous institutions in New Mexico and elsewhere. In 1988, she became a professor in the Drama Department of the University of Houston.

Denise Chávez has won numerous awards and fellowships, including Best Play Award for "The Wait" from New Mexico State University in 1970, the Steele Jones Fiction Award in 1986 for her story "The Last of the Menu Girls," two fellowships from the National Endowment for the Arts in 1981 and 1982, and a Rockefeller Foundation Fellowship in 1984.

Despite Chávez's high productivity as a playwright, it is her published works of fiction that have contributed most to her national reputation. Chávez has published short stories in magazines and a collection of inter-related stories, *The Last of the Menu Girls* (1986), which focuses on the coming of age of Rocío Esquivel. As Rocío compares her own life to that of her mother and as she encounters a wide range of characters in her neighborhood and at work, she begins to formulate her own identity. By the end of the book, we realize that we have been participating in the making of a novelist, and that what we have been reading is the product of Rocío's creative and psychological exploration.

Evening in Paris

Down the aisles of Woolworth's with my other self, Christmastime 1960, three shopping days left, a dollar for each day, and all I had was my awkward youth and one question: "What can I buy for you, Mother, this Christmas?"

The cellophane cannot conceal the rich colors of my dreams, the midnight blue bottles of *Evening in Paris*, the gift package I so long to receive myself. The deep, pungent smell is sealed in silver and blue. Twinkling stars surround me as I ponder the inevitable. But first, "Just looking."

The lady at the counter has brows like a man's, fiercer than a man's. She is someone like Mrs. Limón who lives down the street, with her brown, fish eyebrows and her fleshy, large-pored smell.

I stand while the saleslady, Mrs. Limón Jr., slides a serpentine hand along those clear compartments of ice-cold adulthood, bringing into the light pale lipsticks in pink and white, and small compact circles of Angel Face powder, translucent as the sun. No salves, ointments, colors or creams this time—"Just looking." My hungry lips and young girl's face contemplate an unclear view of potential self.

Please hurry, I haven't time to linger. My mother and sister are somewhere in this store, this circus of objects, searching for opiates, rickrack. I am wonderstruck by the colors behind the glass, by my image in the mirror, by the smell of this blue midnight time. It is as strong as the scent of woman, faraway as Paris and full of lights.

The partitions in the case speak of care, "Now don't you touch," the eyebrows say. Color me Rosy Red, Angel Pink, Hot Rose, Dusty Brown and Heavenly Blue. My eyes are brown. But in the mirror they are Velvet Black, Torrid Blue and Nile Green.

I take out my Christmas gift list, crossing out Father. Mother takes care of him, house shoes and a tie, signs the card "We love you, Daddy." My sister? I don't know. Mother comes first. Perfume is what I want. Limón looks at me, probably thinks to herself: "What help is there?" I wonder myself. Young make-me-beautiful girl, fill my hanging darts with the fleshed-out dreams of a dark, perfumed lady with loves. What help is there for three-dollar realities?

Mother gave me a wallet with Christ's picture on it to give to my sister. He is a Jesus anyone would love. He is so handsome with his long, curly beard and hair and deep-set eyes. He was painted by someone named Sallman, who perhaps saw him in a vision or a dream. It seems removed from me:

Paris, Sallman, men become flesh. It is removed from me, my awkward limbs, uncertain dreams.

I am afraid to be seen looking at myself in the mirror, in my uniform of navy blue, with my white blouse and navy beanie, the center button of the beanie gone. Torn off. I look down to my bobby socks, the only pair I own. I wash them every morning, dry them on the heater, wear them dripping wet to school. I wore them then, in that after-school time of if only this and how to that.

I have decided to buy the gift package of *Evening In Paris Cologne and Bath Water* for my Mother. "I'll take this please," my voice falters. I don't remember how to speak, I am afraid, my clothes all wrong. Can't you cover me up? Shape my doubts, pluck the nervousness away, mask the fear and seal the lips with hope for self. Dynamite Red, of course.

The package lays heavily in my hands. I must not drop it. Oh, what a joyful treasure! This is the nicest gift I have ever given Mother. I know she'll like it, I know she will. Scent of Mother: those lilies she loves in our front yard. *Tabu* no longer her only recourse.

The Paris of Mother's dreams momentarily fused with mine. They were one and the same, child's dreams of happiness, but more. Glory. We revel in it, rich and powdered queens, no worrying about money or any man who goes away, leaving us perfumed, alone.

I am on the edge of that vast, compartmentalized sea, looking across islands of objects, most of them man-made. I give the stranger waves of green. "Here's your change." Mother is the only one I can buy a gift for this year. I'm sorry, all of you, my friends. No one expects a gift from children, except other children. "Where's my gift?" they say, and so you look in your room, in your drawers, for something that is not used, *valuable.* I forgot about the Jesus wallet. And I can slip in a School Day's Picture. I don't know what happened to me that day. I thought I looked so good; I put the hair over my ears so they wouldn't stick out, but they did, and so did the hair.

There is a voice at the edge of this world. It is not the sour one's, she's turned away, shriveled up. The cash register has registered me. The voice calls: "Let's go, Mother's ready," and "What do you have in that package?"

Daylight darkens into dreams.

Most of the gifts under the tree are from Mother's students. We take turns passing them out—this is for you and this one and this one, too. Oh, and this is for *me*! The pile in front of Mother grows, her usual gifts are uncovered: a book of Lifesavers, Avon perfume in a white plastic vase, some green Thinking of You stationery, several cotton handkerchiefs flowered with roses, and a package of divinity, we'll all enjoy that. Most of these gifts will go into the gift box, so next year I'll have something to give my teacher. But for now, they are relegated to a temporary space on the rug, to be covered by the falling needles of our dying tree.

That particular tree lasted into February. It was with great reluctance that it was dispatched into oblivion, which in this case was the irrigation ditch behind the house. The longest tree was flocked, we did it ourselves. The flocking hung from dried bushes and clung to the yellow winter grass, all the snow that would be seen *that* year.

Summer and Dust were the only real seasons. The dry brown grass bespoke winter and any other in-between time. Only farmers and the young, who live dependent upon change, would understand these small consistent movements toward growth. The rest of us are tucked into life's compartments, assigned worth, given shaded colors of illusion with which to arm ourselves against changing mirrors. In days of childhood, our bright, eager faces stared from behind crystalized glass, reflected images tinted with prisms of available light, like the truncated boxes of fabricated well-being found at Woolworth's. All of us now see the edge of this material world, with its objects and playthings. But then, we were stuck! Heavenly Blue with a tinge of sweet cotton candy, little rosettes of illusion. And mine were the proudest, most sustained. They were founded upon hopes.

I recall the smell of our kitchen in those days of Christmas. There was a chicken in the oven, our Christmas "turkey." *Empanadas de calabaza*, indented and grooved into symmetry, lay in what might have been the "turkey tin," alongside *bizcochos* laid out by my Mother's holiday hands.

Most likely there was someone around to help us then: a maid from Mexico, a friend like Ninfa, who told us stories about the overly curious mouse who fell into the stew and was later eaten for his impudence. Or maybe Emilia, who showed me the round, not rectangular worlds of tortillas and how you turn-push-down-turn-keep-turning the rolling pin, her instrument of grace. There was a familiarity of shelves and counters where one perched along blue linoleum expanses and stared into the blocked universe of Emilia's cutting board. Her squat, heavy hands, her Saviour's hands, for once she saved me from sure death on the Tilt-A-Whirl, kneaded circular balls of inanimate masa into future life. Oftentimes Emilia would lean over, and with her flour-covered hands, would search the airways for her favorite station, XELO. "Ay qué lejos estoy del cielo donde he nacido," she sang, as from my Mother's room floated the sound of my favorite Christmas carol, "We Three Kings," sung so effortlessly by Perry Como.

It is enveloped in blue, this time of the past.

The shelf closest to me is one of Mother's miscellaneous shelves, her where-to-put-something-that-I-don't-know-what-to-do-with space. These four large areas contain many parts of my Mother's life. The first holds old dishes, cups and saucers, crystal plates with a thin, slightly greasy layer of moist dust, a bowl in the shape of a duck, its bright orange beak and blue eyes full of constant surprise. Near the back is a small statue of the Infant Jesus of Prague, in a long, red robe, his head awry and held in place with a wadded, previously chewed stick of old Juicy Fruit, his arms extended in benevolent greeting. This memento was the gift of some distressed Anglo woman who had spent several days with us, searching for her Filipino husband who was working in the cotton fields. She was one of the many who passed through our youthful lives, as servers or served. "Can I help you?" Mother said, and so she did, and they in turn left part of themselves with us. There was a constant stream of faces, but it is those few that I remember, like the lady with the unsteady Infant Jesus of Prague who stayed in my room and cried to herself while I slept on the couch.

The other shelves were duplicates of the first, with old dishes, broken wedding gifts, small bud vases and an occasional statuette. Amongst the clutter were other objects bespeaking personality: a twined and dried collection of palms from previous Palm Sundays, a small paper sack of cactus candy from Juárez, a stick of *piloncillo*, a half-empty box of Fig Newtons, a few votive candles left over from last year's *luminarias* and, in the corner, far from prying eyes, an ashtray filled with old cigarette butts left by my Father on his last visit. These inanimate objects assumed a banal ordinariness in full daylight, and yet their internal life danced in the darkness of significance and could never be understood by the casual observer.

Each object on those shelves had its smell and touch and taste. In those days of Sugar, it was the *piloncillo* that I gravitated toward, secretly chipping away rich amber edges and devouring them with delight. The cigarette butts I lifted, touched and pondered, and may have tried to smoke some in some long, solitary afternoon in the back yard, near the garbage can, in that blind space that allowed concealment, freedom.

The dishes were tokens, and each plate was embossed with streams of invisible words, known only to my Mother. How I stared into the crystalline smoothness of those inaccessible and undecipherable emotions, as a small child stands in front of the new, the novel, and as I now stand, an adult, before the sublime fluctuations of an individual heart. My Mother's heart. And so it seemed to me this Christmas that at last I had found the perfect gift for her.

When the time came around for Mother to open the dark blue gift which I had so carefully wrapped in white tissue paper, the anticipation I felt uprooted any commonplace joy I might have felt upon receiving any gifts that stood before me in "my pile."

My sister's face fell as I handed the bright white package to Mother. I quickly gave my sister a smaller unboxed gift. The red Jesus wallet. Mother had signaled Ninfa to start gathering up wrapping paper and to put the bows in a plastic bag. I asked sheepishly, "Aren't you going to open your gift?" for as far as I was concerned, there was only one. "This one, it's from me." "Yes, oh yes," she said, and stooped over to pick up several stray papers.

Later it seemed to me that perhaps Mother had thought the *Evening in Paris* had been given to her by one of her students. I even imagined that she'd been disappointed in my gift. I couldn't understand why. Maybe she actually preferred *Tabu*.

The shimmering star-filled box ended up under the tree, along with the handkerchiefs and the Lifesavers. For a long time it stayed there, unopened, unused. The Avon somehow found its way into Mother's room.

Those nights it was my custom to sit in the darkness of the living room near the tree and watch the lights. The *luminarias*, as seen from the windows from where I sat, hazily burned their way into the black-blue night. As usual, I felt unfulfilled, empty, without the right words, gifts, feelings for those whose lives crowded around me and who called themselves my family. How removed I felt, far away as Paris, no longer glamorous or ageless or full of illusion. The streets outside were dark and long. Much later, when I was older and found myself in Paris, it was the lost little girl who understood so much about its reality. It was the person of the inappropriate gifts who followed hunchbacked old women on winding metal stairways into a greyed, murky expanse of space with no stars. It was a Paris of balding, hennaed heads and odors of sausage exuded by men with polished, black umbrella handles that I knew, as intimately as the painted, illusionary worlds of the postcard Tour Eiffels that said, "Wish You Were Here" and "Sending Love Across the Miles."

That Paris of lights and magic exists, I have seen it, inside the haunting starless nights. And this is what I felt when I sat in the deep, embracing darkness of that special tree, the longest of all time.

Going back is going forward. It is better to give than to receive. All the familiar boring lessons are true.

The Infant Jesus of Prague with his gummed head eventually came to watch over those two ill-fated bottles of perfume. The candy changed shelves, was consumed, replaced, consumed. The wedding gifts were covered in plastic. Time was sectioned off, divided like the little boxes of painted worlds in Woolworth's. Previous intensity became a stale wash of growing up, without the standing back to choose.

I'll take this color here, that perfume there . . . that one. *Evening in Paris*. Dark blue bottle, liquid manifestation of so much hope, of long European nights, of voices mingling in the darkened streets, calling out: Remember me, remember me.

The following Christmas Mother gave *me* the Jesus wallet. She'd forgotten that the year before I'd given it to my sister, who in turn had given it to her for the gift box.

What need had Mother of perfume on those dusty playgrounds?

What need had I of wallets?

That Sallman did a good job. You know the picture, don't you? He is a Christ that anyone could love, with his long brown curls and beard. His deep-set eyes stare out.

Lucha Corpi

Lucha Corpi's bilingual artistry has manifested itself differently from most of the other writers, such as Rolando Hinojosa, who either use English-Spanish code-switching or create two separate-language versions of their works. Throughout the body of her highly symbolic, intimate poetry and in her short fiction for children, Corpi has used the language of her early upbringing and education in Mexico: Spanish. Her prose fiction, on the other hand, is written in the language of her professional life and education in California: English. She was born in Jáltipan, Veracruz, Mexico, in 1945, where she was raised in a household that resounded with music. Corpi received all of her early education in Mexico, and when she came to the United States in 1964 with her husband, who was a student at the University of California-Berkeley, she knew not a word of English. But through classes for foreign students at the University of California, her experiences while raising a child in the United States after a divorce in 1970, and her college education at the same university, she became proficient enough to become a teacher and a writer in her adopted language. Corpi holds both a B.A. and a M.A. in Comparative Literature.

Throughout her college education, Corpi wrote poetry, and in 1976 she published her first short collection of poems in a bilingual anthology, *Fireflight: Three Latin American Poets*. With this collection her relationship with her poetry translator, Catherine Rodríguez-Nieto, began. The relationship has endured through Corpi's two highly applauded books of poetry: *Palabras de mediodía/Noon Words* (1980) and *Variaciones sobre una tempestad/Variations on a Storm* (1990). In 1979, Corpi received a fellowship from the National Endowment for the Arts to produce the latter book.

While Lucha Corpi had experimented with short-story writing earlier, her first full-length novel, *Delia's Song*, was published in English in 1984. Based on her political activism at the university in the early 1970's, *Delia's Song* is one of the very few novelistic representations of an historical period that was so important in the making of the modern Chicano.

Of her novelistic writing, Corpi has said, "I write in English because my dreams are—literally—expressed in that language. Also, I write about the political struggle I have witnessed and have shared with so many Chicanos during my life in California."

Her second novel, *Eulogy for a Brown Angel* (1992), also takes as its background the Chicano civil rights movement. Described as a feminist detective novel, *Eulogy* is fast-paced, suspenseful and packed with an assortment of interesting characters. Her feminist protagonist, Gloria Damasco, is somewhat of a clairvoyant who is able to use more than reason and logic in solving a very puzzling crime.

Following is the first exciting chapter of *Eulogy for a Brown Angel*.

City of Angels

Luisa and I found the child lying on his side in a fetal position. He was about four years old, with curly, soft brown hair falling over his forehead, and partly covering his brows and long lashes. Small, round and still showing those tiny dimples that baby fat forms around the joints, his left hand rested on his head. He was wearing a Mickey Mouse watch on his wrist, marking 3:39 in the afternoon. Four minutes ahead of mine. His right arm partly covered his face, pulling his T-shirt up over the roundness of an over-sized liver. A soft, sleeping, brown cherub, so like my daughter Tania, probably napping back home at that very moment.

As the image of my daughter asleep in her bed surfaced, so did the suspicion that something was very wrong. How could a child be asleep on a sidewalk off Whittier Boulevard in East Los Angeles? Had he gotten separated from his parents during the disturbance, then cried himself to sleep amid the popping and hissing of exploding gas canisters a few hundred feet away from us?

For two hours, we had been hearing the screams and cries of adults and children as they ran from the gas and the shattering of store windows. There seemed to be no end in sight to the violence.

It was August 29, 1970, a warm, sunny Saturday that would be remembered as the National Chicano Moratorium, one of the most violent days in the history of California. Young and old, militant and conservative, Chicano and Mexican-American, grandchild and grandparent, Spanish-speaking and English-speaking, *vato loco* and college teacher, man and woman, all 20,000 of us had marched down Whittier Boulevard in the heart of the barrio. From as far north, west and east as Alaska, Hawaii and Florida, respectively, we had come to protest U.S. intervention in Southeast Asia and the induction of hundreds of young Chicanos into the armed forces. Laguna Park had been our gathering spot.

With our baskets of food, and our children, our poets, musicians, leaders and heroes, we had come to celebrate our culture and reaffirm our rights to freedom of expression and peaceful assembly as Americans of Mexican descent.

In our idealism, Luisa and I, and others like us, hoped then that the police would appreciate our efforts to keep the demonstration peaceful and would help us maintain order with dignity. Surely, we thought, they would realize that we would not needlessly risk the lives of our very old and our very young. How foolish we had been. When a few of the marchers became disorderly, they were subdued by police officers in a brutal manner. People gathered around them and protested the officers' use of undue restraint. A bystander threw a bottle at the police, and five hundred officers armed with riot equipment marched against us. Our day in the sun turned into the bloody riot we were now running from.

I looked at the child again, at the unnatural stillness of that small body bathed in the afternoon sunlight, then felt Luisa's hand on my arm, pulling me away from him. Freeing myself I walked over to the child, hoping all the while that he was asleep or perhaps only slightly injured.

As I bent over, reaching out with a trembling hand to shake him, I became aware of the strong smell of excrement coming from him. Automatically, I pulled up the leg of his shorts and looked in. He was soiled, but not enough to account for such a strong smell. A fly swooped down and landed on his right arm, then another. Resisting the desire to fan them away from him, I watched as they raced over and under his elbow to his mouth, and with a trembling hand I lifted his arm. I was shaking violently by the time I saw the human excrement in his mouth.

I don't know that I understood entirely then what I had just uncovered, but when I realized that the child was dead and his body so defiled, I felt a jolt moving from my chest to the back of my neck, then to my stomach. With my eyes closed I felt my way to the wall. No sooner did I reach it than a burning wave of horror and impotent anger shot up from my stomach and out of my mouth. My body went limp and I fell down in my own vomit, my eyes wide open. For an instant, I felt that I was looking down at the child, at Luisa and at myself from a place up above while the action below me rushed, like an old film over a screen.

I felt I was floating over the rooftops. In the distance, clouds of tear gas rose and mingled with the smoke of a dozen fires burning out of control. The fumes quickly overtook the crowds who then rushed onto the nearest streets that fanned out from Whittier Boulevard.

Two older people were hosing the tear gas off the faces of passersby, among them several eighth-grade students and their teachers who were running towards a school bus. Two teenagers helped a third one, whose leg was bleeding profusely. Over their shoulders or cradled in their arms, some parents carried their children who had been overpowered by the gas fumes.

Policemen and sheriff's deputies armed with riot equipment marched against the crowds, using their batons to strike anyone who crossed their path or dared to strike back. Then they cuffed and filed them into the paddy wagons.

Downtown, brown and black men gazed on the world through the reeky mist of alcohol, while beyond, in Beverly Hills, people gracefully slid in and out of stores on Rodeo Drive, then into chauffeured Roll Royces, Mercedes or Cadillacs. They headed down palm-lined streets towards their mansions, where their dark-skinned domestic staff tended to their every need.

On the horizon, a thin blue layer of haze marked the place where the Pacific Ocean, indifferent to the affairs of men, had met the land indefatigably every instant of every day since time immemorial.

I looked down at myself. There I was—all one hundred five pounds, five-feet-four inches of me—lying fragile next to the dead boy, my dark skin glistening with sweat. How did I get up here? I wondered.

Luisa had her hands on my shoulders and was shouting my name again and again. Despite my desire to stay where I was, I began to descend and suddenly, I was holding on to her hands. I looked into her worried eyes and struggled to stand up.

Surely at least an hour had passed, I thought, as I collected myself and looked again at the dead boy with a cool-headedness that surprised me. I glanced at my watch: 3:45.

"Let's find a phone," I said.

"A phone? My God. Let's get out of here! You just scared the hell out of me. You looked dead, too." Luisa was pulling me by the arm. "There's nothing we can do for him." Her voice trembled and she cleared her throat, pretending to be tough, although I knew she was as affected by the death of the boy as I was. "They're getting closer. Listen," she warned.

I shook my head. "We're too far out of the way. They won't come here. At any rate, I can't just leave him here. You go on. I'll meet you at your house later."

Luisa began to walk away, then changed her mind and faced me. "Okay," she said, in resignation. She pointed in the direction opposite the Boulevard. "My friends Reyna y Joel Galeano live about two blocks from here. Remember I introduced you to them outside the *La Causa Chicana* newspaper yesterday? Joel is a freelance reporter." I nodded and Luisa added, "I'm sure you can call from their house. Go to the corner and turn right, go another two blocks, then left. It's the only blue house, the second one on your right. Number 3345, I think. I'll wait for you here."

"What if they're not home?" I asked.

"I'm sure Reyna is home. She told me she wasn't going to the march. She says she's terrified of crowds. Go on," Luisa commanded. "I'll watch over him." I turned in the direction she was pointing.

As soon as I rang the bell at the blue house, Reyna Galeano looked out the window; recognizing me, she opened the door. Joel was on the phone in the breakfast nook and seemed to be dictating a news report.

"Joel just came in, too," Reyna told me as she invited me to wait in the living room. "Rubén Salazar is hurt. He may even be dead. We don't know for sure." There were tears in her eyes.

"Who is Rubén Salazar?" I asked.

"He's a reporter for the *L.A. Times*. We just saw him yesterday. Joel talked to him about taking photos of the march for the paper."

"Oh yeah, now I know who he is. He also works for one of the Spanish-speaking TV stations here in L.A., doesn't he?" I sat down and looked at Reyna. "What happened to him?"

"We don't exactly know, but he was probably shot. At the Silver Dollar Cafe, where La Verne Street dead ends—oh, my God! I didn't mean to put it that way. Joel just came in and he's trying to get the facts."

"That's only a few blocks from here," I murmured. My legs itched and I started to scratch as I quickly considered and dismissed any possible connection between the shooting of Rubén Salazar and the death of the child. "We just found a little boy a couple of blocks from here," I said to Reyna. "He's dead. I came to call the police."

"You found a dead boy on the street?" Reyna looked incredulously at me. "I'm so glad our kids Mario and Vida are at my mother's in Santa Monica. We figured it was better not to have the children around today. From what you're saying, we were right."

Before I could answer Reyna's quick questions, I saw that Joel had finished with the phone, and I rushed to pick it up. "Sorry, don't mean to be rude but I need to call the police," I explained, then added, "I don't know if you remember me. I'm a friend of Luisa's."

"I remember you." He looked concerned. "Is it about Rubén Salazar?"

"No. I just found out about him from Reyna."

"I really don't think you should be calling the pigs. We're almost sure one of them shot Rubén."

"This isn't about him," I interrupted. "It's about a little boy Luisa and I just found." I wasn't making sense, yet I knew that groping for words and getting the sequence of events right was going to take too long. Joel raised his eyebrows, but he didn't question me further. He sat at the table and began to go over his notes.

I dialed "information," then hesitated. Should I call the homicide division? I was very sure I had found a murder victim, but I dialed the general information number anyway.

Since I was rambling on about finding a little boy dead on the sidewalk in the vicinity of Whittier Boulevard, I kept getting transferred from one section to another of the L.A.P.D. I had been reluctant to mention the excrement in the child's mouth, afraid that I would not be taken seriously. "Somebody listen, please," I pleaded into the static at the other end of the line when I was put on hold once more.

Aware that Joel was giving me an "I-told-you-so" look, I tried avoiding his gaze and turned my attention to the photos and certificates on the wall in front of me. I could see he'd won a couple of awards for photos he'd taken in Viet Nam. I studied a photo of Joel in fatigues with other Marines until a voice came on the phone.

"This is Matthew Kenyon. I understand you have a matter for homicide?" Too late to worry now about having called the police. Joel frowned, shook his head, then left the kitchen.

"A child was murdered this afternoon, I tell you. I found him on the street with *shit* in his mouth. I mean that literally. *Shit*!" I said impatiently to this Matthew Kenyon, no doubt an old cop with a desk job, feeling sorry for himself for not being out there where he could get some action. Immediately, I felt ashamed for blurting out such a crude description of a child whose death had so profoundly disturbed me.

Ironically, it was the crudeness of my remark that made Matthew Kenyon take notice of what I had to say. As I found out soon thereafter Kenyon was a middle-aged detective in the homicide division who had purposely, I suspected after meeting him, not participated in the assault on the demonstrators at Laguna Park.

"What's your name?" he asked me. I hesitated. A Spanish surname always meant a delay of at least an hour in emergencies. He seemed to guess the reason for my hesitation and added, "All right. Just give me your first name."

"Okay," I answered, "my name is Gloria. Gloria Damasco."

"That's good, Gloria." There was no hint of pleasure or displeasure in his voice. "Are you related to the dead boy?"

"No. I just found him." I was losing patience.

"Yes. Now, tell me. Where exactly did you find the boy?"

"On Marigold Street, corner with Marguerite, a few blocks from Whittier Boulevard."

"Are you there now?"

"No. But I can meet you there."

"I'll be there in ten minutes. But I want you to do me a favor. Go back to the place where you found the boy and make sure no one touches him or anything around him."

As I put the receiver on the hook, I realized that somewhere in that city named after Our Lady of the Angels of Porciúncula, a killer roamed the streets or waited at home for news, the knowledge of his crime still fresh in his consciousness.

Roberta Fernández

Roberta Fernández is a well known writer, editor and promoter of Hispanic literature and third-world women's literature. Born in Laredo, Texas, Fernández received all of her early education and her college education in Texas. In 1990, she received a Ph.D. in Romance Languages and Literatures from the University of California-Berkeley. Since the late 1960's, Fernández has served as a teacher, lecturer and researcher at universities around the country, including Brown University, Carlton College in Minnesota, the University of California-Santa Barbara, the University of Houston, the University of Massachusetts and Mills College, where she founded and edited *Prisma*, a literary magazine. Fernández is currently one of the principal fiction editors of Arte Público Press, the nation's oldest and largest publisher of U.S. Hispanic literature.

Through her creative writing, Fernández has embarked upon a two-decade long search for an Hispanic/Third World feminist aesthetic. Her stories have resulted out of this diligent artistic inquiry and ideological commitment. Her beautifully crafted short stories—which have been written in both English and Spanish and published in magazines throughout the country—are comparable in detail and intricacy to the art of filigree. Such stories as "Amanda" and "Zulema" construct a literary style and approach to writing that derive from handicrafts and trades that have been traditionally considered "women's" work in Hispanic culture: dress-making, braiding hair, orally recording the family history. For Fernández, there is art in much of "women's" culture, much that can form the basis of a feminist aesthetic. For her pains, Fernández was awarded first prize for the novel, *Intaglio: A Novel in Six Stories* (1990), by the Multicultural Publishers Exchange. "Amanda," one of the *Intaglio* stories that portrays a model grass-roots artist, is included in the present anthology. The novel itself uses the device of a writer-narrator who is trying to piece together her own adult identity by remembering the women who most influenced her development. The *Houston Post* concluded that *Intaglio* "is a beautiful story of beautiful women who are powerful in their weakness, wise in their ignorance, steady in their volatility. (. . .) These are the women who have, to a great extent, shaped Mexican-American society and therefore have helped shape South Texas."

Amanda

> ¿Dónde está el niño que yo fui,
> sigue dentro de mí o se fue?
>
> . . . ¿Por qué anduvimos tanto tiempo
> creciendo para separarnos?
>
> Pablo Neruda

I

Transformation was definitely her speciality, and out of georgettes, piques, peaux de soie, organzas, shantungs and laces she made exquisite gowns adorned with delicate opaline beadwork which she carefully touched up with the thinnest slivers of iridescent cording that one could find. At that time I was so captivated by Amanda's creations that often before I fell asleep, I would conjure up visions of her workroom where luminous whirls of *lentejuelas de conchanacar* would be dancing about, softly brushing against the swaying fabrics in various shapes and stages of completion. Then, amidst the colorful threads and iridescent fabrics shimmering in a reassuring rhythm, she would get smaller and smaller until she was only the tiniest of gray dots among the colors and lights, and slowly, slowly, the uninterrupted gentle droning of the magical Singer sewing machine and her mocking, whispering voice would both vanish into a silent, solid darkness.

By day, whenever I had the opportunity I loved to sit next to her machine, observing her hands guiding the movement of the fabrics. I was so moved by what I saw that she soon grew to intimidate me, and I almost never originated conversation. Therefore, our only communication for long stretches of time was my obvious fascination with the changes that transpired before my watchful eyes. Finally she would look up at me through her gold-rimmed glasses and ask "*¿Te gusta, muchacha?*"

In response to my nod she would proceed to tell me familiar details about the women who would be showing off her finished costumes at the Black and White Ball or at some other such event.

Rambling on with the reassurance of someone who has given considerable thought to everything she says, Amanda would then mesmerize me even further with her provocative gossip about the men and women who had come to our area many years before. Then, as she tied a thread here and added a touch there, I would feel compelled to ask her a question or two as my flimsy contribution to our lengthy conversation.

With most people I chatted freely, but with Amanda I seldom talked, since I had the distinct feeling by the time I was five or six that in addition to other apprehensions I had about her, she felt total indifference towards me. "How can she be so inquisitive?" I was positive she would be saying to herself even as I persisted with another question.

When she stopped talking to concentrate fully on what she was doing I would gaze directly at her, admiring how beautiful she looked. Waves of defeat would overtake me, for the self-containment that she projected behind her austere appearance made me think she would never take notice of me, while I loved everything about her. I would follow the shape of her head from the central part of her dark auburn hair pulled down over her ears to the curves of the bun she wore at the nape of her long neck. Day in and day out she wore a gray shirtwaist with a narrow skirt and elbow-length sleeves which made her seem even taller than she was. The front had tiny stitched-down vertical pleats and a narrow deep pocket in which she sometimes tucked her eyeglasses. A row of straight pins with big plastic heads ran down the front of her neckline and a yellow measuring tape hung around her neck. Like the rest of the relatives, she seemed reassuringly permanent in the uniform she had created for herself.

Her day lasted from seven in the morning until nine in the evening. During this time she could dash off in a matter of two or three days an elaborate wedding dress or a classically simple evening gown for someone's fifteen-year-old party, which Verónica would then embroider. Her disposition did not require her to concentrate on any one outfit from start to finish, and this allowed her to work on many at once. It also meant she had dresses everywhere, hanging from edges of doors, on a wall-to-wall bar suspended near the ceiling and on three or four tables where they would be carefully laid out.

Once or twice, she managed to make a hysterical bride late to her own wedding. In those hectic instances, Amanda would have the sobbing bride step inside her dress, then hold her breath while she sewed in the back zipper by hand. Somehow people did not seem to mind these occasional slip-ups, for they kept coming back, again and again, from Saltillo and Monterrey, from San Antonio and Corpus Christi, and a few even from far-off Dallas and Houston. Those mid-Texas socialites seemed to enjoy practicing their very singular Spanish with Amanda who never once let on that she really did speak perfect English, and, only after they were gone, would she chuckle over her little joke with us.

As far as her other designs went, her initial basic dress pattern might be a direct copy from *Vogue* magazine or it could stem from someone's wildest fantasy. From then on, the creation was Amanda's, and everyone of her clients trusted the final look to her own discretion. The svelte Club Campestre set from Monterrey and Nuevo Laredo would take her to Audrey Hepburn and Grace Kelly movies to point out the outfits they wanted, just as their mothers had done with Joan Crawford and Katherine Hepburn movies. Judging from their expressions as they pirouetted before their image in their commissioned artwork, she never failed their expectations except perhaps for that occasional zipper-less bride. She certainly never disappointed me as I sat in solemn and curious attention, peering into her face as I searched for some trace of how she had acquired her special powers.

For there was another aspect to Amanda which we only seemed to whisper about, in very low tones, and that was that Amanda was dabbling in herbs. Although none of us considered her a real *hechicera* or enchantress, we always had reservations about drinking or eating anything she gave us, and whereas no one ever saw the proverbial little figurines, we fully suspected she had them hidden somewhere, undoubtedly decked out as exact replicas of those who had ever crossed her in any way.

Among her few real friends were two old women who came to visit her by night, much to everyone's consternation, for those two only needed one quick stolen look to convince you they were more than amateurs. Librada and Soledad were toothless old women swarthed in black or brown from head-to-toe and they carried their back sacks filled with herbs and potions slung over their shoulders, just as *brujas* did in my books. They had a stare that seemed to go right through you, and you knew that no thought was secret from them if you let them look even once into your eyes.

One day, in the year when it rained without stopping for many days in a row and the puddles swelled up with more bubbles than usual, I found myself sitting alone in the screened-in porch admiring the sound of the fat raindrops on the roof; suddenly I looked up to find Librada standing there in her dark brown shawl, softly knocking on the door.

"The lady has sent a message to your mother," she said while my heart thumped so loudly its noise scared me even further. I managed to tell her to wait there, by the door, while I went to call my mother. By the time Mother came to check on the visitor, Librada was already inside, sitting on the couch, and since the message was that Amanda wanted Mother to call one of her customers to relay some information, I was left alone with the old woman. I sat on the floor pretending to work on a jig-saw puzzle while I really observed Librada's every move. Suddenly she broke the silence, asking me how old I was and when my next birthday would be. Before I could phrase any words, Mother was back with a note for Amanda, and

Librada was on her way. Sensing my tension, Mother suggested we go into the kitchen to make some good hot chocolate and to talk about what had just happened.

After I drank my cup, I came back to the porch, picked up one of my *Jack and Jill*'s and lay on the couch. Then, as I rearranged a cushion, my left arm slid on a slimy greenish-gray substance and I let out such a screech that Mother was at my side in two seconds. Angry at her for having taken so long to come to my aid, I kept wiping my arm on the dress and screaming, "Look at what that *bruja* has done." She very, very slowly took off my dress and told me to go into the shower and to soap myself well. In the meantime she cleaned up the mess with newspapers and burned them outside by the old brick pond. As soon as I came out of the shower she puffed me up all over with her lavender-fragranced bath powder, and for the rest of the afternoon we tried to figure out what the strange episode had meant. Nothing much happened to anyone in the family during the following wet days, and Mother insisted we forget the incident.

Only, I didn't forget it for a long time. On my next visit to Amanda's I described in detail what had happened. She dismissed the entire episode as though it weren't important, shrugging, "Poor Librada. Why are you blaming her for what happened to you?"

With that I went back to my silent observation, now suspecting she too was part of a complex plot I couldn't figure out. Yet, instead of making me run, incidents like these drew me more to her, for I distinctly sensed she was my only link to other exciting possibilities which were not part of the everyday world of the others. What they could be I wasn't sure of, but I was so convinced of the hidden powers in that house that I always wore my scapular and made the sign of the cross before I stepped inside.

After the rains stopped and the moon began to change colors, I began to imagine a dramatic and eerie outfit which I hoped Amanda would create for me. Without discussing it with my sisters, I made it more and more sinister and finally, when the frogs stopped croaking, I built up enough nerve to ask her about it. "Listen, Amanda, could you make me the most beautiful outfit in the world? One that a witch would give her favorite daughter? So horrible that it would enchant everyone ... maybe black with wings on it like a bat's."

She looked at me with surprise. "Why would you want such a thing?"

"Cross my heart and hope to die, I really won't try to scare anyone."

"*Pues, chulita*, I'm so busy right now, there's no way I can agree to make you anything. One of these days, when God decides to give me some time, I might consider it, but until then, I'm not promising anyone anything."

And then I waited. Dog days came and went, and finally when the white owl flew elsewhere I gave up on my request, brooding over my having asked for something I should have known would not be coming. Therefore, the afternoon that Verónica dropped off a note saying that *la señora* wanted to see me that night because she had a surprise for me, I coolly said I'd be there only if my mother said I could go.

II

All the time I waited to be let in, I was very aware that I had left my scapular at home. I knew this time that something very special was about to happen to me, since I could see even from out there that Amanda had finally made me my very special outfit. Mounted on a little-girl dress-dummy, a swaying black satin cape was awaiting my touch. It was ankle-length with braided frogs cradling tiny buttons down to the knee. On the inside of the neckline was a black fur trim. "Cat fur," she confessed, and it tickled my neck as she buttoned the cape on me. The puffy sleeves fitted very tightly around the wrist, and on the upper side of each wristband was attached a cat's paw which hung down to my knuckles. Below the collar, on the left side of the cape, was a small stuffed heart in burgundy-colored velveteen and, beneath the heart, she had sewn-in red translucent beads.

As she pulled the rounded ballooning hood on me, rows of stitched-down pleats made it fit close to the head. Black chicken feathers framed my face, almost down to my eyes. Between the appliques of feathers, tiny bones were strung which gently touched my cheeks. The bones came from the sparrows which the cats had killed out in the garden, she reassured me. She then suggested I walk around the room so she could take a good look at me.

As I moved, the cat's paws rubbed against my hands and the bones of the sparrows bounced like what I imagined snowflakes would feel like on my face. Then she slipped a necklace over my head that was so long it reached down to my waist. It too was made of bones of sparrows strung on the finest glittering black thread, with little bells inserted here and there. I raised my arms and danced around the room, and the bells sounded sweet and clear in the silence. I glided about the room, then noticed in the mirror that Librada was sitting in the next room, laughing under her breath. Without thinking, I walked up to her and asked what she thought of my cape.

"Nenita, you look like something out of this world. Did you notice I just blessed myself? It scares me to think of the effect you are going to have on so many. *¡Que Dios nos libre!*"

I looked at Librada eye-to-eye for the first time, then felt that the room was not big enough to hold all the emotion inside of me. So I put my arms around Amanda and kissed her two, three, four times, then dramatically announced that I was going to show this most beautiful of all creations to my mother. I rushed outside hoping not to see anyone on the street, and since luck was to be my companion for a brief while, I made it home without encountering a soul. Pausing outside the door of the kitchen where I could hear voices, I took a deep breath, knocked as loudly as I could and in one simultaneous swoop, opened the door and stepped inside, arms outstretched as feathers, bones and *cascabeles* fluttered in unison with my heart.

After the initial silence, my sisters started to cry almost hysterically, and while my father turned to comfort them, my mother came towards me with a face I had never seen on her before. She breathed deeply, then quietly said I must never wear that outfit again. Since her expression frightened me somewhat, I took off the cape, mumbling under my breath over and over how certain people couldn't see special powers no matter how much they might be staring them in the face.

I held the *bruja* cape in my hands, looking at the tiny holes pierced through the bones of sparrows, then felt the points of the nails on the cat's paws. As I fingered the beads under the heart, I knew that on that very special night when the green lights of the fireflies were flickering more brightly than usual, on that calm transparent night of nights, I would soon be sleeping in my own witch's daughter's cape.

III

Sometime after the Judases were all aflame and spirals of light were flying everywhere, I slowly opened my eyes to a full moon shining on my face. Instinctively my hand reached to my neck and I rubbed the back of my fingers gently against the cat's fur. I should go outside I thought. Then I slipped off the bed and tiptoed to the back door in search of that which was not inside.

For a long time I sat on a lawn chair, rocking myself against its back, all the while gazing at the moon and the familiar surroundings which glowed so luminously within the vast universe while out there in the darkness, the constant chirping of the crickets and the cicadas reiterated the reassuring permanence of everything around me. None of us is allowed to relish in powers like that for long, though, and the vision of transcendence exploded in a scream as two hands grabbed me at the shoulders, then shook me back and forth. "What are you doing here? Didn't I tell you to take off that awful thing?"

Once again I looked at my mother in defiance but immediately sensed that she was apprehensive rather than angry, and I knew it was hopeless to argue with her. Carefully I undid the tiny rounded black buttons from the soft, braided loops and took off the cape for what I felt would be the last time.

IV

Years passed, much faster than before, and I had little time left for dark brown-lavender puddles and fanciful white owls in the night. Nor did I see my cape after that lovely-but-so-sad, once-in-a-lifetime experience of perfection in the universe. In fact, I often wondered if I had not invented that episode as I invented many others in those endless days of exciting and unrestrained possibilities.

Actually, the memory of the cape was something I tried to flick away on those occasions when the past assumed the unpleasantness of an uninvited but persistent guest; yet, no matter how much I tried, the intrusions continued. They were especially bothersome one rainy Sunday afternoon when all the clocks had stopped working one after another as though they too had wanted to participate in the tedium of the moment. So as not to remain still, I mustered all the energy I could and decided to pass the hours by poking around in the boxes and old trunks in the storeroom.

Nothing of interest seemed to be the order of the afternoon, when suddenly I came upon something wrapped in yellowed tissue paper. As I unwrapped the package, I uttered a sigh of surprise on discovering that inside was the source of the disturbances I had been trying to avoid. I cried as I fingered all the details on the little cape, for it was as precious as it had been on the one day I had worn it many years before. Only the fur had stiffened somewhat from the dryness in the trunk.

Once again I marvelled at Amanda's gifts. The little black cape was so obviously an expression of genuine love that it seemed a shame it had been hidden for all those years. I carefully lifted the cape out of the trunk, wondering why my mother had not burned it as she had threatened, yet knowing full well why she had not.

V

From then on I placed the little cape among my collection of few but very special possessions which accompanied me everywhere I went. I even had a stuffed dummy made, upon which I would arrange the cape in a central spot in every home I made. Over the years, the still-crisp little cape ripened in meaning, for I could not imagine anyone ever again taking the time to create anything as personal for me as Amanda had done when our worlds had coincided for a brief and joyous period in those splendid days of luscious white gardenias.

When the end came I could hardly bear it. It happened many years ago when the suitcase containing the little cape got lost en route on my first trip west. No one could understand why the loss of something as quaint as a black cape with chicken feathers, bones of sparrows and cat's paws could cause anyone to carry on in such a manner. Their lack of sympathy only increased my own awareness of what was gone, and for months after I first came to these foggy coastal shores I would wake up to *lentejuelas de conchanacar* whirling about in the darkness, just as they had done so long ago in that magical room in Amanda's house.

VI

Back home, Amanda is aging well, and although I haven't seen her in years, lately I have been dreaming once again about the enchantment which her hands gave to everything they touched, especially when I was very tiny and to celebrate our birthdays, my father, she and I had a joint birthday party lasting three days. During this time, he would use bamboo sticks to make a skeletal frame for a kite, and then Amanda would take the frame and attach thin layers of marquisette to it with angel cords. In the late afternoon, my father would hold on to the cords, while I floated about on the kite above the shrubs and bushes; and it was all such fun. I cannot recall the exact year when those celebrations stopped, nor what we did with all those talismanic presents, but I must remember to sort through all the trunks and boxes in my mother's storeroom the next time that I am home.

Roberto Fernández

Roberto Fernández is in the vanguard of Cuban-American literature, having made the transition from the literature of exile to the literature of the culture and social conditions of Cubans in the United States, and having made the transition from producing works in Spanish to writing in English. Born in Sagua la Grande, Cuba, on September 24, 1951, just eight years before the Cuban Revolution, he went into exile with his family at the age of eleven. His family settled in southern Florida, not in the Cuban community of Miami, but in areas where Anglo-American culture was dominant. This led to periods of adjustment in what seemed like a hostile environment to the young boy, an impression that accounts for some of the cultural conflict narrated in his writings. The Fernández family nevertheless maintained close ties with the Miami community, and this, too, became subject matter for the writer.

Fernández became interested in writing as an adolescent, and this interest led him to college and graduate school. In 1978, he completed a Ph.D. in Linguistics at Florida State University; by that time he had already published two collections of stories: *Cuentos sin rumbo* (1975, Directionless Tales) and *El jardín de la luna* (1976, The Garden of the Moon). At this point, he also began his career as an academic, teaching linguistics and Hispanic literature at Florida State University in Tallahassee.

Roberto Fernández is the author of three open-formed novels which have created for him the reputation of being a satirist and humorist of the Miami Cuban community. In all three, he is a master at capturing the nuances of Cuban dialect in Spanish and English. *La vida es un special* (1982, Life Is on Special), *La montaña rusa* (1985, The Roller Coaster) and *Raining Backwards* (1988) are all mosaics made up of monologues, dialogues, letters, phone conversations, speeches and other types of oral performance that, in the composite, make up a continuing tale of the development of the exile community and its younger generations of increasingly acculturated Cuban-Americans. Through the pages of these books, the author charts the goings on at social clubs, coming-out parties, counter-revolutionary guerrilla movements in the Florida swamps, poetry and art contests, and many other episodes that create a broad and epic spectrum of a dynamic community caught between two cultures, two sets of values, two languages and two political systems. *Raining Backwards*, Fernández's first book to be published in English, became a small press hit, receiving outstanding reviews from coast to coast in major newspapers and magazines (*The New York Times, USA Today, San Francisco Chronicle*). "Retrieving Varadero" and "Miracle on Eighth and Twelfth" are both from *Raining Backwards.*

Retrieving Varadero

It had been raining non-stop for months and Eloy was doing his best to swat the palmetto bugs, mosquitoes and gnats which, drunk with rain and crashing against each other, were emerging from the puddles and trying to nest in Mirta's wavy bronze mane. Eloy had been serving Mirta faithfully for the last two months in exchange for tidbits of the past. He was thirsty for learning about the golden-roofed cities of that enchanted island, places which were so fabulous and sacred that his aunt refused to even mention them.

"Faster! They're driving me crazy. Faster! C'mon, you can do better than that. Fan me faster. Go to the bathroom closet and get the ostrich feather. Maybe it'll help. But be careful with it. It's the only thing my mother left me."

The evenings with Mirta had begun before the deluge. It all started one afternoon when Eloy, tired of folding clothes for his aunt, the laundry woman, and realizing the futility of trying to retrieve any information from her, pressed his ear against the wall and listened in astonishment to the discussion that Mirta was having with the radio on the other side of the wall.

"Why do you go on with your lies? Everyone knows that Varadero was the most beautiful beach, not only in the world but in the whole universe! The waters were forever changing colors, the sand had the texture of baby powder, the breezes were always warm but never hot. So how dare you say that Cancun or Sanibel are better and more beautiful. Liar! Communists! And there you go again. Isn't it enough just to say it once. You're getting me mad. I'd love to turn your program off, but you know I'm waiting for Julio's latest hit with Germán García. But I'm losing my patience! I swear on my mother's grave that I've had it with you. I'm going to silence you forever. Liar! You're forcing me to do it."

Eloy heard a crashing noise and, overtaken by his curiosity, he sneaked out and knocked on Mirta's door. Mirta refused to open, but managed to stick her head through the kitchen window and shout in anguish: "What do you want?" She was afraid of a rapist or, even worse, the Mastercard collector. Quickly, she muttered: "She's in Disney World in Orlando. Very, very far away from here." In her nervousness, Mirta had failed to recognize her little neighbor, the laundry woman's nephew.

After he explained to her who he was, Mirta opened the door and, somewhat surprised by his visit, offered him a few pieces of candy which were left over from Halloween. After this first meeting, Eloy developed the need to talk to her every evening after school and Mirta had finished her daily factory routine. Gradually, Mirta intoxicated his mind with her maze of remembrances.

"Yes. That's right, the water was always changing colors like a kaleidoscope. Each time that wind changed course the water changed color. When the wind was blowing strongly, it turned into an intense violet, and when it was calm, it was as green as Ireland."

"What's Ireland?"

"It's a deodorant soap. But that's not really important. Our ocean was so delicious that even Aristotle, who is a very cultured gentleman, and who can't practice here because he never passed the board, when he tasted a sip of our waters, he left all his knowledge aside and started shacking up with El Cid, who was this enormous black woman that sold coconuts carved in the image of Mary Magdalene, but had the faces made out of bread in El Cid's own image."

"And the sand? Was it like Clearwater's?"

"You must be kidding! In all the beaches in Cuba the sand was made out of grated silver, though in Varadero it was also mixed with diamond dust. And it was definitely finer than Mennen's Baby Powder, the one with the baby inside the rose. I'm going to tell you something no one has ever told you, so you are going to become a very special person because there're only a few people that know this. Are you ready?"

"Yes, ma'am."

"The sun rose in the North and set in the South."

And thus, the days became weeks and the weeks months, and Eloy came religiously every morning at dusk to hear Mirta. Very slowly, Mirta came to realize that her words had a narcotic effect upon the youth, and shrewdly opted to trade her remembrances of memories for practical favors that could ease the burden of living. She would send Eloy to Pepe's Grocery to buy a bottle of Seven-Up, or to Cabrera's Pharmacy to buy librium without prescription or benadryl to calm the constant itching that had plagued her since puberty.

One drenching afternoon, Eloy arrived and, as usual, he wiped off the mud that covered his shoes. Mirta greeted him with a list of errands: buy one jar of Bella Aurora cream; go to Clavo, the numbers man, and place $5 on 5-9-80; stop by the bank and tell them that there's a mistake in my checkbook, that my name is Miss Mirta María Vergara, not Mrs. Mirtha

Verga; and fill out my insurance papers that I don't understand. While Eloy read the list, Mirta promised more tales from her seemingly inexhaustible vein. Suddenly, Mirta sneezed and Eloy rushed to wipe her nose.

"Thank you, child. You are the living image of St. Gabriel the Archangel, because you're more beautiful than all the other angels. And now go and wipe the sofa cushion once more, because it still has a lot of dirt, and then go to my room and vacuum it . . . and the breezes were warm but never hot and there was no need for suntan lotion nor sun screens because the breezes carried the properties of aloe and they even unclogged your nose while moisturizing your skin. Now, let me tell you something very important, I watched everything from the porch. It had the best view of the beach. Besides, my mother never allowed me to go down to the beach because she said I was going to get dirty if I mixed with trash. I remember that at times, when it thundered, El Cid would take off her clothes and, with her two big breasts dancing in the air, stretch her arms, imitating a crucified martyr, and shout: 'Mary Magdalene, blessed virgin. Deliver us from thunder and lightning.' And then the thunder would cease and my mother would come to cover my eyes so I wouldn't see the naked Cid."

"Eloy, Eloy are you in there? Do you want to play some baseball? C'mon out."

"I can't. I'm busy."

"Could you tell me some more, Miss Mirta? I'll bet my friends don't know about El Cid."

"There were giant penguins and white seals that roamed the beach . . . "

"Excuse me, Miss Mirta. I think it's my aunt calling me. I've got to go now. I have to help her."

"If you stay a little longer, I'll tell you about Foquie, the seal with the bright green eyes. Stay, stay . . . "

"Okay, but just a little bit more."

"But could you first squeeze the blackheads on my back, and also those little pimples that are really itching. Could you? I can't see them."

As Eloy groomed her, Mirta felt, without knowing why, a deep pleasure with each exposed blackhead, with each popped pimple.

" . . . and the white seals came around the Cape of Horn only because they had heard about the pleasures of Varadero, the most beautiful beach in the world. Once they got there, they would be driven mad by the one hundred waterfalls that bordered the beach and they would slide and play with the swimmers and dive for fish and pearls in exchange for bananas and papayas and could you pour some boric acid on my back and take a damp towel and put it right on my shoulder blade, and while you are at it, rub my swollen thigh with Ben-Gay."

"Really, ma'am, I've got to go. My aunt is calling me and I have to help her fold the laundry and then do my homework because last year I flunked the seventh grade."

"Why don't you bathe me before you go? I'm so tired with so much overtime at the factory that I can hardly hold the soap. Just a little shower, okay?"

"But Miss Mirta!"

"It's not Mirtha, it's Mirta. C'mon! Be a good boy. I can even be more than your mother. Stop that nonsense and get the sponge, the avocado soap and the cologne. They're in the closet."

"Okay, Miss Mirta, but tell me more. Tell me more. Do you know about my reading aunt's farm, the one that ended where the rainbow ends?"

Mirta could only think about the pleasures that Eloy's hands would exert on her back as he bathed her, and started to tremble thinking that she would have to turn around and face Eloy in order to reach the towel that hung from the door nail. Just this thought made her salivate so profusely that the dribble threatened to inundate her neck. While Mirta was getting undressed to dive into the old tub, Eloy commenced lathering the sponge without realizing that many years later he would forbid his wife to use a sponge to do the dishes, much less to bathe the kids. That strange spongephobia would last throughout his life. Not even Dr. Kings, with her potions, balms and incantations, would be able to cure this malady. Eloy approached the tub and urged her to continue dispensing stories of the by-gone days.

"It was on Varadero Beach that I met my only fiancé. It was a week after the 1943 storm, two days before my fifteenth birthday. He was sunbathing, but he never knew that I was his sweetheart. I treasured our love with all my soul. His hair was the color of mahogany, like yours, but wavier, and when I came over here I sent him love messages in a bottle three times a week. They always read: 'I love you. Yours forever, MV' ... MV is me, Mirta Vergara ... and the breezes were warm ... a little bit more to the right, lather me right down there ... but the breezes were never hot and you didn't need suntan lotion and the white seals would play happily with the swimmers and they slid through the falls that surrounded Varadero and when it rained, it rained molasses and rice so you just needed to open your mouth and eat and if you wanted more to eat you just simply said: 'Sea creatures, I'm hungry,' and the fish and the mollusks would jump from the water to your pan and the sand had the texture of baby powder and the breezes were warm but ... "

"Miss Mirta, you already told me about the breezes and the sand," shouted Eloy, exasperated, as he retrieved the sponge and used it to wipe the sweat drops that covered his forehead.

"I'm tired, Miss Mirta. I'm tired," Eloy kept saying.

For the first time, Mirta realized that the well of remembrances that she had been exploiting was about to run dry at the precise moment when she needed to feel the skeletons of those magnificent corals, which had sacrificed their lives for her happiness, to form that joy-giving sponge.

"Yes, child, continue lathering down there," said Mirta at the same time that she turned around smiling like an old rabbit and exposed her two udders which had sagged with the weight of virginity and were trying to rest on her reddish bush. Eloy looked at her indifferently for the first time and defiantly said, "Tell me more! If you don't continue, I won't either."

Mirta, alarmed by his attitude, tried to lure him again with her all but exhausted memories.

"The white seals then came accompanied by yodelers shouting their yodel-eeps. The women on the beach who greeted the yodelers were dressed in straw skirts and moved their hips incessantly while singing: 'Waha, waha, trum, trum, waha, waha, trum trum.' And the men had wide, bronzed shoulders and were always blowing these enormous sea shells. They were sounding them to appease the volcano which stood majestically at a distance and which would let a plume of smoke escape as a sign of gratitude for the shell sounds which pleased him so much. The name of the volcano was 'Pan de Matanzas,' the Killing Bread. It got that name from the many bakers who had thrown themselves from its summit. El Cid's coconut figurines with their heads made out of bread drove the bakers mad with love, for they wanted to possess the immense maiden who denied them her body. Between the lagoon and the sea there was a mountain all covered with snow. Mamá, after finishing her cleaning duties at Señora Nelia's would swim towards the mountain to pack some snow and make herself a rum ice cream. She died evoking that mountain and whispering my father's name. He was a very rich merchant from Venice whom I never met and ah, ah, ahhhh."

"What's the matter ma'am? What's the matter, Miss Mirta? You're sweating! Are you okay? Do you want me to call my aunt?"

"It's nothing. It's just that I get excited when I remember so many beautiful memories. But please, please don't stop lathering me, but now a little bit toward the left . . . please."

"But Miss Mirta. I'm too tired and my aunt . . . "

"I'll tell you more, my love. I'll tell you so much . . . and when a visitor arrived they placed leis around his neck and would whisper in his ear: 'Tiare, tiare haere mai, haere mai,' and at that same time their hips would go crazy and they would take him to a heavenly hotel all made of ivory, gold and coral called El Oasis. There they would take their skirts off and, with only hibiscuses on their heads, would dive into the waves carrying with them bananas and plantains for the white seals, yodelers and penguins. Keep lathering, please keep lathering me and I will tell you how the white seals came up to the beach and how they ate from your hand and how Mamá followed Señora Nelia when she left for Miami and Mamá embraced each room in the house, telling them that she had loved them more than her own family and as a souvenir she plucked an ostrich feather from a hat which the Señora had left forgotten on her bed and how the sand had the texture of baby powder and how the breeze tanned your skin and the waters were technicolor and Aristotle and El Cid were wrestling naked on the sand. Why don't you stay to sleep with me?"

Eloy didn't answer. Mirta got out of the tub, ready to force him to stay if so required. Then a cloud of palmetto bugs landed on her body, covering her nakedness like a robe. This time Eloy didn't even try to swat the gnats that were trying to invade her nostrils. Worn out, he grabbed a folding chair and sat quietly observing and listening to the emerging Mirta who, screaming madly, told him that his mother was a tramp, that his aunts slept together with his uncle in the same bed, that his father had been in jail for being a drug-pushing cuckold and that above all he was ungrateful, for if it weren't for her he would never have known about the past.

Eloy, baffled, used the sponge which he was still holding in his hands to wipe his sweaty face once more. Mirta misinterpreted his gesture and immediately started to salivate again. She knelt and told him that she would constantly talk to him about the past and the beach, and that there were still many things that he didn't know about, like his reading aunt's (as he called his other aunt) silver boat and rainbow ranch, the singing palm trees and the queen of the lizards. She implored him to stay, promising to buy his aunt a dryer and find his father a good job.

He just smiled, caressing with his right hand the peach fuzz growing on his upper lip, and hiding the sponge behind his back with his left hand, he nodded murmuring, "Tell me more, Mirta. Tell me more, baby."

Miracle at Eighth and Twelfth

Me and Manolo were walking toward Eighth and Twelfth after we left Pepe's Grocery 'cause I needed a few things for Sunday when the grandchildren would be over. I know what you are thinking, but it's my very own shopping cart. I'm no thief. Well, I was guiding my Manny and thinking how hard life had got ever since he went blind after lighting that old kerosene kitchen. I warned him, but he's always been so hard-headed. You want some coffee? It's not American coffee. It's not watery. So the kitchen exploded right in his face, and my poor Manny pretended for weeks that he could still see, and he even tried to drive the car and ended up smashing it against Mr. Olsen's porch. Mr. Olsen never knew Manny did it 'cause he was vacationing in Georgia at the time. Let me tell you, life then was a lemon, and I didn't have no sugar to make it a lemonade.

So we were walking and it was good Friday. Wait a second, I think something is burning in the kitchen. Manny, is that you, my little heart? I wonder what he is doing in the kitchen. Last week, he turned on all the burners and nearly burned the house down. Now that he can see again he still likes to pretend to be blind. I guess he enjoyed all that extra attention. I always took care of him, like the king of this house he is. So we were walking along Eighth and Twelfth and it was Good Friday. It must have been around a quarter to three since it was really getting dark and windy. I was saying a rosary, just to do something, and I was admiring this huge mango when I noticed next to the mango tree, near the fence, Mr. Olsen's sea grape crying. It wasn't really crying, but sap was oozing from its branches. Somehow I was inspired and I helped Manny jump the fence and then I jumped. Actually, it wasn't really that easy since Manny's privates got tangled in the fence and I had to help him. I remember he screamed: "Barbarita, they are useless. Let's leave them there."

I went straight to the tree, gathered some sap in my hands and rubbed it all over my poor Manny's sightless eyes. At first, he cursed me, but then he knelt, lifted his arms and shouted: "Coño, I can see. Barbarita, I can see!" I thought he was kidding, so I asked him what color my blouse was. "Red, white and blue," he said. I wasn't convinced yet, so I asked him again what color his shoes were. "Blue sneakers," he said with a grin. I quickly knelt and was beating my chest in gratitude when Mr. Olsen came out with his shotgun and threatened to kill us for trespassing. I tried to explain, but he wasn't interested.

Finally, I had to bribe him with some bubble gum. You know how Americans go crazy for stuff like that. He let us go, screaming that only Superman could save him from this foreign plague. While he was shouting, I was trying to scoop up some more holy sap in case Manny had a relapse, but he saw me and placed his gun right in my nose and said, "Lady, put that sap where it belongs . . . you . . . you tropical scum, or I'll blow your head off."

We were very scared of Mr. Olsen, but very thankful for Manny's sight, and now we go every day at a quarter to three to pray across the street from Mr. Olsen's house, facing the tree, while a watchful Mr. Olsen keeps his gun cocked. "Scuse me, just a minute. Manny is that you, my little heart?" It's Manny, all right. Every time he goes to the toilet he closes his eyes like he's blind and misses. I always have to go clean up after him. I want you to promise me by your mother's body lying in her funeral casket that you will tell everybody you know about this divine happening, so the faithless can become believers. But what I told about Manny's privates, keep it to yourself.

> ATTENTION PLEASE. MAY I HAVE YOUR ATTENTION PLEASE: WOULD YOU PLEASE DISPERSE AND GO HOME. GO CASA! THIS AREA IS BEING CORDONED OFF BY ORDER OF THE POLICE. POR FAVOR, GO AS QUICKLY AS POSSIBLE. ¡PRONTO!

That sure is a big helicopter up there! Please, ma'am! Please, ma'am, don't push. Let me go by, please. Please don't push, don't you see I'm carrying a sick child! Who pinched my ass? Mima, where are youuuu? Hail Mary full of grace, the gentleman with the green shirt please get out of the way. Excuse me, please. Forget it, honey. I ain't moving, I saw this spot first. Out, out, out! This is private property, propiedad private! Hot dogs! Hot dogs! Get your hot dogs and cockfight tickets here. Oh, my tree! Oh Julia, if you could only see what they are doing to my tree. My beautiful sea grape! Who pinched my ass? The mother who pinched my ass! Hail Mary full of get your Bud, get your ice cold Bud here. This butt's for me. Ouch! If you touch my tree again, I'll kill you! Shut up, old man. Lois, Lois call the police! I am not. This is so much fun, olé! I swear by my little boy that I saw everything from my bathroom window. She was pushing the shopping cart with a man inside. The man had no legs. Then I saw her jump the fence and gather something from the sea grape tree and spreading it all over his stumps and the next thing I saw was the man sprouting a new pair of legs. I swear by my mother's grave that I saw everything from my bathroom window. That's why I'm here. You spic English? Yes, a little. What the police saying from the helicopter? They said that the Virgin is coming real soon. How they know she is coming? They are gringos, my friend, they know everything. If Superman could only hear me, but I can't get to my watch now. Holy cards, with the Pope blessing the holy tree, with your order of a small pizza and a Bud. Number, numbers, bolita. Coke, coke. Get your coke here. Snort, excuse meee, drink your Coke here. C'mon, Manny, rub a little bit of sap on your pipi, it might make it work again. Do it for me, Manny. Okay, Barbarita, but just a little bit! Let me go by, I have arthritis. Connie, just chip off a piece. It'll keep Bill at your side. And her royal highness for the Queen Calle Ocho Festival is, may I have the envelope: Lovee Martinez, a modeling student. Hey, don't take that whole branch. Shut up, viejo. My country tis of thee sweet land of liberty. And then he sprouted two legs and an arm. Caridad, our lady, is landing. She's landing upside down on top of the tree! Who pinched my ass? Oh, Manny, that's incredible. It's so big and hard!!!!

Lionel G. García

Lionel G. García is a novelist who has created some of the most memorable characters in Chicano literature in a style that is well steeped in the traditions of Texas tall-tales and Mexican-American folk narratives. Born in San Diego, Texas, in 1935, García grew up in an environment in which Mexican Americans were the majority population in his small town and on the ranches where he worked and played. His father, a paint-and-body man, and his mother, a teacher, García was reared in a middle-class home and did so well in school that he was one of the very few Mexican Americans admitted to Texas A & M University, where he majored in biology but was also encouraged by one of his English professors to write. After graduating, he attempted to become a full-time writer, but was unsuccessful in getting his works published. He served in the Army and, after being discharged honorably, he returned to Texas A & M and graduated from that institution in 1969 as a Doctor of Veterinary Science. Since then he has developed a successful career as a veterinarian.

Throughout this time and to the present he continued to write. In the early 1980's, he once again attempted to publish, and he found that there were many more opportunities at hand. In 1983, he won the PEN Southwest Discovery Award for his novel in progress, *Leaving Home*, which was published in 1985. This and his second novel, *A Shroud in the Family* (1987), draw heavily on his family experiences and small-town background. In part, *A Shroud in the Family* also demythologizes the "great" Texas heroes, such as Sam Houston and Jim Bowie, who have become symbols of Anglo-Texans' defeat of and superiority over Mexicans. His latest novel, *Hardscrub* (1989), is a departure from his former works; it is a realistically drawn chronicle of the life of an Anglo child in an abusive family relationship. *Hardscrub* has won two of the most important awards in the Southwest: the Southwest Book Award and the Texas Institute of Letters Award for the Novel. García has also published short stories in magazines, newspapers and anthologies. The bittersweet tale of "The Day They Took My Uncle" was first published in *The Americas Review*.

The Day They Took My Uncle

The day they took my uncle, I had been under the house playing all morning long with a little girlfriend older than me and she had shown me her female part. I was amazed, seeing it for the first time, at how simple it was. At that age I could never have imagined it as I had seen it that morning. Afterwards, I could never get her, teaser that she was, to show it to me again. So the memory of it faded from me and I was left with a blur, a blur much like the pictures of female pubices in nudist colony magazines that I had a peek at as a child. I imagined that these magazine pictures had been true and that these female parts were constantly moving at a great rate of speed. Why else would they create a blur on a photograph? But that was not what I had seen that morning. What I had seen was standing still. I had been educated. But that in itself is another story.

My uncle was insane, crazy. He was also missing, but I knew where he was. His insanity was well known throughout town. He had been insane for many years. His problem was that, at a spur of the moment and without forewarning, this lean and sallow man would rise to his feet, if he was sitting or squatting on his haunches, and start walking desperately. Then he would grab his ears, the lobes, and start yanking them down violently, as if trying to shake some diabolical voices from his ears. Then he would begin to curse violently. He cursed at people, naming names. He had the indelicate habit also of bringing up pasts that were better left behind and he would talk about the people and about what they had done. I don't know where he got his information, but a lot of it was not true. It was all right as long as he stayed within the family and in our yard or in the immediate neighborhood. But, for no apparent reason, he began to set off in his tirade to the mayor's house: cursing, yanking at his ears, impugning the mayor's ancestry, calling him a sonofabitch and a son of a whore, plus a bastard. The mayor's wife was not spared. My uncle stoutly proclaimed that she was fucking the mayor's cousin. The poor mayor's wife was a frail little dried up person of a woman who probably didn't even do *it* with the mayor. He also called her a whore and a bitch. I knew he had done this for sure. I was with him that day.

I was, for some reason, his favorite, and he tried to do things for me. He would whittle away with his knife, occasionally having these fits, the knife in his yanking hand, until he would finish some little wood carving for me. He made a great fuss when giving me these carvings as if he were really giving me something of great value. He was not a good whittler. In fact, he was not good for anything except for drinking and causing the family trouble.

He was an alcoholic. Which brings me to the supposed cause of his bedevilment. He had been possessed, my grandmother told us, when he accidentally drank the dregs of a bottle of beer that had been laced with a special potion, a potion so powerful it would cause insanity. It was, she said, a potion meant for someone else. I cringed at the thought that some day I would encounter the potion accidentally as my uncle had done and that I would be rendered into that same state. Therefore, I resolved at an early age never to drink left-over beer.

His life consisted of whittling or drinking from early on in the day and coming home, but there was always someone who would buy him a beer. He was a source of entertainment in these taverns, for no one knew when he would get these cursing attacks. No one knew when he would explode. When he did, inside the tavern, he would walk round and round among the men pulling violently at his ears and cursing. The fun was that no one knew whom he was going to curse. In this small town it was usually someone everyone knew, and the men would hoot and holler, as my uncle went round and round screaming his insults. Soon, after a few minutes, he would come to and stare blankly for a while, gather his thoughts and sit down and mumble to himself. The men would laugh, and then my uncle would start laughing with them. Sometimes, when he had a fit in town, the children would run behind, taunting him.

Whether he remembered what he did or not I never knew. I never asked him. In fact, after he was through with his maniacal episodes, I would try to change the subject—talk of something else, something more cheerful. And it seemed as if he preferred it.

But he loved me most of all and that was my problem. He involved me, at a very early age, in things that I never should have been involved in. I can't believe to this day that my parents allowed me to walk the streets with him.

One day, drunk as usual, he took me by the hand, and we went to get the milk cow which he had tied across from the mayor's house. As we came by the house, I could feel a slight trembling starting in his hand. And suddenly, as if a demon had possessed him, he started cursing and running toward the mayor's house, towing me along with him. This time he jerked only at one ear at a time. His other hand was holding mine. I was barely touching the ground as he swung me around on his rampage. He started with the mayor and cursed him, and then he continued with the mayor's wife. I could see the poor lady, worried as she was and scared, peeping through a crack in the curtain, watching all this: a deranged man yanking at his ears holding a little boy by the hand and running, menacingly, toward her house.

It was embarrassing to have an uncle like this one around the family. Your friends needed to be very tolerant. My sister didn't like him too much. She could never invite anyone over.

One time a young man came uninvited to call on my sister, and, as he was walking to the front door, my uncle started having a fit inside the house and ran out, bursting through the front door, screaming, just as the man was coming up the stairs, and my uncle ran right through him and knocked him down. The man got up fast and started running away, but everywhere he tried to run it seemed he'd run into my zig-zagging uncle. He never came back to call on my sister. He was known to have said that he would never call on a girl who had heard so many curse words in her young life.

He didn't stay with us at night. I guess he realized the inconvenience it would have caused. He lived next door in a small house with no electricity, no heat and no water. Later on when he became sick and right before he died, my grandmother moved him into the dining room that we never used and set up a small cot for him. It was interesting, as I was told, that in his last days the doctor told him he couldn't drink anymore unless he wanted to die. So he quit drinking and died within the week. What he died of no one knew and no one cared. That was the beauty of life in a small town. People died and that was that. There was no need for heavy medical expenses or lengthy hospital stays or exotic diagnostics. If a person got sick and then got well, that was a cause for joy. If a person got sick and died, well, they buried the person and everyone kept on living. So when he died, he just died. Even the doctor was not particularly interested as to why a person had died. He was there to treat well people.

The mayor was not home when we were trampling his front yard, but his wife told him about it and, rightfully so, the mayor became very angry. He had already been angry before, since that was not the first time my uncle had gone on a rampage against him and his wife.

That night the mayor came over and talked to my grandmother, my mother and my father, and they had assured the mayor that they would scold my uncle. My uncle, in the meantime, was at the tavern begging for beer and getting drunk and forgetting to bring the cow home.

You see, my uncle had only one job to do. He was to take the cow to a pasture in the morning after milking her and then he was supposed to bring the cow back before sunset, milk her, and put her up for the night. He was able to do the morning part of the job well and with consistency, but bringing the cow back presented a problem to him. If he was in the middle of a fit, he would forget what time it was or whether he had already taken the cow home or, if he were drinking steadily, if someone was buying him beer, he didn't want to quit just to bring a cow home.

So frequently, as we did that night, my father and I went to look for the patiently waiting and confused cow to bring her home. I say we had to look for the cow because we never knew for sure where my uncle had tied her that morning. The tethering of the cow and it's location was left entirely up to him. If he found a lush grassy place by the cemetery, he would tie her there. The next day he would tie her somewhere else. Usually the cow was never at the same place on two successive days.

My father and I would go looking for the cow and I would hold the lantern as we walked the dusty streets and, when we thought we saw the huge bulk of the animal in the darkened field, he would take the lantern from me and raise it above his head to see if we had located the cow.

My father never got angry with my uncle. He would scold him lightly and in a very gentle way. My uncle would look at him with his large sorrowful eyes and would promise to do anything that my father wanted him to do. Then he would walk away, the halter rope in his hand, the cow walking slowly behind him. Sometimes he would start his fit at this time and let go of the cow and he would walk hurriedly away, tugging at his ears and cursing at the sky. The cow would stop, look at him stoically, as if she knew this was the cross she had been given to bear, and wait patiently for him to complete the fit.

He had another one of his fits while he was walking through downtown main street and this time everyone there heard him curse the mayor and his wife.

The sheriff's car came slowly by the house, went slightly past it and I could see from under the house the sheriff straining to see if he could spot my uncle. He stopped the car and backed up and parked in front. He got out. He was a formidable man, over six feet with a large belly, his gun belt hidden by the bulge in front. He carried a large long-barreled revolver and a pair of hand-cuffs were tucked under the belt at one side.

My girlfriend and I looked at each other. I suspected why he was here. You see, a week before, the doctor and the sheriff had come by the house and I overheard them telling my parents about what my uncle had done and that my uncle had to be placed in an insane asylum. My parents were law-abiding people and they agreed that, if that was what was best for my uncle, then that's the way it had to be. The sheriff said it was the legal and proper thing to do. He said that my uncle was a menace and a constant source of embarrassment to the community. Even the Sister's of Charity, the three nuns who were left behind after the parochial school closed, were demanding that something be done. The priest, of course, was in complete agreement. Since the school and the rectory and the church were across the street, they, the priest and the nuns, could hear my uncle shouting obscenities. The priest said he had condoned it for some time, but he figured it was time to do something now that the mayor and the sheriff and the doctor were in agreement. He hadn't wanted to be the first one to complain, being a priest and all. The solution, of course, was to get my uncle into an insane asylum in Galveston.

We could see the sheriff come up the dirt path, the path bordered by lime-covered rocks. He came up the stairs and walked above us onto the little porch and he knocked heavily. The whole house seemed to shake under his heavy fist.

We could hear the footsteps above us as my mother came to answer the door. "Coming, coming," my mother said.

"María," the sheriff said in his gruff voice. "I've come for Mercé. It's time. This is the day we agreed on."

"Come in, come in," my mother was saying to him.

To us eavesdroppers under the house, it seemed that everything that was said had some humor in it. My girlfriend placed her small dirty little hand over her mouth to cover up a giggle. I was smiling at the thought that no one knew we were there.

"Sit down," my mother said, "sit down." She had the habit of repeating everything when she was nervous.

"I don't have time to sit," the sheriff informed my mother. I could tell he was angry. "We need to get him out of town and put him up somewhere, like Galveston, where someone who knows about these things can help him."

"My husband and I agree," my mother replied. "We'll cooperate in whatever way we can."

"Well it's been a long time. I mean he's been hanging around town cursing at everybody for a long time. It's just come to a head recently, that's all. Maybe we should've done it sooner. It's just that we all treated it as a joke."

"He's always been harmless," my mother said. "He wouldn't hurt a fly."

My uncle and I often went hunting but we never killed anything. He carried the rifle and I walked by his side. Once in a while he would hold me up as I stopped to pick a burr out of my foot. He would wait patiently, much like the cow had done for him, as I balanced on one leg and dug out a goat-head from the sole of my foot. When we came upon a rabbit, I would whisper excitedly, "There's one. Can you see it? Can you see the rabbit?"

My uncle would look close at the little animal and act as if he were going to shoot it, then he would say, "We'd better save him. We'll kill him on the way back."

We could hear the sound of leather as the sheriff adjusted his gun belt. "Don't be too sure," he said. "He could be violent under certain circumstances."

"That's strange," my mother said. "I've never known anything, *anything*, that makes him violent, except being violent on himself. God only knows what voices he hears or what pain he gets, but he yanks at his ears like he's going to pull them off."

"Well, enough of this," the sheriff said, and we could hear him walk around our little house opening doors. "Where is he?"

"He's probably at the beer hall," my mother replied, "where he normally goes every day. Don't you think?"

"No, he's not there," the sheriff informed her. "I've looked everywhere except here."

"Well, I'll be," my surprised mother said. From under the house I could imagine her putting her fingers to her mouth like she always did when she felt surprised.

"You don't have any idea where he's at?" the sheriff asked.

"No," my mother replied. "But have you seen the cow? He may be close by."

"I didn't see the cow," the sheriff said. "But I wasn't looking for her either. Where was he supposed to take her?"

"I have no idea," my mother said, "but I think that lately he's been staying close to the mayor's house on that open pasture."

"And you're sure you haven't seen him?" he asked my mother again to make sure she wasn't lying.

"I'm sure," she answered and she was telling the truth.

We could see my grandmother coming across the yard. She lived next door. We could see her long black dress moving from side to side as she strode over to see what was going on.

"Are they here for Mercé?" she asked my mother as she stood outside.

My mother came to the window by where we were sitting and she talked to her. My grandmother was telling my mother where he was hiding. Of course, I knew where he was hiding all along. He was under an old rug in a corner of the toolshed behind my grandmother's house.

In the morning he had come to the window by where I slept and he had scratched on the screen and awakened me. Today was the day they would take him, he said. He didn't want to go. "You've got to," I said to him. "Where are you going to hide?"

"I'll hide," he said and he thought for a moment, as if he didn't know, "in the toolshed."

I felt sorry for him at that time. I wanted to cry. I didn't want them to take him away. And yet I knew that he needed help. Just think, I had told him, if you can come back normal how much better off you'll be. He still wanted to hide.

"And what if they find you?" I asked.

"They won't," he said. "What do you think?"

"If you think you can hide there forever, then give it a try," I said, although it scared me to think that I would have to lie about his whereabouts. What I didn't realize at the time, young as I was, was that they would find him very quickly and that there was no escaping the law.

Unknown to anyone, my uncle had panicked and fled the toolshed. The sheriff had already come outside and he was checking the yard. When he stood in front of the toolshed door, my grandmother and my mother screamed, "Don't hurt him! Don't harm him! Please don't hurt him! He's a very gentle man."

The sheriff kicked the door open and had his hand on his pistol ready to draw it out if he needed to. He disappeared into the toolshed and we could all hear the commotion inside. My mother was screaming, as was my grandmother, imploring the sheriff not to hurt my uncle. From the noise inside it appeared that my uncle had been discovered. The sheriff seemed to be tearing the place apart. Finally, the old rug came flying through the door and my grandmother and my mother both screamed. They thought it was my uncle flying through the air. My grandmother fainted and fell to the ground, like a rag doll. The sheriff kept crashing into things and I wondered how the place would look like after he got through. My mother ran inside the toolshed and my grandmother, who had gotten up and recovered, followed her, and my girlfriend and I could hear all three thrashing about and the greatest commotion I ever heard.

Then, suddenly, from behind me I picked up the faint smell of stale beer. It was my uncle's breath. He was under the house with us! He had escaped from the toolshed while the sheriff was inside our house.

I couldn't very well talk to him. My mouth was so dry and I was so scared, but the words finally came out and I asked him what he was doing. He didn't seem to know. He had the look that I had seen wounded rabbits have right before you step on their heads, as if they were pleading for help and knowing they can't have any. It was the sight of fear in his eyes, the feeling of being tracked down for the kill that haunts me still. What could I do? I was too little to do anything. He put his arms around me and we both fell to the ground and he started crying, sobbing. He didn't know what to do. He didn't want to go. My girlfriend started crying, too.

The sheriff had come out of the toolshed and he looked like he had been in a terrible fight. My mother and my grandmother tried to fend him off with ropes and tools and whatever they could find. You see, they thought that he had killed my uncle. They were chasing him down the yard when, as luck would have it, my uncle began his trembling and started one of his crazy fits. He hit his head on a floor joist and he started bleeding. And thus he came out from under the house, crawling sideways like a fast crab, bleeding from the head. He straightened out, grabbed his ears and began yanking and pulling them as he started his walk, shouting obscenities at the world. This time he included not only the mayor and the mayor's wife, but he also said some bad things about the priest and how the priest was fucking the nuns. And as if on order, the windows of the rectory closed as fast as possible.

Once he had shed the two women, the sheriff ran up from behind and tackled my crazed uncle. He caught my uncle completely by surprise, blind-sided him, and my poor uncle, in the middle of his cursing, gave out a loud grunt as the wind was knocked out of him. The sheriff quickly put my uncle's hands behind his back and handcuffed him. Still, my uncle persisted and yelled and screamed, and he rubbed first one ear and then the other into the ground until he caused them to bleed.

Once they realized that my uncle was alive, that the sheriff had not killed him, my mother and grandmother stopped beating on the man. And once they realized my uncle had been found and restrained, they ran over and tried to help the sheriff and my uncle to their feet.

My father arrived running. He had been at work. We could see that he was helping the sheriff get Mercé up and they had gone to the other side of the house to the water faucet. The sheriff cleaned himself up and my father, mother and grandmother cleaned up my uncle. He had quieted down now and was into the mumbling stage of his fit.

"Look at what you did to yourself," my mother said to my uncle. "You could really hurt yourself doing all this."

"He can't help it," my father told her.

"Well, he wasn't so hard to catch," the sheriff said.

"And yet I feel sorry for you," he told my uncle.

"Come, we'll help you get him to the car," my grandmother told the sheriff.

"I'd appreciate it," the sheriff replied.

"Now, Mercé," my mother lectured him, "be good in Galveston. You're going to Galveston, did you know that? Maybe somebody there can help you. And it's very pretty in Galveston, did you know that? They have a beach."

My uncle shook his head.

"Well, that's where you're going. Be good over there and behave. Try to control yourself and maybe you can come back soon."

When they helped the sheriff put my uncle in the back seat, he looked toward us under the house. I could see him plainly, but I could tell he was trying desperately to find me, so I came out a little ways to where the sun was shining under the house, and I could tell he saw me. He gave a terrible cry.

As the car drove away, my father kept yelling for the sheriff to stop, but the sheriff never heard him.

"What did you want?" my mother asked him, crying, as the car with my uncle disappeared from view. He replied that he wanted to find out what my uncle had done with the cow.

And my mother and grandmother cried some more. At first they cried every time they saw the cow. The poor cow could never figure out what there was about her that made them cry. She would look inquiringly from one side of herself to the other, as if looking for some clue.

My uncle came back a year later, uncured and ready to go. He did, though, carry a little card in a billfold my father bought him saying that he was not a menace to society.

Genaro González

Genaro González has had to steal hours from his busy career as a professor of Psychology at the University of Texas at Pan American to further his career as a creative writer. González, born in McAllen, Texas, in 1949, was a participant in the early Chicano literary movement as a student at Claremont College in California. One of his early stories, "Un hijo del sol," had the distinction of being included in a mainstream press's first anthology of Chicano literature in 1970: *The Chicano: From Caricature to Self-Portrait*, edited by Edward Simmen for New American Library. His subsequent stories appeared in such national magazines as *Nuestro*, *Denver Quarterly* and *The Americas Review*. As a scholar, González has been the recipient of National Endowment for the Humanities and Fulbright/Hayes fellowships. As a creative writer he has been the recipient of a National Endowment for the Arts Creative Writing Award (1990) and a Dobie Paisano Award from the Texas Institute of Letters (1990).

The success of Genaro González's first novel, *Rainbow's End* (1988), actually catapulted him back into an active creative writing career, a career that had languished somewhat all of those years that he had been studying psychology and working his way toward tenure as a professor. *Rainbow's End* was selected "Editor's choice" by *The Los Angeles Times* and received favorable reviews far and wide. *Rainbow's End* charts generations of a Rio Grande Valley family as its members gradually leave migrant farm work behind to become drug smugglers. The novel is enriched with the detail from the geographical and cultural environment of the Valley and a broad array of interesting characters. *Only Sons* (1991) is a collection of interconnected stories that develop the theme of the generational differences of characters who live along the Mexican-American border. As in the story, "Too Much His Father's Son," selected for this present anthology, the greatest and most troubling differences are about values that are held by fathers and sons. *Multicultural Review* concluded that González's stories "are fueled by genuinely felt emotion and a vision broader than any border, without barriers. *Only Sons* belongs on that shelf of good books about modern family relationships."

Too Much His Father's Son

In the middle of the argument, without warning, Arturo's mother confronted her husband point-blank: "Is it another woman?"

"For heaven's sake, Carmela, not in front of—"

"Nine is old enough to know. You owe both of us that much."

Sitting in the room, Arturo could not help but overhear. Usually he could dissimulate with little effort—being a constant chaperone on his cousin Anita's dates had made him a master at fading into the background. But at that moment he was struggling hard to control a discomfort even more trying than those his cousin and her boyfriends put him through.

The argument had already lasted an hour and, emotionally, his mother had carried its brunt. Trying to keep her voice in check was taking more out of her than if she had simply vented her tension.

His father, though, lay fully clothed in bed, shirt half-buttoned and hands locked under his head. From his closed eyes and placid breathing, one would have thought that her frustration was simply lulling him into a more profound relaxation. Only an occasional gleam from those perfect, white teeth told Arturo he was still listening, and even then with bemused detachment.

"Is it another woman, Raúl?"

His father batted open his eyes only to look away, as though the accusation did not even merit the dignity of a defense. His gaze caught Arturo and tried to lock him into the masculine intimacy they often shared, an unspoken complicity between father and son. But at that instant it simply aggravated Arturo's shame.

"Who is she, Raúl?"

His smile made it clear that if there were another woman, he was not saying. "You tell me. You're the one who made her up."

Arturo had seen that smile in all its shadings—sometimes with disarming candor, but more often full of arrogance. When his father wished, his smile could become a gift of pearls, invigorating all who saw his teeth shining with their special luster.

Yet at other times his father needed only to curl his lips, and those same teeth turned into a sadistic show of strength. Well aware of his power over others, the father seemed indifferent as to whether the end effect exalted or belittled.

Out of nowhere, perhaps to add to the confusion, he ordered, "Bring *abuelo*'s belt, Arturo."

Instead of strapping it on, he pretended to admire what had once been his own father's gun belt. The holster was gone, but a bullet that had remained rusted inside a middle clasp added a certain authority. The hand-tooled leather, a rich dark brown, had delicate etchings now too smooth to decipher. His grandfather Edelmiro had been a large, mean-looking man in life, and Arturo still remembered the day his father received the belt. He had strapped it on for only a moment, over his own belt. Later that day Arturo opened the closet for a closer inspection and had come upon his father, piercing another notch for his smaller waist.

His mother continued to confront his father, who idly looped the belt, grabbed it at opposite ends and began whipping it with a solemn force. At first the rhythmic slaps disconcerted her, until she turned their tension into punctuations for her own argument. Suddenly the belt cracked so violently that Arturo thought the ancient cartridge had fired. He was startled, as much from the noise as from the discovery that his father's legendary control had snapped. For an instant both parents, suddenly realizing how far things had gone, appeared paralyzed.

No, his father would never strike her, he was sure of that. But nobody had ever pushed him that far, least of all his mother, whose own strength had always been her patience.

He wondered why his eyes were suddenly brimming. Perhaps trespassing into the unknown terrified him, or perhaps he was ashamed of his father's indifference. That confusion—crying without knowing why—frightened him even more.

"See, Carmela? Now you've got the boy blubbering."

He was hoping to hide his weakness from his father, and the unmasking only added to the disgrace. Desperate to save face, he yelled, "I'm leaving!"

As always his father turned the threat in his favor. "That's good, son. Wait outside and let me handle this."

"I'm going to *papá grande*'s house!"

Arturo had never been that close to his mother's family, and that made his decision all the more surprising. But if his father felt betrayed he did not show it. "Fine, then. You're on your own."

It took him a while to catch his father's sarcasm and his own unthinking blunder: he did not know the way to his grandparents' house. He had walked there only once—last Sunday—and that time his mother had disoriented him with a different route from the one his father took.

But now, standing there facing his father, he had no choice. Rushing out the kitchen door, he ran across the back yard, expecting at any moment to be stopped in his tracks. When his arms brushed against a clothesline, he almost tripped as if his father had lassoed him with his belt. Not until he reached the alley did he realize he had been hoping his father would indeed stop him, even with a word.

He crossed the alley into an abandoned lot. There he matted a patch of grass and weeds reaching his waist and settled in, so as to give his heart time to hush. He sat for a long time, wondering whether to gather his thoughts or let them scramble until nothing mattered.

From Doña Chole's house came the blare of a Mexican radio station. Two announcers were sandwiching every song with a frenzied assault. Farther away David's father continued working on his pet project—a coop and flypen for his game cocks: four or five swift whacks into wood . . . silence . . . then another volley. For a while he lost himself in the hammering. If he listened closer he could hear the cursing and singing that gave the neighborhood life. Only his own home remained absolutely still.

Soon the sun began to get in his eyes whenever he looked homeward. A cool breeze was blowing at his back, and as he waited in the weeds a sun-toasted aroma penetrated his corduroy shirt.

Someone was coming up the path, making soft lashing sounds in the weeds. His intuition told him that the person was Fela the *curandera* and when he finally dared peek he immediately dove back into his hiding place, wondering whether to congratulate or curse himself.

A part of him scrambled for a rational explanation: who else could it be? Fela the healer was the only grown-up unconcerned about snakes in the undergrowth. In her daily forages for herbs she was used to cutting swaths through the weeds. Yet another side of him was forced to side with the barrio lore—that she had special powers, that she appeared and disappeared at will, that she could think your thoughts before they occurred to you.

The brushing got closer, so he lay very still, trying to imitate his father's self-discipline. When the rustling suddenly stopped, he swore the waft of his corduroy shirt had given him away.

A voice called out: "Since when do little boys live in the wild?"

His heart began beating wildly, but her tone carried enough teasing that he half-raised his head.

"You're hiding from someone?"

All at once, he had a clear image of his father sprawled across the bed, amused, almost bored. Arturo answered her question with a nod, afraid that if he spoke, his rage might leap out and injure them both.

"You did something bad?"

He managed a hoarse, determined vow: "I'm going to smash my father's teeth."

He expected the violence in his words to stun her, but instead she disarmed him with a kind smile. "Whatever for? He has such nice teeth. Some day yours will look just like his."

For a moment, in place of the familiar habit of his own body, he experienced an undefined numbness, followed by the fascinated terror of someone who has inherited a gleaming crown with awesome responsibilities. He stood speechless, repulsed yet tempted by the thought of turning into his father.

"Anyway," she added, "before you know it he'll be old and toothless like me."

She picked a row of burrs clinging to her faded dress, then said as she left, "And tell your mother she's in my thoughts and prayers." Watching her walk away, he tried without success to retrace the route he and his mother had taken to her father's house at the time of their secret visit last Sunday.

That Sunday morning, while his mother talked to Fela in the living room, he had sat on a wicker chair on Fela's porch, entertained by Cuco, an ancient caged parrot with colorful semi-circles under his eyes. Arturo was feeding him chile from a nearby plant to make him talk. "Say it," he urged between bribes: "*Chinga tu madre*." But the chile only agitated Cuco's whistling.

"Come on, you stupid bird. *Chinga tu madre*. Screw your mother."

Suddenly there was a raucous squawk. "Screw your *padre* instead!"

As he wheeled about and felt the blood rush to his face, Fela was already raising her arms in innocence. "Who says he's stupid? That's an exotic, bilingual bird you're talking to."

From there, he and his mother had gone to his grandparents' house. Her route through alleys and unfenced back yards led him to ask, "How do you know all these shortcuts?"

She had paused to dry her forehead on her sleeve, and for the first time in days he had seen her smile. "I grew up in this barrio. This is where I used to play."

Trying to imagine her at the same age he now was, he had to smile to himself.

When they got to his grandfather's house, they had to wait until his grandfather Marcelo finished his *radionovela*. Then, after hearing where they had been and why, his grandfather shook his head. "I knew your marriage would come to this. But going to Fela was a mistake. If he finds out he'll claim you're trying to win him back through witchcraft."

"I had to know if he's seeing another woman."

"And what if he is?"

Arturo had never seen her as serene and as serious as when she answered, "Then he's not worth winning back."

"But a *curandera* . . . Why not see a priest?"

Arturo's grandmother took her side. "What for, Marcelo? He'd only give her your advice: accept him as your cross in life."

"I wouldn't in this case. An unfaithful husband is one thing, an arrogant s.o.b. is another. Still, a priest could say a few prayers in your behalf."

"Fela offered to do that herself."

"And no doubt offered good advice," his grandmother added.

His mother's fist clenched his own. "Yes," she said, and her firmness made it obvious that was the last word.

His grandfather, deep in thought, held his breath without taking his eyes off him. Then he closed them and exhaled a stale rush of cigarette smoke, as if unclouding his thoughts. "I've always said your father was a *cabrón*."

"Now, Marcelo. Don't turn him against his own father," his grandmother interjected.

"Mamá's right. None of this is Arturo's fault. He's going through enough as it is."

"True. But I still wouldn't give a kilo of crap for the whole de la O family, starting with Edelmiro."

"May he rest in peace," said his grandmother.

His grandfather stood up. "Not if there's a devil down below."

"Marcelo! He was your *compadre*."

"I had as much choice in the matter as the boy had in being his grandson." He turned to Arturo's mother. "Remember, if there's a falling out, don't ask that family for anything. Your place is here."

His grandmother added, "And of course that includes Arturo. He's as much a part of the family as the rest of us."

His grandfather had simply said, "Let's hope he's not too much his father's son."

By now the late afternoon sun was slanting long, slender shadows his way, but he was determined to spend the night there if need be. He began counting in cycles of hundreds to keep his uncertainty in check.

Suddenly the rear screen door opened and his father leaned against it, his belt slung over his chest and shoulder like a bandoliered and battle-weary warrior.

"Arturo, come inside." Whenever he wanted to conceal something from the neighbors, he used that phrase.

Arturo slowly stood up but held his ground, as much from stubbornness as dread.

"It's all right, son." His father sounded final yet forgiving, like a king who had put down a castle uprising, regained control and had decided to pardon the traitors.

Arturo blinked but once, but his pounding heart made even something that small seem a life-and-death concession.

Then his mother appeared alongside his father, and for an instant, framed by the doorway, their pose reminded him of their newlywed portrait in the living room: his hands at his sides, her own clasped in front, both heads slightly tilted as if about to rest on each other's shoulder. In that eye blink of an interval before she stepped outside, he felt like an outsider looking in.

She was halfway between him and the house when his father said, "Your mother's bringing you back."

He could not believe her betrayal. After all that, she had surrendered and was bringing him in as well. He wanted to cry out at her for having put him through so much. But another part of him understood he shared the blame, for not helping her, for being too much his father's son.

"I forgot the way," he said. Although she was quite close he could not tell whether she heard—much less accepted—his timid apology. He managed his first step homeward when she blocked his path, gently took his hand and guided him in the opposite direction.

He heard, or perhaps only imagined, his father: "Come back." He tugged her arm in case she had not heard. She tightened her grasp to show that she had. Then, intuiting his dilemma, she paused, saying nothing but still gazing away from the house. He realized then and there that the decision was for him alone to make. Hers had already been made.

Unable to walk back or away, he felt like the only living thing in the open. Then his father called out, "Son," and he knew it was his last call. His spine shivered as though a weapon had been sighted at his back, and he imagined his father removing from his belt the cartridge reserved for the family traitor.

There was no way of telling how long he braced himself for whatever was coming, until he finally realized that the moment of reckoning was already behind him. It was then that he felt his father's defeat in his own blood. With it came the glorious fear of a fugitive burning his bridges into the unknown, or a believer orphaned from a false faith. And in that all-or-nothing instant that took so little doing and needed even less understanding, his all-powerful father evaporated into the myth he had always been.

He felt a flesh-and-blood grasp that both offered and drew strength. He began to walk away, knowing there was no turning back.

Rolando Hinojosa

Rolando Hinojosa is the most prolific and bilingual of the Hispanic novelists of the United States. Not only has he created memorable Mexican-American and Anglo characters, but he has completely populated a fictional county in the Lower Rio Grande Valley of Texas through his continuing generational narrative that he calls the "Klail City Death Trip Series."

Hinojosa was born in Mercedes, Texas, on January 21, 1929, to a Mexican American father and a bilingual Anglo-American mother. Hinojosa was educated at first in Mexican schools in Mercedes and later in the segregated public schools of the area where all of his classmates were Mexican Americans. He only began integrated classes in junior high. It was in high school that Hinojosa began to write, with his first pieces in English published in an annual literary magazine, *Creative Bits*. Hinojosa left the Valley in 1946 when he graduated from college, but the language, culture and history of the area form the substance of all of Hinojosa's novels.

Although he continued writing throughout his life, Rolando Hinojosa did not publish a book until 1973, his *Estampas del Valle y otras obras* (which he recreated in English and published as *The Valley* in 1983), winner of the national award for Chicano literature, Premio Quinto Sol. From that time on, he has become the most prolific Chicano novelist, publishing one novel after another in his generational narrative that centers around the lives of two of his alter egos, Rafa Buenrostro and Jehú Malacara, in individual installments that vary in form from poetry and dialogue to the picaresque novel and the detective novel. His titles in English alone include *Korean Love Songs* (1980), *Rites and Witnesses* (1982), *Dear Rafe* (1985), *Partners in Crime: A Rafe Buenrostro Mystery* (1985), *Claros varones de Belken / Fair Gentlemen of Belken County* (1986, bilingual edition), *Klail City* (1987) and *Becky and Her Friends* (1989). His original Spanish version of *Klail City*, entitled *Klail City y sus alrededores* (1976), won the international award for fiction, Premio Casa de las Américas, from Cuba in 1976.

Hinojosa has been hailed as a master satirist, an acute observer of the human comedy, a Chicano William Faulkner for his creation of the history and people of Belken County, a faithful recorder of the customs and dialects in Spanish and English of both Anglos and Mexicans in the Lower Rio Grande Valley. "Coming Home I" and "Coming Home V" have been excerpted from *Klail City*.

Coming Home I

It should come as no surprise that Belken County's largest, best known, and certainly most profitable whorehouse is to be found in Flora. Flora people have convinced themselves that they invented sliced bread; this goes for Texas Mexicans and Texas Anglos alike. For their part, the Flora Mexicans have also come to think of themselves as an integral part of the Flora economic establishment. No such thing, of course; at best, they've stopped resisting, have become acculturated, and, delusion of delusions, have assimilated. All this up to a point, of course, but still, they're an energetic folk and hell to deal and live with.

Flora is also the newest of the Valley towns; sprang up during that war the Anglos had between themselves in the 1860's; truth to tell, though, Texas Mexicans fought on both sides of that one. So, Flora was born yesterday and thus not as old as Relámpago or Jonesville or Klail; Klail City's real name is Llano Grande, the name of the grant. (General Rufus T. Klail came down here, took over the name, and then thought he'd swept away the traditions with the change. And so it goes . . .)

Anyway, the Texas Anglo and Texas Mexican citizenry of Flora are identical in many ways: noisy, trust God and give Him credit on Sundays, and believe in cash on the barrelhead from sunup to sundown. They also believe in other important things: leap years, for one. To their credit, Flora is unlike the other Valley towns in other respects and thus so are the Mexicanos who live and die there.

As for whorehouses, this is a lamentably recognized universality, but the Flora-ites claim it as a native invention. Just like that: judgment without explanation. To compensate, perhaps, the town of Flora also boasts of more churches per capita than any other Valley town. See? Admittedly, there is a cure for hiccups (water, air, a good scare); for polio (Drs. Salk and Sabin); but there's nothing you can do about stupidity. Takes more than a pill or a shot for that one. But the Flora-ites don't know this, and if they do, they choose to ignore it. Secure, then, in their ways.

Don Manuel Guzmán, Klail's lone Mexicano cop, was rolling himself a flake tobacco cigarette as he sat with some of the *viejitos*—the old men; men his age, then. He'd risen from the sidewalk bench, walked to the curb to stand under the corner lamplight. He spit-sealed his roll, lit it, and looked at his pocket watch: ten after twelve; a warm, foggy, December night, when out of the fog and walking straight at him, there came a woman, gun in hand.

Why, it was Julie, a young black whore from Flora. "Mist Manyul . . . c'n I talk to you?" And then: "Mist Manyul, I done shot Sonny . . . shot 'n killed him, Mist Manyul."

Don Manuel nodded, listened some more, and handed her his cigarette. She stared at it as if she'd never seen one before in her life. Don Manuel opened the front car door, and she slipped in and waited for him as he walked over to see the *viejitos* (Leal, Echevarría, and Genaro Castañeda), those old, well-known friends of the former revolutionary.

"What is it? You leaving now?"

"Got to." Pointing with his chin: "I'll see you here in about an hour or so; and if not here, I'll just drive on to Dirty Luke's."

"What'd she do?"

"She says she shot her husband . . . at María Lara's house . . . in Flora."

"She works there, does she?"

"Aha . . . but she lives here, in Klail. I got them a room at the Flats."

"Hmmm. What happened out in Flora this time?"

"You think the pimp held out on her?"

Don Manuel, slowly. "It's possible; I didn't ask her much, and it's probably best to leave her alone for a while."

"I think you're right there, don Manuel."

Old man Leal: "*I* know who she is. Her man works for Missouri Pacific; a switchman, right? Sonny . . . yeah, he plays semi-pro ball for the Flora White Sox . . . Yeah."

Echevarría: "Now don't tell me he didn't know about his wife workin' over to Flora?"

Don Manuel: "Oh, he knew all right. They've been married five-six years, I'd say."

Castañeda: "Married." Bland.

Leal: "Do black folks marry? Really?" Curious.

Echevarría: "Yeah, I think they do, once in a while." Not sure.

Castañeda: "Man was probably drinking." Abruptly.

Leal: "Why not?" A hunch of the shoulders.

Echevarría: "Yeah, why not?" Resignation.

Castañeda: "Did, ah, did Sonny pull a knife on her?"

Don Manuel: "Yes; that's what she says."

Leal: "How'd she get over *here* from Flora, anyway?" Admiration.

Don Manuel: "Took a bus, she says."

Echevarría: "A bus? There's a lot-a guts in them ovaries, yes *sir*."

Don Manuel: "I'm taking her to jail; I'll go ahead and drive her on over to Flora tomorrow sometime. She killed her man and they're probably looking for her about now. I think it's best she be alone for a while; cry herself to sleep, think about what she's done; sort things out, you know. But, she needs to be left alone for now; she'll have enough to do tomorrow with that Flora crowd, poor thing ... Look, I'll see you all here or over to Dirty's."

With this, don Manuel got into his car—his, not the city's which didn't provide him with one, anyway—and then drove Julie Wilson to the Klail City workhouse.

"We goin' to jail, Mist Manyul?"

"Yes."

"I din mean to do it, Mist Manyul. I din mean to kill Son ... you know that, Mist Manyul? But I kill him. ... Oh, I shot that man. ... I say, Son, don't you do it ... I say, you back off now, you hear? But he din back off none. ... He din 'n I shot him ... got him in the chest I did 'n he plop down on the bed there. ... I kill Son, Mist Manyul, an' you know that no one come to the room when I shot him? ... Oh, I shot him and killed him, Mist Manyul. ... He was drunk ... all out drunk Sonny was and then Ijustupandshothim. ... You taking me to Flora jail, Mist Manyul?"

"Takin' you to Klail City jail, Julie."

"Oh, thank you, Mist Manyul. I don't want to go to no Flora jail tonight, no I don'. ... You takin' me there tomorrow? That it, Mist Manyul?"

"Yes ... tomorrow ... one of my sons will bring you hot coffee tomorrow morning and then I'll take you to Flora."

"Thank you, Mist Manyul. ... I won't cry no more ... I up 'n shot that man and he dead and he deserve it ... he say he gonna cut me an' I say you back off, Sonny, back off ... don' come over to here, Sonny, but he did and then I did ... Mist Manyul, can I go to the bathroom now?"

"There's a bowl in the room."

"Oh, thank you, Mist Manyul."

Don Manuel Guzmán drove out to the corner of Hidalgo Street and, since his old friends weren't anywhere to be seen, he did a U-turn in the middle of the deserted main street and headed for Dirty Luke's. Beer time was over and now it was time for the coffee crowd to take over. The *viejitos*'d be there, waiting for him, and then he'd take them home, as always.

Tomorrow, early, *mañana muy de mañana*, after bringing Julie a pot of coffee, he'd drive her to Flora; first though, he'd stop at María Lara's place and get some firsthand news.

He and María Lara had known each other for over forty years, and although there'd been an arrangement between them when both were in their twenties and healthy and vibrant and ready-to-go, their long friendship and a shared place of provenance (the Buenrostro family's Campacuás Ranch) was what kept them in close contact. He thought of the old ranch house and its Texas Ranger-burned-down-to-its-ashes church … The ashes were still there, fifty years later. The man shook his head slightly.

But now, headed for Dirty Luke's, he parked any old way and walked into the place; he sat and waited for Rafe Buenrostro to bring him his cup of coffee.

"Boy, turn the volume down; you're going to have the neighbors down on you."

"Yessir."

Coffee over, don Manuel says: "Going back to Hidalgo and First; when y'all get ready to go home, let me know."

The oldsters thank him, as always, and don Manuel leaves the car in front of Dirty's; he's going for a walk, and he'll eventually wind up on Hidalgo Street in Klail City; a town like any other in Belken County in Texas's Lower Rio Grande Valley.

Coming Home V

Don Orfalindo Buitureyra is a quadrilateral lump of Valley loam and shit. Buitureyra is also a pharmacist, thanks to some pretty lax laws in the Lone Star State; there are other weaknesses in Orfalindo Buitureyra's arsenal: he's a sentimentalist and so much so that he goes on three-four day drunks (we call 'em *parrandas serias*), and then, later on, he wonders where those King Kong-sized hangovers come from; as said, forgetful, as most sentimentalists.

Anyway, the man will break out two or three times a year and here's the pattern: he'll drink alone for a while, and then he'll drink with some friends, and *then* comes the dancing (a solo effort) and then la pièce de résistance: He sings.

"I like to," he says. To tell the truth, he's so-so in that department.

On the other hand, there's no oratory, no public crying, declamations, patriotic speeches, etc. "That's for queers; get me?"

Sure, sure, don Orfalindo; no need to come to blows over a little thing like that, is there?

"Good! Just so's we understand each other. Know what I mean? Now, where was I?"

Singing.

"Right! Almost forgot . . . "

And he does. Actually, what he does is to sing along with the Wurlitzer. The following is tacit: if an Andalusian *pasodoble* breaks out, the floor belongs to don Orfalindo. The reader probably thinks people stop and stare; the reader is *wrong*. And no, it isn't that the drinkers are bored stiffer than the Pope; not at all. It's more like this: live and let live. Man wants to dance? Let him. Man wants to dance alone? Who's he bothering? Right!

To put it as plainly as possible: People simply leave him alone.

"They'd better; what if he poisons them, right?"

Jesus! I'd forgotten about that . . .

"Tscha! I'm just talking."

Don Orfalindo Buitureyra, it so happens, is a cuckold. A *cabrón*, a capricorn, antlered. You with me? This makes him the lump he is. And, he's a nice old guy, too. None of this is incompatible, and why should it be? A bit of a fool, like all of us, then, *but* he *is* a cuckold; in his case, a cuckold Made in Texas by Texas Mexicans.

"And the kids?"

"Oh, they're his, all right."

"Damn right they are: they got his nose, all-a them."

"And that lantern jaw, too; even that girl a-his has it."

"Hmmm; but he's a *cabrón*, and that stain won't go away."

"We—ell now, that's something that don't rub off with gasoline. Goes deeper than that, you see."

This is all talk. Don Orfalindo is, *a la italiana, cornutto*, but not *contento*. If anything, he's resigned to it. A bit of Islamic resignation that.

"Look, his kids like him and love 'im. Isn't that enough?"

"Yeah, what the hell. Tell me this: just how long is that wife a-his gonna remain good looking? There's no guarantee of longevity, you know."

"Well, nothing lasts one hundred years, not even a man's faith, let alone his wife. Truth to tell, though, he'll wear those horns to his grave."

"How long she been running around now? Five? Six years? Give her two, three more; tops."

"Well, Echevarría, you ought to go into counseling and fortune-telling, ha!"

"Tscha! A matter of time is all. Look at him: dancing that *Silverio Pérez pasodoble* . . . Who's he bothering?"

"Well now, if it comes to bothering, you're right: he's not bothering anybody, but look out in the sidewalk there: there's some youngster watching him."

"So? Those aren't his kids; his are all grown up."

A newcomer said that; and he really doesn't belong in that table with the *viejitos*: "Out with it, then . . . who's his wife fooling around with?"

This is a breach; the inquisitor should know better.

The Wurlitzer blinked once or twice and then some *norteño* music came on: don Orfalindo went to the bar.

Not a peep at the table. Don Orfalindo's at the bar and orders another Miller Hi-Life. The men at the table look away, and the inquisitor excuses himself; to the john, he says.

Don Orfalindo takes a swig from the Miller's and then, without fail, he caps the bottle with his thumb. Conserves the carbonation, he says.

The *viejitos* at the table wave; he waves back. They're all friends; good men, really. The man who went to the john is still out there. It's hoped he doesn't ask many more questions. What would be the use?

First of all, being a cuckold isn't a profession; it's hard, cruel, but then it can happen to anybody: Napoleon, the President of the United States, one's best friend. No telling. There's don Orfalindo, for ex. Except for the oldsters at the table, few know and less remember *the reason* for don O.'s binges. As my neighbor says: "Who cares?"

"Don Manuel Guzmán ought to be dropping in pretty soon."

"Right as rain. Rafe! Rafe, boy, better heat up that coffee; don Manuel ought to be coming in any minute now."

"Yessir."

Don O. pulls away from the bar; on his way to the john. But here comes the Grand Inquisitor; they almost run into each other.

At the table, Esteban Echevarría, Luis Leal, don Matías Uribe, and Dirty Luke, the owner of the place, throw a glance at the pair. The four men, the *viejitos*, shake their heads; the inquisitor shouldn't even be at this table, he's forty years old and out place with these men. He invited himself, then. Worse, it's don Manuel's chair.

Enter don Manuel. "Son, cut the volume, you're going to get the neighbors down on you."

Don Orfalindo is back at the bar, bottle in hand, thumb in cap. He spots don Manuel at the table.

"Begging your pardon, don Manuel, but I've been drinking."

"You want me to take you home, don Orfalindo?"

"Well, no; ah . . . not this minute. I just started this morning."

"Well, you take care now."

"Yessir; I'm going back to the bar now."

There'll be no dancing by don Orfalindo as long as don Manuel is in there. (A note of respect acc. to don O.) For his part, don Manuel sips at his coffee and, as he finishes, says to the others: "My car's out front; let me know when you're ready to go." He rises and walks out the front door.

The inquisitor is back, too, but the chair is no longer there.

As don Manuel walks out, don Orfalindo hits the floor: *Besos Brujos* (*letra de* R. Schiammarella; *con música de* Alfredo Malerba). Libertad or Amanda sings out: "Déjame, no quiero que me beses . . . "

Un tango, tangazo! Eyes closed, don Orfalindo Buitureyra glides away. Years, miles, and more years: it's that woman again: young, hardbodied, once married to a former military surgeon from Agualeguas, Nuevo León; the surgeon died as a result of a prescription handed him by the apprentice pharmacist Orfalindo Buitureyra years and years ago . . .

Besos Brujos; bewitched kisses, in English, doesn't cut it. Another long glide by the man and *then* a sudden severe cut to the right! *Bailando con corte*! Eyes closed, harder now. A smile? Is it? Yes!

The eyes remain closed. Yes; he smiles again, and one could almost say, almost say, that don Orfalindo Buitureyra is contented enough to be happy. And alive, and older, too.

But above all, happy; *y eso es lo que cuenta*. And that's what counts.

Max Martínez

Max Martínez's career as a writer spans the full course of the development of contemporary Chicano literature. In the late 1960's he became active in the Chicano literary movement in San Antonio. By the early 1970's, he began publishing his stories in the short lived *El magazín* and the seminal pulp literary magazine, *Caracol*. Having lived the life of a sailor, a stockbroker and freelance writer, Martínez attempted to settle down into a more stable intellectual environment by studying for his Ph.D. in English at the University of Denver and pursuing a career as a college professor at the University of Houston. But it turned out that neither was for him: he never wrote the dissertation and he abandoned the tenure track by the mid-1980's to continue to dedicate himself to serious writing.

Aside from numerous stories published in a variety of literary magazines—as well as hundreds of "man on the scene" commentary and thought pieces that he writes for a trade journal—the fruits of Martínez's labors have been three very different books. The first is a collection of his early short stories, *The Adventures of the Chicano Kid and Other Stories* (1983), in which he experiments with a variety of styles while depicting the various types of Chicano lives: a farmworker, a middle class suburban businessman (today what would be called a yuppy), an educated self-confident modern Chicano in a face-off with traditional rural prejudice in the person of a Texas "redneck," an old man snoozing on a park bench and recollecting how things have changed, and others. The title story is a satire of nineteenth-century dime novels. "Faustino," included in this present anthology, is an outrageously inventive tale that portrays the various levels of oppression in a rural, stratified setting, very similar to Martínez's own place of rearing in the central Texas farm country.

Martínez's novel, *Schoolland* (1988), chronicles a single, critical year in the coming of age of the child narrator in the Texas farm town of Schoolland during the 1953 drought, the same year that his role-model grandfather dies. And, Martínez's latest book, *Red Bikini Dream* (1990), is another collection of lives as recreated in the short story genre, Martínez's forte. Here the lifehistories and angst of a variety of Chicano and non-Chicano characters are deftly drawn, again giving us glimpses of Martínez's own life as a struggling writer in New York, as a sailor, as a child growing up in a fatherless home. *The Review of Contemporary Fiction* concluded that the stories in *Red Bikini Dream* "offer a disturbing glimpse of the complex relationship between self and culture that underlies modern life," while *The Bloomsbury Review* stated that Martínez "knows how to twist a wicked smile out of his characters, while making marvelous statements on who we are and where we are headed."

Faustino

I

The truck clang-banged over the bumpy dusty road which half-circled the house. Faustino held on to the wheel, partly to steer, partly so he would not bounce out of the cab. He maneuvered the truck recklessly but expertly around the house, coming to a noisy, clattering, dust-filled stop beside the withered, unpainted toolshed.

His face was a blurred image through the film of dust and splattered bugs on the windshield. Faustino was smiling, almost laughing, exhilarated by the ride. His smile revealed a set of even, white teeth offset by the dark sunburned brown of his face. He raced the engine a few times feeling the cab sway back and forth. He hooped and hollered and yelled as though he had just declared his independence. The sound of the popping mufflers, like distant gunfire, made Faustino shudder with glee. He felt good.

He switched off the ignition, feeling his body continue to quiver and shake as the motor sputtered rebelliously and was finally stilled, emitting a vicious reptilian hiss from its bowels beneath the rusting hood.

Faustino did not step down from the truck immediately. He slouched a bit and reached inside the breast pocket of his denim jacket for the crumbled blue bag of Bugler cigarette tobacco. After smoothing the half-empty bag, he opened it, buried his thumb and forefinger in the contents, pinching enough of the stringy brown tobacco to roll a cigarette. He smoothed a crumpled cigarette paper, cupped it in his hand lengthwise to accept the tobacco. Satisfied that the paper was in proper position, Faustino began to cautiously sprinkle the pinch of brown strands, bending his head, his tongue draped over his lower lip, oblivious to all else, intent upon rolling a perfectly round smoke.

Faustino was very proud of the way he rolled his smokes. He manipulated the paper and the tobacco so that he spilled only a few errant strands, rolling it continuously, twisting it, squeezing it, smoothing the lumps, inspecting it all the while, until the degree of roundness and firmness was achieved.

The cigarette finished, he looked at it one last time before he gingerly licked the glue-coated flap of the paper. He wet his tongue-tip, slid it out of his mouth, touched it to a corner and smoothly ran it along the glue. That finished, he twirled it between his forefinger and thumb, proud of his workmanship. Satisfied, he twisted one end to contain any loose tobacco and stuck the other end between his dark maroon lips.

Faustino relaxed, leaned back on the cracked, imitation leather seat, allowing the cigarette to dangle from a corner of his mouth. He searched for a match, first in the jacket, then in his jeans, brushing some tobacco strands from his lap as he did so. He found a match, raised a thigh, touched the head of the match to the canvas material of the jeans, and slid it forward in a swift, violent motion. The match did not ignite the first time he did so. He repeated the arched motion several times until it caught fire.

The match-tip flared into a yellow flower, then subsided to a steady flame, producing a sulfurous stench inside the cab of the truck. He touched the flame to the twisted end of the cigarette, inhaling deeply, drawing the smoke into his lungs with a long, laborious gesture.

The exhalation through his nostrils was abrupt, fierce, almost as if he expelled a noxious gas. Positioning the cigarette comfortably in the corner of his mouth, he was ready to step down from the truck. Through the dim haze of the windshield, Faustino could be seen with the smoke swirling around his head.

So intent had been Faustino on the ritual of rolling his cigarette that he had not looked to the back yard of Buster's house, in front of which he was parked. As he grabbed the door handle, he chanced to peer through the dusty windshield toward the ranch house. Mrs. Crane, Buster's wife, was in the back yard, hanging the contents of an aluminum washtub on the taut wires of the clothesline. Faustino had seen her before often enough, had noticed her, had been aware of her presence, but never without Buster at her side or within range of her. Now Faustino noticed her as something other than a faceless, shapeless, voiceless extension of her husband. Mrs. Crane appeared different to him now.

Faustino thought better of stepping down just yet. He released the door handle and settled back on the seat to enjoy his smoke. He continued to observe the woman under the clothesline facing away from him. Her actions were monotonous, single-minded, repetitive. Stooping to the tub, straightening to the line, shaking the article of clothing, pinning it to the wire. Then again and another, then again and another. As she stooped, on the downward motion, her long brown hair fell along the sides of her face, shielding the narrow profile she gave him. As she did so, the hair fell in a long, graceful swing, almost touching the rim of the tub. Then, suddenly, the hair would erupt, shudder out of its stillness, and became wild in the wind as her head jerked upward and Mrs. Crane stood erect. Once again, the hair glided softly around her neck and shoulders, smooth, flowing, finally becoming feathery still in the sun.

Faustino only briefly noticed the woman's hair. Of more interest was the outline of her buttocks under the thin housecoat she wore. When she bent over, the housecoat draped itself snugly over her back, ballooning in front. It expanded, flowed and flushed itself over and around the buttocks like a multicolored waterfall. The housecoat slid between the flesh of her buttocks as they parted, then the material was sucked in as she stood up, imprisoned, the swallowed part becoming a thin, jagged, puckered line. It would burst forth and become instantly smooth when she lifted her arms to the clothesline.

Faustino did not know her first name. Mrs. Crane was all the address required of him should he ever have occasion to talk to her. Although he did not know her first name, Faustino was not at a loss, thinking to himself, the sound of his words exploding in his head, *¡ay, mamacita, güerita, empínate más!*

Buster Crane and she had been married for a year. Rumor among the hands had it that she came from San Antonio, but Faustino would have no business asking about such a rumor. The affairs of his employer and of whites in general were not the concern of Faustino and the other Chicano ranch hands.

¡Qué nalgas, güera! Muévete un poquito más para ver mejor, que no se hace nada. ¡Mamá, mamá, me meo!

From the talk in the fields and the few times he had seen her, he calculated she was at least ten years younger than Buster. That Buster looked so much older than she would be enough to start rumors. Now, as Faustino noticed her, as if for the first time, she did look young to him, pretty in a *gringa* sort of way, but not too pretty.

He saw that she was already becoming stocky, heavy around the hips, with the thick thighs and bulging calves common to Anglo farm women of European peasant stock. Buster, on the other hand, was balding, his once young ruddy face already losing its battles with age as if it were no longer a battle, and age pranced about proudly over the lines and crevices and puffiness of the vanquished gringo face. Buster had a perfectly straight back, no buttock line. In front, his thin chest swelled at the bottom into a full-flowing belly which spilled over his belt, cozily snuggling his accustomed large belt buckle in its folds.

¡Chingao! ¡Chingao! ¡Qué cura! ¡Qué puerta! ¡Si te empinas un poquito más, mamá, qué sonrisa me darás!

Faustino yelled inaudibly, feeling the tightness in his temples. He became agitated in his seat, squeezing his thighs together, curling his toes.

Because of the difference in their ages, Buster had to suffer a great deal of good-natured, but irascible, joshing on account of his wife. The ribbing came from those who knew him well and who felt confident of their equality with him. Casey, the ranch foreman, was largely the cause and instigator of this field sport at Buster's expense. Others present might join in, but they would be just a little more restrained than Casey. Casey had a special relationship with Buster, allowing him privileges which no other ranch hand could enjoy. The ranch had been started by Buster's father and Casey. Since the old man's death, Casey felt himself to be a second father to Buster.

If the Anglo hands joked at all about Buster's marriage, they did not do it to his face. The Chicanos, who largely made up the work force on the ranch, never joked about it out of respect for the sanctity of the man's marriage. The whores and loose women to be found in the Gonzales bars were fit topics for ribald conversation, but not a man's wife. Besides, if Buster had been known to fire an Anglo hand for such an impudence, there was no telling what he would do to a Chicano for something similar.

Mrs. Crane turned from her laundry to notice Faustino sitting inside the truck. A faint smile crossed her lips, almost a smirk, which said nothing at all, which gave no indication that she knew he was there, had known he was there, watching her, had been watching her. She placed her hands on her hips, stretched her bones, pushing her breasts forward, before continuing her work.

When she stooped over the next time, she seemed to go slower and lower than necessary, allowing the housecoat to ride up higher over her hips. Faustino could not be sure, but it seemed she raised the housecoat with her elbows, briefly, fleetingly, mysteriously. This time, he saw more than before. There flashed before him a thin, white glimpse of her panties as a comet streaking across the expanse of pink universe.

Faustino had not had such a *cura* in the few moments he had been watching her. He could not have missed one as he had not blinked at all, his eyes wide, clear and intent. The possibility of a *cura* did not allow for blinking.

He could not be sure, could not be certain that she was not now performing for him, that she had made him an audience and she, conscious of being seen, knowing his eyes were draped over her body, prepared a slow, long, undulating movement. Faustino continued to watch, unable, unwilling to leave the truck at that moment, frozen in his vision, unconcerned about the errand that brought him to the house.

Mrs. Crane, instead of rapidly bending down as before to pick up a garment for the line, anxious to finish the chore, now measured and calculated her movements, doubling at the waist, lingering over the tub, lifting first one garment, than another as if she required long, thoughtful deliberation on which article to hang on the wire.

Faustino's throat swelled. He tried to swallow, his mouth, throat, dry. He felt an uncomfortable, dry, rasping sensation as he swallowed. His jaw slackened to relieve the pressure on his teeth. He had no other conscious thought except the vision of the slightly overweight woman in front of him.

Faustino's father had worked for Buster's father, and with the passage of the ranch to Buster, Faustino, who had been born on the place, grew up to work there, it being the only world he had ever known. Faustino, without thinking it, without so much as admitting it, felt an obligation to his father's memory, to the memory of Buster's father, who had been a good man, to continue to work on the ranch, for Buster. He had a strong sense of tradition in the best way of tradition which does not require the saying of it or the knowing of it, it being what is done and what has always been done.

Faustino had a sense, something as palpable as the callouses on his hands, that he belonged on the ranch, that he belonged to the ranch; that he must give of himself and of his labor to it; knowing all the while but never thinking that he did not own the land, that he would never own the land; that finally the land was neutral, that what happened upon it was something else; that his devotion to it was one-directional, that Buster used him, that Buster hired his sense of obligation, his sense of tradition, his sense of loyalty in the same way he hired his body to plow the fields, to care for the stock, to mend the fences, to do the hundreds of tasks that kept the ranch going, that made more work for the hands, that made Buster a profit.

Faustino lived with the exploitation without ever knowing it for what it was, accepting the wages he earned, accepting the fact that there was no further obligation on the part of his employer toward him. And Faustino knew that the money—the wages paid for work completed, the wages withheld on account of rain or because of the slack seasons of the year—was never enough. He knew that the money only sparingly provided for his needs and the needs of his family. That the Chicanos were paid only when they worked and that the Anglo hands were paid weekly, whether there was work or not, did not bother Faustino. He had accepted his position in the scheme of things, he recognized his situation. Except for the hardships which befell him and his family from time to time, he was content with his life, with the life he had been born to lead. He did not concern himself with the rest.

Faustino loved the ranch, he knew every inch of it. Since he had been old enough to be placed on the payroll, at the age of eight or nine, he had sprinkled his sweat over every square foot of the ranch. He was satisfied to work for the low pay and the long hours because it was his home, the only home he had ever known, and it was his wish that it be the only home he would ever know. All of this in spite of his not owning a single clod of earth over which he stepped, a single tree against which he peed or rested, a single drop of the water in the streams from which he drank.

Buster owned the land. To him it was property, the subject of a compact between him and other men that they not trespass upon it. To Buster the papers he kept locked away in the bank were proof of his ownership, they bestowed title to him and his heirs, should he have any. Beyond that, it was only a means to provide for himself and his wife.

Faustino had a special relationship with the land. He had risen from it, he had grown tall on it; and because the land belonged to Buster, because the land was Buster, Faustino felt an especial allegiance toward him. The two were interwoven, threaded through the black richness of the land, interdependent, and finally joining to become an indistinct shape, inseparable from one another.

Buster perceived the scheme of things differently. To Buster, the fact of Faustino's birth on his ranch meant that he could expect more from Faustino, extra work for which he did not have to pay. When Buster spoke of Faustino, he spoke of him as his nigger, his Meskin, and there was a ring of authority in his voice, a self-satisfied sense of proprietorship, a pride and a satisfaction that comes from a bond so strong that one human being can claim ownership of another. And this bond is further cemented when the one owned cannot, will not, break the bondage, when he who is owned dare not, for reasons petrified in the bond, annul and rupture the perverse union.

Buster knew of, realized, his hold on Faustino, a hold connected long before either of them knew of it, and he used him, exploiting his skills and knowledge of farming and ranching; paying him half the salary he paid the lazy and incompetent Casey, and less than he paid Anglo high school kids who worked summers.

Casey, who attached himself to Buster parasitically, exploited the friendship with Buster's father, using Buster in the same way Buster used Faustino. And Casey, knowing he could not ranch, knowing he had neither the will nor the skill to hire working hands, remembering his two ranching starts ending in bankruptcy, clung to Buster, playing upon Buster's weakness in the memory of his father, retelling the anecdotes of the beginning, the friendship begun as roughnecks, the stakes they pooled, omitting the buying out the one of the other, the years together, the forging of a ranch, an identity, where once there had been only brush, mesquite trees and rattlesnakes. And just when Buster, in the throes of a grown man's tantrum made up his mind, decided once and for all, to fire Casey, to force Casey away just as he would any meddlesome hand, to rid himself of the spectre of his father who loomed still over the terrain in a constant disapproval of all that Buster did, Casey would interpose the spectre of the father between him and Buster, make flesh through his words what Buster most hated and what he most feared. Because the memory, the spectre of the father that stretched the length and breadth of the ranch, was larger and more powerful than Buster could contain or deny. It was as if Casey was indeed the father, spoke in the cadence of the father, brought the father's wishes from a tomb that Buster was too weak to seal once and for all. And Casey would stay, year after year, not relishing his power over Buster, never over-playing his hand, never taking more than he needed. Buster resented the hold Casey had over him, he hated knowing it, feeling it, giving in to it.

Faustino, at the urging of María, his wife, had approached Buster to ask about more wages for working Saturdays and Sundays. Faustino had gathered his strength, had summoned his courage, had brought himself to the full fore of what he was, formulating the words over and over again even before they became speech, assuring himself, reassuring himself, the words finally clear and unmistakable and irretrievable. Buster had heard ingratitude and impertinence; had become indignant, furious, and had yelled, mentioned, questioned Faustino's presence as part of the ranch, the rent-free house, the work always available, the paycheck always on time, the loans secured by work undone. Faustino had taken the step backward, ashamed, angry; had recognized the tenuousness of things; had sensed but did not know the injustice of the refusal; had turned and left with an apology unsaid.

Home again, he faced the house he had to enter, he thought of the wife he had to face. Faustino, bitter at his failure, kicked in the door, the question in María's eyes hitting him between his eyes, and he, taking out his fears and frustrations and bitterness, blackened María's eyes. He resolved never to ask Buster about wages again. No matter what Buster chose to pay, the hope of more was not worth what he had gone through.

Buster did try to be nice to Faustino, did on occasion yield to a sense of distant responsibility toward him. Perhaps it was because he had grown up with Faustino, the two of them playing together as children. Buster would visit Faustino and María, early in the morning, the day following a holiday, to bring a left-over turkey dinner or a piece of baked ham, poured indiscriminately, disdainfully, into a brown paper sack in the same way that scraps are gathered and tossed to dogs baying at the kitchen porch. The meat would be coated with creamed corn, gravy, peas; sometimes, a half-eaten piece of bread would be tossed in. Faustino and María would thank Buster politely, agree with him that it was good food, that it always was good food; neither of them knew how to be rude, not to Buster, not to anyone; they did not know how to refuse; and they would wait until Buster's pick-up turned onto the main highway, see the top of the cab sink beneath the roll in the land, and then they would feed the scraps to their dogs without making comment to each other, not acknowledging what it was they did for fear of offending an unseen, unhearing master.

Mrs. Crane gradually, languidly, came up to her full height, bending backward a little, holding a blue work shirt in her hands. She shook the garment, spread it wide between her arms, examined it. She knew Faustino's eyes were on her as are a worshiper's eyes riveted upon the sacrificial victim before the altar. Raising herself on tiptoes, making the offering before an imaginary tabernacle, she pinned one shoulder of the shirt to the line, then the other. As she did so, the housecoat rose up, loose and billowing around her upper thighs. The wind made it flap suddenly and again Faustino caught a glimpse of her white underwear.

While he had been looking at Mrs. Crane, the cigarette in Faustino's mouth smoked itself, the ash-covered ember inching its way toward his lips. He had not felt its initial warmth and it was not until his upper lip was burned that he grabbed it quickly and tossed it out the window. Momentarily distracted, he opened the truck door, adjusted his trapped, erect, straining penis inside the tight Levi jeans before stepping down.

Once on the ground, with a determined effort, he forced himself not to look in the direction of the clothesline. Inside the truck he had been protected as if he really had not been there. Outside, he knew himself to be vulnerable to the distance he must keep between them. He could not stare at her as before. In the open nothing would be between them, and the brief pretense to which they both tacitly agreed was over.

Faustino walked directly to the toolshed a few steps away from the truck. The door was held in place by a length of manila twine. He tried to untie the two knots, having an unexpected difficulty as his fingers trembled and could not maintain their grip on the twine. Finally and feverishly he unsecured the door and entered the shed to look for the wrench Buster and Casey wanted.

It was musty inside the shed, with its odors of old leather, dust, grease and rusting metal bluntly and heavily snaking their way into his nostrils. He felt hot and sweaty. The shaft of light coming in through the door, along with slivers of light coming in through the cracks in the walls, helped his eyes adjust to the hazy gray inside. He pulled on the string attached to the light switch overhead. The impotent clicking signaled the bulb was burnt out. He found a block of wood and used it to wedge the door open in case the wind started up and shut it. He began his search for the wrench.

As he searched, Faustino thought of Mrs. Crane outside, a few yards away from the shed, hanging her wash. He wondered whether she continued in the same way now that she knew he was in the shed. He could still spy on her through the cracks in the wall. His erection was subsiding, he felt a drop of liquid moist against his thigh. He pressed the palm of his hand against his pelvic bone, squeezing the bulge of his crotch, numbing the residual erection.

His thoughts were centered on her wide, mottled pink buttocks and the white flash of her panties. She must have known I was watching, he thought, *curándome*. And didn't I see more of her, more of her ass after she saw me there? Didn't she change her position and didn't she perform for me?

There was a resurgence inside his trousers. The bulge grew larger, stiffer, more aching. There was nothing he could do to ease himself. To relieve the strain, he repositioned the tumescent organ, but that did little for the deeper, more insistent ache within. He made a sweeping motion in front of his face as if to wipe away his thoughts and he began to look for the wrench with renewed and frenzied interest.

He soon found the wrench, stuck it in his back pocket, and came out of the shed to a cool breeze that had started while he was inside the stifling shed. The sweat on his face, glistening blisters of moisture, was cooled by the gentle rushing of the wind and he felt better. The tension in his upper chest relaxed, the dryness in his throat eased as his body cooled. The flesh of his penis lost its tautness, becoming tangled in his loose underwear. He was about to smooth his clothing when he heard his name called.

"Faustino!" Mrs. Crane yelled in the thick, nasal twang of South Texas that he was accustomed to hearing from Anglos and which, had she not used it, would have seemed strange to him.

"Yes, m'em," Faustino said in a low, husky voice, unsure whether she heard him, but certain that having stopped his movement, having turned in her direction, she would know he had heard her. He stood with his hand frozen on the door handle of the truck, looking in her direction, his eyes not raised high enough to meet hers. Had he looked up, higher than is permissible, had he the temerity to face her squarely—something which Chicanos did not often do to Anglos—he would have seen her standing under a row of her underwear, a fluttering rainbow of colors and shapes, each with a panhandled, wrinkled crotch. It was an erotic cross-bar under which Mrs. Crane purposely stood.

Faustino's eyes were fixed on the region of her knees. He was uncomfortable at being called, but he could not keep his gaze from devouring her deep, splotchy skin, the outline of her fleshy thighs under the material of the housecoat, the recessed, sunken, almost bashful V at the juncture of her legs as the wind pressed the housecoat against her; and he took in the steep, rising mound directly above the V, which impertinently curved upward, then slightly downward, finally disappearing into the folds of a beginning paunch.

Mrs. Crane relaxed one leg, bending it slightly forward, bringing her thighs tightly together as she did so in a slow, fluid movement unmistakably for Faustino, brazenly inviting him to look at her, appealing to his eyes as she repeated the movement several times before she spoke again.

"Faustino, com'ere a minute," she said at last, letting her tongue slip slowly out of her mouth, snaking it upward in the direction of her nose, wiping her upper lip with it. Her thigh continued to move forward and backward, her hips moving to and fro.

"The boss, m'em, he want this wrench," said Faustino, nervous, embarrassed, overcome by a sexual confusion he had never before experienced. In his world, it was man the aggressor and woman, a certain kind of woman, submitted. This was different for him. He told her again that Buster wanted the wrench, taking it from his hip pocket to show her as if to demonstrate the truth of his words.

Faustino sensed a situation he would not be able to control. Immediately, he felt a chill scurry throughout his skin like a lizard scurrying into a gopher hole. There was a danger in remaining, if only because he could not be sure what it was she had in mind. He did not control very many of the events of his life, that he knew, but he could sense trouble and he could control whether or not to participate in it. He was not in complete ignorance of Mrs. Crane's gestures, they being the source of his confusion. He knew that white women did not entice Chicanos, of that he was sure.

He pointed the wrench at Mrs. Crane, shaking it a little to be sure it caught her attention, wishing desperately that the wrench could speak and confirm the truth he spoke, that if she did not believe him, she would believe the inanimate object. Faustino lifted the wrench in the air as if offering it to her.

"I don't care about no wrench, Faustino. I said come here. I got somethin' for you to do." Saying that, she turned without waiting for a response, walking rapidly toward the house. She walked awkwardly trying to keep her house slippers on her feet, losing her balance once when she stepped on a stone hidden by a tuft of grass.

A thought crossed Faustino's bewildered mind. Of course, he said to himself. She knows I was watching her, *curándome*, and this is her way of punishing me. She wants me to look at her while she looks at me. Like the time my mother caught me taking a piece of *pan dulce* and made me eat and eat and eat until I got sick, to teach me a lesson. But, he could not be sure that this was what Mrs. Crane had in mind. It was all very strange to him.

Faustino watched Mrs. Crane walk away from him. He started to follow her as she had ordered. When she reached the porch, she turned to the side to open the screen door. Just then, a gust of wind blew into her housecoat, filling it out like the sails of a schooner. The two buttons holding it together could not withstand the force of the wind. The bind slipped as the wind died down, the cotton material gently coming to rest along the sides of her body. Mrs. Crane held on to the door not bothering to fasten the coat, not bothering to conceal her body.

Faustino trembled as he caught the glimpse of her naked, pendulous, bobbing breasts. She stood on the porch steps looking at him. He took a longer, more leisurely look at her nakedness, down to her waist and below, the pink whiteness of her skin interrupted only by the tight white bikini panties she wore which seemed to be stretched to the point of tearing and which so compressed her flesh that the side panels produced an indentation in the flowing outline of her body.

"M'em," Faustino said, trying to recall her words from what seemed an eternity before, trying to make them echo inside his confused, struggling brain. It was the vision of the siren in front of him, its song echoing, bouncing off the flesh of her body, beckoning him to come closer, to obey. Faustino, like the mariners off Amphitrite, was powerless, beguiled, unable to turn away.

Faustino walked forward a little along a narrow path where grass would not grow. He stepped off the path to one side in the direction of the clothesline, his boots crushing some brown weeds and withered grass, victims of the late summer sun. He felt the hard-packed ground beneath his feet refusing to give and cushion his footfalls. He stood with the wrench in his hand, reluctant to go any further.

Mrs. Crane took one flap of the housecoat and covered her left breast, the other still exposed, its nipple beginning to swell. She turned and went inside the screened porch. Faustino did not, could not, avert his gaze until she was completely swallowed by the cavernous blackness of the house. He was afraid, confused by a dangerous desire, but he knew to obey.

The wind picked up again and opened the unlatched screen door. The gust twisted and swirled, slamming the door shut. The sound of it reverberated through Faustino's body as though a thousand bits of shrapnel were stinging him with hot pinpricks, forcing him from the trance he was in. He gripped the handle of the wrench, momentarily grateful for the hard reality of it. Faustino replaced the wrench in his hip pocket and continued to walk toward the house.

In a brief flash, he looked up in the direction of the clothesline and saw the blue, black, red, green, pink and yellow panties; some small, dainty, bikini-shaped, mere wrinkled wisps; others large, flowing, nylon parachutes with leg openings warped by the distended elastic. Some had large, wide puckered crotches, others flat and proud, smooth and pristine, and still others with crotches so thin they could not contain side-tufts of pubic hair. A few had shriveled, wrinkled, dark brown crotches from menstrual overflows, worn monthly and then hidden as if they were a reminder of something unspeakable.

These, the monthly underpants, speaking of unproductive birth cycles, seemed in particular to stare at Faustino. They presented an image of defiance, unashamed and wanton. They were pinned side by side in another row, apart from the others. The crotches were aligned as though they were giving him a leering, obscene, brown smile, as if they were in possession of secrets they would not tell and which he would never know. Faustino walked slowly, deliberately, his gaze still on the line.

The panties waved in the wind, palpitating now rapidly, swaying, now gently fluttering like the guidon of some chivalrous regiment enticing its members to exotic adventures in far away never before heard of places. Faustino tried to recall if any of them resembled the underclothing that María wore, but he could not conjure up an image of his wife in underwear.

Faustino finally reached the edge of the porch steps. His head ached, his erection dissipated as his fear of the situation increased, looming as dark as the house he had been ordered to enter. His penis wilted against the cold but soothing emollient of thwarted secretions. He stood on the porch, the screen door at his face, reluctant to go any further.

Presently, she opened the wooden door and said, irritably, "Will you come in here!"

"I don't know, m'em," Faustino said, his reluctance tossed between them onto the wooden floor of the porch worn smooth by dust, wind and rain. He was grateful he was wearing his newer, darker jeans. The dark splotch of wetness to the left of his crotch did not show.

"Well, you have to come in the house, Faustino. There is something in here I want you to move for me because it's just too heavy for me to lift. I can't bring it to the door for you, you have to come in and get it."

"Yes, m'em," Faustino said, not moving, still reluctant to enter the house.

Faustino knew instinctively that it would not be possible for him to simply leave, to avoid entering the house, to hurry to Buster with the wrench. He could not trust Mrs. Crane. If he refused and she became angry, there was no telling what she would say to Buster, what story she would tell, what horror she might invent. Faustino wished to return to the safety of the fields, to his skill at work, where a man was judged according to what he produced.

He took a few steps forward and sideways, shuffling, trying to go toward the door and away from it at the same time. Mrs. Crane held it open for him; it was an invitation and a command. She released the door and disappeared inside. Abruptly, he swung it open all the way, walking past her into the kitchen.

Faustino could smell her perfume forcing its way into his nostrils, invading his sense of smell. As he stood in the middle of the kitchen, with Mrs. Crane further away from him, the perfume became entangled with the heavy cooking odors which clung just above his head as an invisible cloud.

Had he touched her at the door? he wondered. It felt as though he had, but he insisted lamely to himself that it could not be true, that the stinging sensation on his elbow was imagined, that it was caused by the confusion of the situation. Faustino was aware that he was very much alone in the spacious kitchen, that something cold and forbidding was nudging against him like the wet nose of his mare pushing at his bare back.

Mrs. Crane leaned against the wall, her hand on the doorknob. She held it, swinging it to and fro; played with it, letting it swing as if to slam shut only to break the contact; drawing it to her again, teasing it. She did not speak, she did not seem to be in any hurry. She shifted her gaze between Faustino and the broad expanse of South Texas outside.

Faustino waited for Mrs. Crane to show him what she wanted him to do. His mouth was open, his lower jaw loose as if he were unable to control it. There was a question on his forehead. There was worry there too.

Time seemed to freeze at a moment lost to him, even though he had been in the kitchen only a few seconds. The ongoing processes and rhythms to which he was accustomed suddenly stopped. He stood outside of the cycle of his life, marking some other time, not his own, strange and new to him. The anticipation he felt, the anxiety that made his flesh crawl, all of it was not in time; in drawing its being, its movement, from some other extra-temporal dimension where he the subject was not the knower of the world, rather, he was something to be known, but not yet understood.

Faustino felt a panic compressing the muscles of his chest, crushing his ribs, drawing his belly tight. He felt the tips of his fingers tremble, he felt an itch crawl inside his arms and legs. This he felt whenever he sensed a rattlesnake nearby, long before he saw it. The question on his forehead remained and he waited.

Gradually, the weight of the panic eased. A peaceful and cleansing flush spread throughout his body, opening his pores, his tension evaporating like the film of sweat coating his skin. Faustino began to feel some control of the situation. He started to relax. His eyes started to survey the kitchen, careful to avoid looking directly into Mrs. Crane's eyes. She was still by the door, biting her lower lip, not moving except for the hand swinging and stopping the door. Her face was only partially visible to him on the periphery of his vision. She stared at an object outside, something she could not distinguish and which caused her to squint.

Looking around the kitchen, Faustino realized it was the first time he had been inside the house. For all the years and in all the years he had worked on the place, Buster had never invited him inside. He usually came by on Fridays to pick up his paycheck when Buster did not distribute checks in the fields. It was understood that Faustino and all of the Chicano hands would stand at the foot of the porch steps while Buster remained inside reviewing the days worked in the ledger he kept before determining the amount due in wages. It was not a matter of concern to Buster that the Chicanos stood outside waiting for him in all weathers. When it was cold or it rained, Buster would invite the Anglo hands to come into the kitchen while leaving the cold and wet Chicanos to stand and wait or to scurry to their cars and trucks for shelter.

Faustino could remember standing outside at dusk in a cold rain, the wind cutting through his wool coat. He would be looking through a partially steamed kitchen window, seeing the Anglo hands inside drinking coffee, surrounding Buster, laughing with him, leaning over him, making all manner of obsequious gestures. Faustino did not feel what Buster did as a personal insult or that Buster diminished him in any way. All he remembered, all he could say happened, was his standing in the cold, listening to the tattoo of raindrops on his hat, peering through the blurred window into the warm yellow glow inside.

Faustino did not wish to be a part of the group of white-skinned men inside; he merely wished to be out of the rain and in the warmth. When he thought of quitting Buster, the few times he had thought of gathering his family together and moving on to another place, it was this moment that returned, cold and wet, clear and painful, filling him with a rage that, once subsided, made him gentle and loving toward his wife and children; and finally, when the pull of the land made contemplation of the matter useless, he was more respectful to Buster, atoning for having sinned.

There was a gringo odor about the house, an odor of stale, unimaginative cooking, odd and repulsive to Faustino. In his house, with few utensils and less money, there would be the smells of meals past which clung to the walls, giving the entire house a fragrance of garlic, comino, chile, oregano; from outside, the impertinent smell of the *chile pitín* plants wafted in fresh and saucy. It was a reminder of meals enjoyed, lingered over, mixed with conversation, laughter and sometimes sorrow.

In Buster's house, the kitchen smelled heavily of air fresheners, detergents and other antiseptic fluids which were sprayed, poured and spread into and on every surface, every crevice, every utensil; their purpose to destroy any and every reminder that this was a house in which people lived, to erase the slightest suggestion of living. The stale odors would not be vanquished. The air fresheners tried in vain to route them, but they remained and combined themselves with the heavy, nauseous scent of Mrs. Crane's cheap perfume. All of the indistinct but oppressive smells created a leaden atmosphere inside the kitchen which made Faustino at first gasp for air, his lungs constricting. It smelled of vomit.

Mrs. Crane walked past Faustino, suddenly roused from her trance.

Slowly, lethargically, she began what seemed a long journey from the door to the sink. As she passed Faustino, she purposely brushed his chest with her shoulder.

She stopped in front of the sink, raised a forefinger to her lip. With her back to him, she bent over to inspect a grease can full of water as if by doing so she justified asking him in. Still bent over, she twisted her body, raised her head to face him. The housecoat came open, the mischievous button again slipping through the careless buttonhole. She brushed it back, pinning it to her hip with her closed fist, exposing her breasts. Her nipples were erect and thick, blood pink, set in a wrinkled circle of discolored skin about the size of tarnished silver dollars.

"Come here," she said, and all Faustino could hear was the sound of her voice in the room exploding around his head, coming from no certain direction. The buzzing in his ears prevented him from understanding her words; later he remembered, vaguely, something about a leak in the pipes and something about a can used to catch the spill, and something about Buster emptying it each morning, and something about Buster having forgotten to do it. Faustino's attention was concentrated narrowly and exclusively on her gaping breasts, large, dangling, moving with each word she uttered, quivering like jelly as she struggled with her balance.

Mrs. Crane moved around to grip the handles on the can. Finding that the housecoat was in the way, she hiked it over her hips, bunching it in front.

"Come on," she said, "help me move this."

Faustino did not hear and did not move. Mrs. Crane pulled on the can, her breasts bobbing wildly as she did so. It was too heavy for her, but Faustino stayed where he was. His eyes were riveted on the broadness of her buttocks, his vision pinpointed on the double-crotch corona of the panties, noticing the bruised wet welts made by the elastic bands of the leg openings.

Small, curly, kinky tufts of dark brown pubic hair escaped the double layer of synthetic material. Underneath the panty-crotch, pressured by it, snuggled against it, mashed by it, her vagina reposed, surrounded by the canyon walls of her thighs.

"I want you to take this," her lips parting suggestively into a smile, "out," she said in conclusion.

She let go of the can and stood up, wiping her forehead with the back of her hand. The housecoat fell along the sides of her body, her fists pinning it against her hips.

Faustino walked over to the can. She had not moved away from it and as he stooped to grab both handles, his elbow, covered by the denim jacket, pressed against her breast. This time he was sure. She inched forward toward him, pressing his naked hand with her knee. She placed her hands on his broad back and began rubbing in wide circles.

He lifted the can off the floor and moved it away from under the sink, drawing two steps backward. He set it on the floor again, secured his balance to get a better grip on the handles. Mrs. Crane came to stand in front of him, with the can between them. The juncture of her legs was directly in front of his head. She thrust her hips forward, the V of her panties inches away from his face. He could smell the concentration of feminine odors emanating from the region, a mixture of crystal secretions, urine, soap, deodorants and stale perfume. The underpants were much too small for her and Faustino could see pubic hairs overflowing the top ridge of the material. Through the webby lattice of fake lace, shoots of hair poked like porcupine quills.

Before he could right himself, he felt Mrs. Crane's hands move across his shoulders, caressing the base of his neck, lingering there, squeezing roughly, massaging maniacally. She had leaned over to do so, her pendulous breasts swaying easily, brushing his temples and cheeks. From the corner of his eye he could see the erect, purple, distended nipples. He felt a tremor go through his fingertips as she moved her hand up and down his neck swiftly, uncontrollably, urgently.

Mrs. Crane removed one hand, leaving the other like a hot *comal* searing his flesh. The free hand pressed against her breast, first one then the other, kneading them, mashing them against his head, pinching, tweaking the nipples. She moved forward, straddling the water can, rhythmically pumping her hips toward his face. Her smell was stronger. All he had to do was move his head upward and his nose would be buried in her crotch.

Faustino, still bent over, backed away as if crawling out of a low, narrow cave. He straightened slowly, shakily, maintaining his balance with difficulty. There was a tremor in the back of his knees. Desperately, he tried not to touch her, drew in his hard stomach to avoid contact with her body. She had matched him step for step and stood close to him.

She now placed both hands on his shoulders in imitation of beginning a slow dance. When Faustino did not move, standing there frozen, she slid her hands down his shoulders, along his hard muscular arms. When her hands reached his wrists, she tried to encircle them with thumb and forefinger, making rapid upward and downward motions. Then her fingers glided over the backs of his hands, her fingers slipping between his fingers, making the same in-out urgent movements.

She drew him closer to her, the length of her body touching him. She moved her arms around his waist, pressing first her breasts against his chest and then her pelvis against his crotch. She released her grip on his waist only long enough to move the housecoat aside, pressing her naked flesh against the rough material of his denims. She now slipped her face against his shoulder and began to rotate her hips, pushing, mashing, bumping her pelvic bone hard against the erection that swelled inside his jeans.

Mrs. Crane brought her hands around to Faustino's chest, brushed the jacket aside, hurriedly, nervously, pulling on the snap button on his blue-checked shirt. She pushed him back, spreading her fingers, running them over the hairs on his chest. She inclined her head and began to kiss him, starting with his lower neck, her lips traveling an erratic, jagged trail over his chest, pulling on the black curly hairs with her wet lips, gathering them in sparse tufts; her tongue darting out to pierce his brown skin, penetrating through to his muscles and bone; he could feel the tongue sliding over his entrails, teasing his maleness. Eagerly, hungrily, she tugged and bit his nipples, moistening them, flattening them with the flat part of her tongue. A low, hoarse moan started deep in her chest, rising up into a whimper, vibrating her lips, tingling the loose skin around his nipples.

Faustino was thoroughly aroused, wanting her but not wanting her, his tumescent maleness stretched beyond the point of prudence and fear, the confusion he felt becoming a counterpoint to the desire for the lubricious female enveloping of his member. He had allowed her to go far enough. The demands of his penis had not risen to the point where he would become the aggressor. He was perilously close but he still could not be sure it was what she wanted. He feared this might be part of an elaborate tease, that if he made a first move to join in what it seemed she wanted, she would laugh, push him away, throw him out the door. He stepped away from her.

He spoke in a pained voice full of phlegm. "I better go, m'em. I can take the can," he said, pointing behind her.

"Faustino," she started, her voice deep, husky, urgent. "Don't go. Not just yet." Her face was vulnerable, now as unsure as he was. "All those things people say about Buster are true. I know you've heard them. Everybody knows about it. He ain't a husband to me." There was a suggestion of a tear in her high-pitched voice as she lowered her head.

"I never heard nothing, me'em. I don't know nothing."

"Faustino, I'm telling you he ain't no good to me!" she said, almost snarling a threatening edge to her voice, insistent, unwilling to stop what she had started, her upper lip curling slightly.

"I need a man," she continued. "Right now! It's been so long. Faustino, please. I don't want to have to beg. I could be good to you, very good to you, Faustino. And this don't have to be the first and last time, you know. You could come visit me. I know you can do it. Nobody would have to know. Not Buster, not your wife, not nobody. I could fix it so Buster could pay you more money, or, I could give you some of my money. I have my own money. Faustino, listen to me, please."

With that, she stepped forward and grabbed his engorged penis through his tight jeans, the tautly stretched material preventing her from wrapping her sweating, trembling fingers around it.

"Jesus Christ, Faustino!" she yelled, leaning against him. "I want this! I want you to fuck me, Faustino."

Faustino pushed her away again. He felt her fingernails trying to scratch his penis.

"I got to get back to work m'em," he said. Mr. Buster, he wants this wrench real bad." He showed her the wrench once more.

"Oh, the hell with that god-damned wrench," Mrs. Crane said, yanking it out of his hand. She grabbed his penis with the other hand. She tossed the wrench toward the door where it fell with a dull clunk and at the same time she squeezed the erect throbbing organ in his jeans. The metal instrument slid on the floor and rested mute.

"I want this wrench," she said. She flattened her hand and pressed the palm of it in a circular motion over his penis.

"Maybe all you need is some encouragement. I saw you looking at me outside and in here. I know you want it, Faustino. I'll make you want it."

Mrs. Crane slid down to kneel in front of Faustino, keeping her hands behind his back, sliding them along his buttocks as she went down, resting them in back of his upper thighs, drawing his crotch to her face. She pressed her cheek against the bulge of his crotch. She shoved her chin between his legs, opened her mouth wide and tried to swallow cock, balls and bluejean. She pushed upward, mashing her nose against the base of his penis, her cheekbone against his pelvic bone.

She slid her tongue inside the flap of his fly, running it upward along the jagged copper teeth of the zipper. She took the zipper tab in her teeth and pulled down, bringing her fingers up to help.

Her mouth insinuated itself inside the trousers, moving along the under-clothed shaft, her hands now in front of his waist, undoing the belt, tearing the waistband apart, pulling it down, her lips and teeth searching for the glans penis.

She took a mouthful of underwear and penis. She let go, leaving a wet round spot on his shorts. "I can't swallow all of it, Faustino," she cooed. "It's so big. You're so big, Faustino," she said in a little girl voice.

Mrs. Crane slipped a hand inside his shorts, cupping his testicles, gently scratching the tender patch of skin behind them. The sensation startled his throbbing penis and make it jerk. She then brought her hand around his balls and under the aching shaft, drawing it out. The penis, finally free of the cloth constraints, surged outward and upward, secreting a small drop of fluid which welled on either side of the seam of his foreskin. Mrs. Crane stretched the loose skin back, bending the stiff shaft, hurting Faustino.

"Stay here, Faustino," she said. "You can tell Buster you couldn't find the wrench. You can tell him it took you a long time to find it. Stay here, Faustino. He'll never miss you. I need you."

The tip of her tongue touched the moist tip of his penis, drawing an ever-increasing wet circle around the aperture. As the circle became larger, her lips touched it, lingering longer each time; she sucked on it more and more each time.

Faustino was unable to move; did not want to move; and he would have stayed standing still until she finished. However, she stopped abruptly, gave his penis a pat and stood up to face him.

"See what I mean, Faustino?" said Mrs. Crane, smiling, as if saying, I told you so. "Follow me."

Instead, Faustino backed away from her. He noticed the wrench on the floor and walked toward it, intending to pick it up. She followed him. Near the door, where the wrench lay, Faustino tucked his penis in, zipped up his trousers and fastened his belt.

Mrs. Crane came to an absent-minded stop. She was confident of her victory. Faustino, she thought, had a lapse of nerve. She tossed the collar of the housecoat back, over her shoulders, shrugging it loose, letting it slide down her back; it slid smoothly down the curves of her arms, noiselessly around the ample hips and thighs, until it at last came to rest in a soft billowing pile around her ankles.

Faustino had some difficulty breathing as he was assaulted by the fullness of her breasts, as he saw them in the door light: now not so mysterious, devoid of shadows, nothing hidden. Their udder-like massiveness flattened them against her torso. Mrs. Crane's were the biggest breasts Faustino had ever seen, much bigger than María's, bigger than the pictures in the girlie magazines Casey kept in his shack. He took another step toward the door and she stepped back toward the bedroom.

As the distance between them increased, the desire he felt earlier, the blind demand of his erection, his confusion, all of it became less intense. He realized that her breasts were entirely too large, too bovine, too evocative of nourishment than of pleasure. Her waist was narrow but the curve ballooned out to her hips. Mrs. Crane, standing in front of him naked except for her panties, was oddly shaped, disproportionate, outside of what he knew of the female body.

The suggestive glimpses he had caught of her, pieces of body, partially obscured, hidden and highlighted by shadow, had caused his arousal, had produced for him an unwanted erection. It had been the erotic thought of possibility, something created altogether in his mind, the fear and terror and confusion being as much a part of it as the physiology of it.

Looking at the nakedness of Mrs. Crane, Faustino felt as if he were looking at another woman. In the fullness of the light, he confronted the unadorned flesh of a woman who was not attractive in the least. Faustino became calm. He felt like smiling, laughing; he had now regained full control of his mind, his body, his penis, his situation. The danger which had hovered over him like a vulture was gone, there was no longer a threat, and he could now avoid trouble. She was repulsive to him.

Mrs. Crane was not aware of Faustino's thoughts; she noticed the change in him, the smoothing out of the brown face, the relaxation of his fuzzy moustache; she thought he was ready for her, having overcome his reluctance.

"Faustino," she said, "follow me." She kicked the housecoat away and turned, walking the full length of the kitchen to a small corridor leading to the bedroom. He watched her with an odd curiosity, feeling his stomach turn queasy. Her tumultuous hips quivered like flan, sending shimmers through the flesh and fat, up and down and around the clearly massive buttocks. Her tight bikinis slid over one buttock and disappeared in the crack between them. He was embarrassed and sorry for her. In another time, before her body started to sag in resignation, he might have gone through with it, he might have been unable to contain an orgasm.

She walked into the dim corridor. At its end, the bedroom door was open and the windows poured bright blinding sunlight into the room. She stopped in the frame of the bedroom door. Faustino could see her, his view only slightly blocked by the refrigerator. Mrs. Crane peered seductively over her shoulder at him and began the labored negotiation of the panties down her ample buttocks, a movement which she had to interrupt over and over again as the waistband rolled and became trapped in the flabby flesh. Faustino was morbidly fascinated. He could leave at any moment but he was fixed in place.

When she had pulled, twisted, rolled, churned, wiggled and teased the panties midway down her thighs, Mrs. Crane stopped. She took a sidestep with one leg, stretching the material of the bikinis which became a white rope digging deeply into her thighs. She then bent over so that her upside down face was framed by thighs, bikinis and the hairy V of her crotch. She smiled.

She brought her hands around, spreading her buttocks. Her vagina had been hidden primly under the thatch of thick pubic hair. As the skin stretched, its wet pink inside opened. A little above, nestled within a gash of dark brown, her puckered anus stared at Faustino. She remained in the position for a few moments. Faustino did not move.

She straightened, lifted one leg to shake it out of the bikini bind and kicked them away with the other leg. She went further into the bedroom. She stacked her and Buster's pillows and reclined slowly in the center. She slid down off the pillow until her face was almost hidden by her breasts. After she spread her legs and raised her knees, she pressed her breasts together, her small pudgy hands unable to contain the ooze of breast that pushed between her fingers. She slid her hands down, combing her pubic hair with her spread fingers, lowering them on either side of her vagina. She parted the pubic hairs, searching slowly until she found the fleshy skin on either side of the vagina. Gingerly, she clasped the vaginal lips in her fingers, pulling them apart, exposing the inside that hungered for Faustino, that yearned for any man. She waited.

Faustino turned and ran out of the kitchen.

II

The truck came alive with the first turn of the ignition key. He narrowly missed a corner of the toolshed, but he swerved around the house and was quickly moving on the mile of gravel road leading to the highway. The road had not been graded or surfaced since Buster convinced a Texas Highway Department crew to do it on two weekends, using state equipment and materials. Faustino held on to the steering wheel as the truck leaped high into the air. Normally he would not have gone as fast, but he was in a hurry to get on the highway and as far as he could from Buster's house and Mrs. Crane.

The distracting noise and clatter of the truck had a soothing effect on Faustino, forcing him to concentrate on the truck and the road. He flew past the cattleguard, the front wheels of the truck going over the two-inch pipes embedded in concrete, only the rear tires thump-thumping over it. The truck slid briefly out of control on the loose gravel shoulder, the tires spinning a cloud of white dust before he jerked onto the smooth blacktop and felt the roaring hum underneath him. The black ribbon of highway undulated and snaked its way between the pale green-brown of the chaparral before piercing the horizon and going out of sight.

The smooth road and the steady hum of the wheels lulled Faustino, relaxed his concentration, the truck speeding forward by itself. He thought, *vieja chingada, nalgona.* The images inside Buster's kitchen returned, oscillating between clear and blurred, sharply in focus and then as indistinct phantoms. Against his will, the grotesque sight of her naked body pulsated in his mind, making his temples ache. His thoughts became images of the clothesline with the panties hanging like jagged teeth; a ghost-like flowered housecoat flowed and billowed about him; Mrs. Crane's body, hidden and mysterious, freely floated in and out of the housecoat, up and around the panties, fleetingly revealed itself, beckoning to him, inviting him into a black vortex.

As though overtaken by an uncontrollable spasmodic reaction, Faustino flipped the steering wheel, aiming the truck at the road shoulder. His body had tensed, his penis was rock hard pushing against his jeans. He braked, bringing the truck to a stop but did not turn off the ignition. He liked the feel of erotic vibration coming from the idling engine.

¡Chingao! he yelled at the top of his lungs, the sound of his voice rising with the heat from the black pasture soil. He gripped the steering wheel until his knuckles whitened. He felt his penis consuming, channeling, drawing, sucking all of his body's blood into itself, becoming larger, packed harder than he had ever felt it before. The engorged member throbbed and ached, straining inside his trousers, yearning for the denied release. *¡Chingao!* Faustino yelled once more, the sound exploding out of the cab of the truck, echoing and reverberating in the bushes, tumbling about the brittle chaparral, slithering into the brush where it became a whimper, finally dying in the short distance.

Voy pa' 'trás, he thought. *¡Se la meto, vieja jija de su chingada madre! Conmigo no juega. Le voy a enseñar. Vieja culera, de veras quiere coger, pos aquí mero. Aquí estoy. Se la meto. Se la meto hasta en el fundío.*

Faustino raced the engine into a deafening revolution, overheating it, straining the thick metal of the engine. He mashed the clutch and violently jerked the transmission into gear. He braced himself on the wheel ready to release the clutch and surge forward, his mind made up to return to the ranch house, no other thought on his mind, determined to relieve himself inside Mrs. Crane's white waiting body. The roar of the engine rattled away any other sensation.

Faustino lifted the shift level and released the clutch and eased up on the gas pedal. He knew he would not go. The soft, diaphanous, seductive image of her under the clothesline, unaware of being seen, gave way to a sharper image of the flabby Mrs. Crane in the kitchen, a lewd, repulsive mass of flesh abused by a man, knowing only that abuse, seeking to abuse in return, wanting to swallow his maleness, to negate the thwarted sexuality she had known. Faustino could not go back.

Still, his arousal lingered, his excitement remained; he needed a woman, a sexual coupling to restore the sense of himself to himself. His manhood had been threatened, challenged, made separate and apart from himself in a way he had not known before. He needed to be restored into a whole man.

It was true that Mrs. Crane was ready, available, nearby, in desperate need of a penis, any penis. It was true he had not emptied the grease can full of water; he could go back on that pretext, he knowing and she knowing the reason for his return. His arousal drove him to contemplate what he knew he would not do. Mrs. Crane offered a sexual embrace for which he was not prepared.

Faustino had had his share, more than his share, of whores and clumsy couplings in the back seats of automobiles and in the woods. Mrs. Crane presented him with a kind of sex beyond what he knew. To him sex was as natural as anything a man did. It was understood that a man looked for more than he was apportioned. As times changed, it was not rare for a Chicano to go to bed with a white woman. Some of his nephews who lived in the city had Anglo wives. There, in Buster's kitchen, was something altogether different.

He tried to shape the events into an order which made sense to him. It was not a fear of anything physical which Buster might do. Only his penis made sense. He weighed his erection against the repulsion he felt.

He thought of Mrs. Crane, revolting though she had been. She could after all service him, assuage the incessant pleading of his penis, draw from his body the maddening fluids that made him lose control of himself. To return to the ranch house meant he would walk along the short corridor, follow her into the lair of the bedroom. Once there she would drop upon the bed, poise herself to receive the extension of him, her dark pubic hairs bent in segments like spiderlegs, her vagina stalking his penis, preying, eager and patient to close in around the shaft, her thick arms and legs pinning his body to hers, clutching him, drawing him into her baneful center. No, he could not return to the ranch house.

Faustino gently pulled the gear shift into first and slowly released the clutch. The truck eased evenly forward. As he drove, he tried to roll a cigarette with one hand, as his grandfather had taught him. His hand shook, spilling more tobacco than usual. When the cigarette was finished, it was loosely rolled, lumpy, unfit to smoke. In disgust, he violently tossed it out the window.

The clothesline loomed ahead of him on the horizon as the truck rose up the slope of the land. The breasts with each nipple large and purple, the misty image of the succubus spinning her charm around him, speaking in voices that made his scalp tingle and his cheeks itch, the strange incantations crying out of the quivering flesh. His excitement was again in full force, stronger than before, more demanding; the dull aching pain of his engorged penis radiating outward from the base of the penis into his thighs and lower belly. He massaged his crotch trying to soothe the pain, but the palm of his hand could not penetrate through the denim material, could not ease what he felt inside past all skin, all flesh. The speedometer rose to seventy, eighty. The truck shook. Only his erection mattered.

As he approached the crossroads, Faustino saw the road signs flash by rapidly, bright green sparks in the corner of his eye. The white and black signs identified the road he traveled and arrows pointed ahead to roads yet to come. He slowed the truck as the red stop sign came suddenly upon him.

Across the road, a little beyond the intersection, was the aluminum breadloaf-shaped mailbox with his name crudely painted on the side in large black letters. He waited for a tube-shaped milk truck to go by before he crossed the road. He stopped adjacent to his mailbox. He seldom bothered to check for mail as he seldom received any. Normally, he felt good when he saw the mailbox; it signaled the nearness of María and his children. He could see the rooftop of his house in the distance, seeming to have sank into the drying Johnson grass.

Ahead of him, Buster and Casey waited for the wrench. No doubt Buster would be angry. No matter how long it took him to run an errand, Buster would be angry when he returned.

There was an ominous anticipation in his body as he thought about María. He imagined she would be inside the house watching those television programs she did not entirely understand. *Mis historias*, she called them. When he came home for lunch, it would be prepared, but she would not take her eyes off the slow-speaking characters on the screen who were seldom photographed below the neck.

Buster would have to wait. Faustino knew he had to see María. He had been gone a long time, but Buster, the wrench, Mrs. Crane, none of that mattered. He had to see her. Only she, María, who sensed things in him even before he knew them himself, only she could help him rid himself of the ache that bulged in his trousers. Only she could be the receptacle for the welling fluids undammed by the incident at the clothesline, now that he was convinced Mrs. Crane had had little to do with it.

Faustino inched the truck forward and carefully turned into his driveway, a winding, rutted pair of clay ribbons worn smooth by his truck tires, separated by intermittent patches of sparse grass down the middle. The weather-beaten gate lay at a twisted angle, one hinge torn off. He reminded himself to fix it; he would be moving some cattle to graze in the pasture surrounding his house.

Once he turned in, he was sure of what he wanted to do. He accelerated to the top of the hill and killed the engine, gliding down the slope. He aimed the hood of the truck directly at the porch of the house. There, in the house nestled by a clump of mesquite trees, would be María, unaware that he was coming, unaware of his need of her, sure to question why he came.

As the truck gathered speed in the downward roll toward the house, Faustino saw María standing beside the porch, under the muted shade of the large ancient mesquite tree. Years before, he had put a water tap near the tree so she could do the wash. As he approached, she stood in front of her washtub. For him, the scene coming up to him, of his wife performing a similar chore had no suggestion of the previous scene with Mrs. Crane standing and bending over her washtub. María dressed plainly, wore longer skirts, and would have protected her modesty even though there could not be anyone to see her. María would no more expose herself in private than she would in public. It was a habit acquired as a young girl and required no further thought.

María was wringing one of his shirts, twisting and twisting, letting the water drip, drop by drop, back into the tub; some of it, as she shook the shirt turned into a wrinkled rod, fell on her toes. She then walked to the clothesline and pinned it. She took another from the soap tub and sloshed it in the rinse tub before wringing it damp. That batch finished, she dumped another into the soap tub, swirling the clothing in the foamy water. María took another of his shirts out, squeezed it, shook it loose and draped it evenly over the ribbed, brass surface of the scrubboard. She dipped her hand in the water for the scrub brush and applied it vigorously to the shirt. She scrubbed so furiously that she did not hear the approaching truck.

Faustino parked the truck adjacent to the porch, which he did when he would soon be going out again. He jumped out, slammed the door shut. The crash of the door on the truck's body startled María from her work. She straightened up from the scrubboard to look at Faustino, her eyes wide and questioning. María placed her hands on her hips and bent backwards slightly to ease her taut back muscles.

Faustino did not look in her direction, but went straight to the house in long strides which seemed to suppress a run. He threw the screen door open, shaking the hinges, sending the wooden frame crashing against the wall. He went inside, permitting the door to swing shut by itself.

His was a one-room house. In a rear corner, to the left, stood an iron frame bed, once painted in a dark walnut color. Now, most of the paint was gone, leaving a smoothly worn metal which rusted only in spots. The kitchen corner was immediately to the right as one walked in. A large, two-burner camp stove stood atop a linoleum-covered table. Next to the table, partially shielding a small window, was a fat, bulky refrigerator, its white enamel aged to a yellow, almost brown tone, dotted with rust pocks like flyspecks.

Just off the center of the room was the only furniture Faustino had bought during the time of his marriage. It was a dinette set. The table top was made of a scratch-proof surface which had many scratches on it and the chairs were constructed of a thin, fragile, tubular metal and upholstered with a synthetic material. He had bought the set in nearby Nixon, on credit; the store owner unsure Faustino could pay for it, finally agreed only if Buster co-signed the credit slip and guaranteed the payment of ten dollars a month for two years.

In the corner to the right of the entrance, a television set was lodged precariously upon a wooden crate. The channel selector nob had long ago disappeared. In its place, wedged into the metal slit, was a nail, its center filed flat to fit. The picture tube was old, oval; the transmitted images would appear as swiftly moving clouds. The set had belonged to María's mother, and she had made a present of it when María's father died. Her mother did not want it to remind her of the deceased. Whenever she came to visit, María made sure to drape a cloth over it.

The house, the room, gave a cluttered appearance because everything seemed so close together, but María had arranged all of the items neatly, each carefully located in its special corner, its proper place, as if separated by walls only María could see. Once, long ago, soon after their marriage, when Faustino had brought her to her new home for the first time, María had shaken her head in dismay. She was not one to be defeated without a struggle. Soon enough, she nailed two criss-crossing wires to the walls just below the ceiling, and then threaded long cloth panels in an effort to create four rooms out of the space. The first morning, Faustino rolled over on the hem of the wall, pulling all four nails from the walls. The cloth walls came tumbling down, the heavy wire landing on Faustino, startling him awake. María cried and he cursed under his breath. He put the wires back up, tighter this time, and María was pleased. Then, his cousins came for a visit. They were their first guests. María worked long and hard scrubbing the floor, arranging some old chairs he had, even finding some flowers to put in a bowl of water. His cousins had made the trip to *La Tacuachera* bar before coming over. They had a few beers and a guitar with them. Upon entering and seeing the arrangement, they began to laugh. Faustino had been embarrassed and furious. After the cousins had gone, he sat in a chair drinking the last of his beer. In his silence. he was seething, letting it build up until he could stand it no longer. Then, Faustino erupted. He yanked the wires from the walls, gouging bits of wood as he jerked. Afterward, he went outside to smoke a cigarette, calm himself, before coming to bed. María had been awake when he returned, afraid of him. He undressed, got in beside her and took her hand in his. Neither of them said anything.

Over the years, María had become accustomed to the one room. When the two children arrived, she had kept them in a crib near the bed. As they grew older, she prepared a pallet for them each night next to the corner table. The lack of privacy, particularly when she and Faustino made love, bothered her. The first child had ended their nights of carefree, giggling intimacy. When they made love now, which became more and more infrequent, they did it softly and gently so as not to wake the children.

It was hot inside the house. Faustino paced around the dining table. He took three steps to the refrigerator, threw open the door, shaking the rust-eaten appliance along with the floor under it. María had left her wash after seeing him slam the door. She had followed him onto the porch and stood in the doorway watching him. Her features and the outline of her body were hazy through the rusting, dark brown screen. She was somewhat angered by his strange behavior and bewildered that he would be absent from the fields so early in the afternoon.

Faustino did not turn to see María at the door. He searched inside the refrigerator, moving his head from side to side, craning his neck to look over jars and left-over food wrapped in wax paper. His anger rose as he could not find what he looked for. He kicked the door shut. He slapped his thigh and brought his hand up, making a fist which he shook in the air.

He turned to call María and saw her standing on the porch.

"¿Quién chingaos," he yelled, "se tomó mi vironga?"

María shook her head. "Pos' tú, ¿quién más?" she said.

She raised her hand to the red bandana which contained her hair, pulled on the knot, and drew it downward. Her hair fell in black glistening cascades, bouncing on her shoulders. She opened the screen door quietly and stepped inside.

"¡Chingadamadre!" said Faustino.

He collapsed a haunch on top of the table, keeping one foot firmly on the floor. The other, he let swing nervously. He had the appearance of a caged animal. The veins of his neck bulged in thick ridges, his lips were compressed tightly, leaving only a thin line for a mouth.

"¿Qué andas haciendo? ¿No tienes trabajo?" she asked.

"¿Cómo chingaos que no tengo trabajo, pendeja?" said Faustino, his teeth packed together.

"¿A poco viniste a comer?"

"¿Quién chingaos te dijo que vine a comer?"

"Oyes, andas bravo, ¿no?"

"Oyes, andas bravo, ¿no?" he mimicked her voice unpleasantly, turning the sweet musical sound of it into a harsh, biting, imitation.

"Bueno, así no vamos pa' ningún lado," she said. "Entonces, ¿qué quieres? ¿A qué viniste?"

"¿Quién chingaos te dio permiso pa' hablar?" He took the blue bag of tobacco from his jacket pocket. He was unable to smooth the cigarette paper, wadded it and the bag, and threw it against the refrigerator.

María remained where she was, looking straight at him, her eyes never leaving his face. She was concerned, worried, about the strange man in front of her who did not seem to be her husband.

"Yo no necesito permiso para hablar en mi casa, ¿oíste?" she said.

"No me salgas con tu pinche pedo, ¿oítes?" Faustino was ugly, his face covered in sweat, his desire for sex surging as he felt an overpowering need for violence. The two desires rose together, mingled, became inseparable.

"Pero, ¿qué te pasa?" she said, taking a step toward him.

"Nadien te dijo que me preguntes nada," he said.

"Debes de andar en la labor, trabajando. ¿Te dio el día el Buster? O ¿no más te fuiste como baboso?" She ended sarcastically, changing the dark, delicate, pretty face into a grimace which betrayed an inability for cruelty.

Faustino became furious.

"Oyes, tú de veras quieres que te dé un chingazo, ¿no?" He jumped from the table, landing solidly on his feet, clenching his fists, shaking the both of them at her. He took a tentative step toward her.

María ignored his threat. She moved around him and went to sit on the bed.

"Estás bien loco tú. Eso es lo que tienes. A ver cuando aprendes a meterte del sol. Parece que andas asoleado," she said.

Faustino went to the foot of the bed. He began to unbutton his shirt, noticing for the first time that he had not finished buttoning it after being with Mrs. Crane. He yanked the shirt tail out of his trousers, pulled it off his shoulders, threw it across the table, sending a salt shaker crashing to the floor. His hands went to his belt buckle, but before unclasping the leather, he lifted his head toward her.

"Ándale, pronto," he said.

María left the bed, went over between the dining table and the refrigerator to pick up the salt shaker and his shirt. She draped his shirt over a chair. Faustino had his back to her.

"Pos', ¿qué traes tú?" she asked.

"¿Qué crees? Te digo que te quites la ropa," he said.

Faustino unbuckled the belt, undid the metal button of the jeans, slid the zipper down, jerked his trousers over his legs, all in one motion. The stovepipe trouser legs bunched at the knees, held there by his boots. He hopped around the bed, leaning toward it in case he lost his balance, and sat. He had some difficulty, but grunting and jerking, he managed to yank trouser leg and boot off at the same time. He took a couple of deep breaths before doing the other leg.

"Tú andas bien loco, oyes," said María.

Faustino lifted up to slide his underwear into a pile on top of his jeans. He lay on the bed. His penis flopped limply to one side, draping itself over his thigh. He grabbed with his right hand, flicking the ridge of the glans with his thumb, and then he pulled the foreskin all the way down, aiming the dark purple knob at María.

"Ándale, pronto," he said, "me tengo que ir."

"Oye, no," said María. "Eso no. Por ahí vienen los muchachos de la escuela. Todas las puertas y las ventanas estan abiertas. ¿Qué pendejada es eso? ¿No te da vergüenza? ¿No te puedes esperar hasta la noche? Mira . . . cómo eres . . . "

"Cállate y hazte pa'ca," he said.

He leaped off the bed in a single bound, landing on his feet. He stared at María, fully naked in front of her, something rare in their reserved intimacy. María averted her eyes, a little embarrassed by his brazen display, unaccustomed to her husband's nakedness. There was confusion and irritability on her face. He spoke to her in a cold voice, exaggerating the control of his rage.

"Te digo que vengas pa'ca," he said. The command had a finality to it, he would not ask her again.

Faustino lay again on the bed, reclining on his side, his torso supported on one elbow. His testicles rolled over on his thigh. His penis was semi-hard. He pulled on it with a half dozen frenzied jerks and brought it to its full extension. The penis twitched spasmodically in anticipation, as if knowing María could not refuse, could not deny an obligation she had accepted as part of her life with him.

María stood where she was, making no move to go to him.

"¡Chingao!" yelled Faustino, flying from the bed, running to where she stood, grabbing her arm. "¿Estás sorda?" he screamed.

Faustino half-pulled her, half-dragged her to the bed and threw her on it. She landed on a hand and an elbow, bruising her ankle on the bed frame. The bed squeaked from the impact of her weight. María crawled over the bed, bouncing to the other side. She brushed the hair from her face, leaned her shoulder against the wall. She cried noiselessly.

With three long strides, Faustino rounded the corner of the bed and was next to her. He twisted María and struck her with the back of his hand, landing the full force of his knuckles on her ear. He tipped her without much effort onto the bed. She started to cry audibly as she made a move to get up again. She stopped her crying and lay still when she saw Faustino, his arms outstretched, poised, anticipating her move, waiting, inviting her to do something, ready to strike at her again. She lay back on her pillow, no longer wishing to resist. Her hair became a black halo around her head. She closed her eyes and crossed her arms corpse-like over her bosom.

Faustino walked slowly around the bed to the other side and sat on the corner of it, María's head at the opposite end. Her feet were pressed together,

her toes pointing directly to the ceiling. He looked at her bare ankles. He unclasped the buckles on her sandles, tossing them at his feet, patting a few grains of dirt off the coverlet. He rubbed her ankle up and down with his left hand. His eyes were intent on the hidden juncture of her legs which was covered by a faded green cotton skirt. He rubbed her ankle higher, slipping the tips of his fingers under the hem of the skirt.

His body trembled, his shoulders shook; small beads of perspiration formed above his eyebrows and on the bridge of his nose. He squeezed her kneecap and ran his open hand up María's smooth, brown thigh, feeling the soft, feather-like fuzz burn his palm. His hand continued upward, meeting a slight resistance in the material of the skirt. María rolled over so he could overcome it. He pushed upward and upward until the skirt bunched over her belly.

María's loose-fitting, blindingly white panties shone before him, their waistband high over her belly button, under her skirt. Faustino noted thread-bare patches from repeated launderings. The leg elastic was warped and tattered. They had a round hole to one side of the curved crotch panel, through which poked a shock of wavy pubic hair.

In a rough, hungry manner, Faustino forced her thighs apart with the scoop he made out of his hand. As he reached the point where her legs joined, he swiveled his wrist, snaked out his fingers, slid his hand over the flat of her stomach, and made an arc in the air to the bodice of her dress. He pinched the covered breasts repeatedly trying to find her nipples. It was one of the few things María enjoyed in sex. He could not find them.

Clumsily, breathing heavily, he could not manage to unbutton the top part of her dress. The more difficult it seemed, the more enraged he became. María placed her hand over his. Faustino whimpered.

"Espera," she said, quietly, caressing his arm down to his side.

She sat up, her face level with his, and began to unbutton her dress. Faustino rubbed his thigh nervously, impatiently. When it appeared to him that María was taking more time than necessary to unbutton her dress, in a rage, he leaned forward and with both hands, he ripped open the bodice, popping off the buttons as he pulled. He grabbed her brassiere in the middle and yanked. He shook María, but the garment remained in place. He took a handful of dress at the top of each of her shoulders and tore the back down the middle.

María, seeing the fury in Faustino's face, reached behind her to unhook the bra, letting the straps float uneasily down her arms. Instinctively, as though she were in the presence of a stranger, she crossed her arms to shield her breasts. Faustino moved closer to her. He lifted her arms, tossed them away and began to kiss and slobber on her chest. María's breasts were small and firm, perfectly round and proportioned to her body, with small, sloping nipples which, when touched, became flat, mesa-like eruptions on her soft mounds. She had breast-fed the children but her breasts did not sag. They remained as round and as firm as the virginal pair she had offered to Faustino on their wedding night. He bit into her nipple which became distended from irritation and pain and not from passion. As his teeth sank into the brown nipple, she took a quick breath but did not cry out, choosing to endure the hurt and humiliation lest Faustino become angrier.

Faustino crawled on the bed. He hovered over her body on his hands and knees. He hunched back, placing all of his weight on his knees, his body arched, kneeling in obscene piety. His wet hands rested on his thighs. He took the waistband of her cotton panties in both of his hands and pulled them down over her hips and buttocks. María lay still. He got them past her thighs, over her knees and down to her ankles. He slipped one foot through the leg opening and simply turned them aside, leaving them to bunch around her ankle. He grabbed her heels and lifted, throwing her legs in opposite directions. María remained limp, moving only when what he did jolted her.

María looked into Faustino's face. It was hard, animal-like, his lips tightly sealed, lines of anger streaked across his forehead in jagged irregularity. His lower jaw kept twitching, causing abrupt movements of his head to one side. Each twitch made his jugular burst forth, distorting the lean smoothness of his neck.

He crossed over one of her legs. Straddling it, he lowered himself to her kneecap, positioned the intersection of his testicles and the base of his penis and humped, dropping his face into her stomach, his mouth coming to rest on top of her belly button. He sucked, swallowing it and the flesh around it. The bunched-up dress at her midsection hid the top of his head from María. All she could see were his brown buttocks, rising and falling, appearing and disappearing, and she felt the on and off pressure on her kneecap.

Faustino's mind was not on María's body. Her tense, dusky body, with the skirt in a pile at the center of it, did not interest him any more than a surrogate. María was nothing more to him than a lump of indistinct, shapeless meat. María had a reasonably snug opening to receive the fluids that boiled within him and that was all he needed. Faustino recalled the image of the clothesline, remembering an earlier, distant excitement. His memory of what happened was all the more exciting because of the danger it had presented, the peril it had posed for him. The subsequent repulsion he had felt at Buster's house did not quell the tumult which Mrs. Crane had aroused in him.

María would receive him, not with passion or desire or encouragement. She would submit and accept his penetration of her. She would quiet the storm that seemed at every moment about to unleash its fury. María would draw from him the poisons that made him delirious. Inside her body, the familiar flesh would engulf him and bathe him with secretions that would be an antidote. She would drain the wellspring that his fear and his limited knowledge had uncapped.

The hard, erect penis nudged his belly, as if to remind him to continue with what he set out to do. He positioned himself between her legs. Supporting himself on one arm, he brought the other up to the hair-covered juncture of her legs. He touched the soft flesh. It was dry. Faustino poked his forefinger, deeper and deeper until it slid in all the way, taking one or two pubic hairs with it. It hurt, but María made no sound. He jerked the finger in and out, up and down, violently, demanding the mucous response. Faustino was aware that María was not helping at all. He paid no thought to that. Just as Mrs. Crane had been able to get his penis hard even though he had not been interested. Faustino was sure he could prepare her against her wishes.

"Pareces un animal," María said softly, describing what he did in a matter-of-fact voice.

"Cállate el hocico, pendeja," he hissed.

Faustino slumped upon the length of her body, burying his face between her neck and shoulder; the stubble of the day-long beard rasped her skin. He thrust his pelvis at her blindly seeking the entrance. With a harsh, brutal shove, he slid down her silky pubic hair and poked the mattress.

"Chingao," he said huskily, arching on his elbows and knees. "Ábrela."

His hair was wet and stringy, cold, as it fell into her face. His thighs were touching hers and the contact was clammy and slimy. María reluctantly, slowly, brought her hands around her hips. She chastely, careful not to touch him, pulled the labia of her vagina aside. Faustino lowered himself. When his penis was in the chute made by her fingers, he intruded her body. He did not put it in a little at a time as he usually did. He rammed it in as far as it could go, his pelvic bone smashing cruelly into hers.

He shoved and withdrew in rapid-fire fashion, feeling the muscles of his groin tense as he was so close to an orgasm. He changed his rhythm into long, deep strokes to make it last a little. His muscles relaxed and he heard María crying in his ear.

With each slithering lunge, his excitement subsided. He was pounding away what was left of his erection. He could feel it going limp inside his wife.

Faustino became frightened for his maleness. He started to hump with renewed vigor, increasing the frequency of his strokes. It did not help. It was becoming more and more difficult to shove it in once he drew it out.

The muscles of María's vagina reflexsively tried to grip the penis, contract to increase the friction; however, Faustino's penis was becoming so flaccid that the constricted muscles were an impediment. Faustino raised up on an elbow. With his free hand, he slapped María's face. "No hagas eso, cabrona," he said. He was determined to orgasm inside, for now it had become a point of honor with him.

His final lunge resulted in his penis becoming a useless wad of human flesh pressed against her body, unable to go in again. Faustino expelled a long sorrowful sigh. He was suddenly tired, his entire body blanketed by a musky sweat. He lost all of his energy and slumped over María, breathing heavily. María opened her eyes, which were red and swollen. The sun coming in through the window glistened on Faustino's back. She embraced him with one arm, wiping her wet cheek with the other. The two of them lay quietly on the bed.

After what seemed a long time, Faustino raised his hips. He looked at his limp penis, which had shrivelled to the size of a small cork. It dangled in the air as a useless, impotent appendage. A drop of sweat fell from his face onto María's breast. His face contorted into a fierce, wild mask of anger and frustration. Had she only helped him ...

"¡Haz algo!" he shouted at her in a shrill, frenzied scream as if fearful he might not be able to have another erection. María's tears flowed like a continuous crystal down her temples, seeking refuge in the lustre of her long, black hair.

She did not know what to do; Faustino had never had any trouble with his erections. She grabbed his penis and tossed it up and down in her hand. He brushed her hand away. "¡Así!" he said and showed her how to masturbate him. She tried to do as he showed her, but it had no effect. The penis was stubbornly limp. It remained a tiny extension from his body, a wrinkled, defeated protuberance dwarfed by his fat testicles.

Faustino looked about the room as if searching for something to revive the erection. He masturbated himself furiously until her body juices became gummy in his hand. His own, more experienced, ministrations did not help.

Everything seemed wrong to him now. He realized the brutality of his actions. Out of pity for her and anger toward himself, he began to curse her, to beat her, slapping her face with his open hand and striking her body with his fist. He screamed at her not to shield her face from the wide, swinging slaps. He wanted to hit her face. He cursed her and beat her with renewed force each time he struck the back of her hands. It was not until he saw blood splatter upon the white pillow that he stopped. María's teeth, nose, cheeks and hands were covered with blood. He looked at his hands, saw the blood on them and let them drop limply and impotently down his naked hips.

All expression left his face. He stepped off the bed quietly as if she were asleep and he was afraid to wake her. He dressed noiselessly after he wiped his hands with his underwear. The only sound in the room was his labored breathing and María's whispered sobs.

Without saying a word, without turning to look at his wife, Faustino went outside to sit on the porch. He wanted to be away from her crying. He opened a new bag of Bugler for a smoke. He did not care whether it was well-rolled or not, and he was oblivious to the ochre fingerprint he left on the cigarette paper.

He sat on the porch, elbows on his knees, smoking. He wanted to blot out the memory of everything that had happened to him. The events of the afternoon flashed before him in an image that took in everything. He dropped the cigarette and poked his eyes with his knuckles, trying to blank out what he saw with his mind. He clasped his hands together. The blood under his fingernails was already dry. He tried to roll another cigarette, but he trembled too much. Finally, he let go and watched the tobacco and paper float away.

He felt he should go inside to see María, to say something to her. Maybe to just sit next to her and touch her gently without saying anything. He felt he should explain to her that he himself did not understand what he did, that there was something driving him that he could not resist. To explain meant that he would have to start with Mrs. Crane. In the end, it would only make things worse. No, he could not go inside to her. He could not face her with any part of the truth. Of the little he understood, he knew she would forgive him and things would return to normal. Everything would be back the way it was. There was too much of importance between them and what he had done would not destroy it. Things are only the same if a man knows how to wait.

He stood up. All of him ached. He walked slowly, deliberately, to the truck, as if measuring or counting his steps. The spring in his step was gone, his head inclined forward.

The truck roared to a sputtering clatter quickly. As he swung the truck around his front yard, he looked out of the cab window and saw María standing in the doorway behind the screen door. He started to wave to her out of habit but checked himself. She would not want him to just yet. He eased the truck away, afraid to give it more gas, something which María might misinterpret. He felt drained and confused but he was not angry with her.

Instead of driving up to the highway, which was faster, Faustino turned into a dirt road. It was a short-cut to the fields where Buster and Casey waited for him. He had been gone more than two hours. The wrench he had been sent for was not in his back pocket and neither was it on the seat. He could not remember leaving it in Buster's kitchen, although he might have. Or, it might have dropped out of his pants at home. In either case, he could not go back to either place.

The sloping land near his place gave way to flat black dirt. He followed the tractor road. On his left was a field of sorghum which appeared as a copper-colored sea as far as his eyes could see. He was reminded that they would begin cutting in a few weeks. He had seen the advance man for the harvesters already contracting with Buster. He was glad he no longer had to drive the combine.

To his left was Scudder Robertson's pasture. As a younger man, Robertson raised and pitted fighting cocks. As he refused to farm his land, the birds supplemented the income from his cattle ranching. Then, he struck oil. His only son married another man, his English teacher in college, and the both of them moved to New York where they wrote poetry. Each month, an accountant in a bank in Chicago sent the boy a check. The checks would continue so long as the boy stayed away. Each month, the same accountant sent Scudder a check for a lot less. With it, he fed himself and his four hundred fighting cocks. He no longer pitted them and he raised them because they were more of a nuisance than cattle. He had sold all of his cattle as soon as he received his first royalty check. He sold all of his horses, too, keeping only one, a one-eyed sorrel who, according to Scudder, he would shoot one day when he had enough of him.

At the end of the sorghum field, Faustino slipped the truck into neutral and coasted to a stop in front of a gate. He would cross this pasture, which belonged to Buster, to get to a brown gravel farm road that would take him back to work.

He drove into the pasture. The spindly branches of the mesquite brushed lightly over the cab of the truck. There was only the suggestion of a road left, but he knew it well, maneuvering around the trees, heading in the direction of the farm road. About midway there, he came to the water well with its abandoned cistern. Buster kept the well in repair for the cattle and the trough was always full of water. Faustino pulled over to have a drink.

He opened the spigot and bent down, turning sideways, to drink the fresh, cold water. After he finished his drink, he took his handkerchief, soaked it, and draped it over his face. With one hand, he gathered it off his face and ran it along the back of his neck. He returned to the truck and leaned against a fender, intending to roll a smoke.

Faustino threw his head back, closed his eyes. As soon as he shut out the sunlight, the clothesline appeared along with the apparition who pinned underpants to the wire. At first it seemed a mere wisp of an image floating in the vast blackness of his mind. Gradually the image became larger until he could distinguish the sliver of white panties tucked in between the ghost-like thighs. As Faustino leaned further back to rest his head on the hood of the truck, he saw one mammoth breast, its nipple coming straight at him.

His previous unresponsive, dead body began to revive. He felt his blood begin to flow, rushing through his veins. His mind pursued the image of Mrs. Crane stooped over, willed it back into focus. He held the picture, so clear he could almost reach out and touch the plump body. His penis was beginning to strain against his jeans.

He moved away from the truck, walked around it and across the rutted road to a clearing surrounded by cactus. He avoided going near the red ant hill in the center. He stopped beside an enormous cactus pad which jutted well into the clearing, its needles long and sturdy.

Faustino unzipped his trousers and released the flushed and throbbing penis. He encircled it with the fingers of his right hand. He stretched his uncircumcised skin forward over the glans, releasing it finger by finger, twisting his hand so his palm rubbed the underside of it. He then pulled back on the skin until the organ arched, enjoying the sensation. He saw the fat, erratic veins pop out, coursing their way along the shaft-like elongated warts.

Faustino spread his legs, planting his boots firmly on the drying grass, assuring his balance. He found a pumping rhythm with which to begin, varying it by rolling and twisting the loose skin of his penis on the forward and backward motions. He loosened and tightened his grip, maintaining the slow, predictable, expected stroke. He tightened and loosened his sphincter, tensing and relaxing all the muscles in his groin area, rechanneling the flow of his blood, concentrating all of his energy at the base of his penis, gathering it from all points of his body, storing it. The stroking of his penis cleared his blocked passages, rearranged his blood vessels; with all that, he was soon pulsed in anticipation at the base of his organ.

He leaned back slightly, rolled his head backwards, closed his eyes to get a better view of the clothesline. One by one, the panties appeared before him, fluttering, the crotch dangling below his nose unclean, female musk wafting into him. A woman stooped over a washtub. She had Mrs. Crane's body—plump and thick, white and pink—and María's angular, coffee-colored face. He squeezed his eyes together to dismiss the image. Instantly, round, ample buttocks inserted in a pair of bikini panties appeared. That was better. He held on to what he saw, increasing the pumping rhythm.

Faustino now quickened the jerking movements of his hand. He shook his wrist furiously as one after another he saw breasts, thighs, buttocks, bikinis, housecoats. He would catch a wave of orgasmic flush flow into the shaft and he would pump faster as if to evacuate right away; and just as the flow reached the brink of orgasm, he would stop, squeeze tightly, relax his sphincter, open his eyes, enjoying the sensation of the ebbing orgasm. Before it withdrew too far, he started again: gently at first, coaxing it around, massaging the kinks caused by the abrupt reversal, drawing it forward, gathering speed, building momentum, pumping faster and faster, doubling over his body, his chin against his chest, his eyes pressed tightly shut.

He repeated the process several times until his testicles ached, vibrating with the beginnings of a dull pain. On the next surge, the sperm welled again, the pressure behind it built up. This time the flicking wrist did not stop. This time he humped his pelvis forward, thrusting into a phantom vagina in the air. His body jerked uncontrollably, ejaculating massive gobs of milk-white viscous semen. The first drop shot far into the air. Its arc splattered it against the cactus pad, into a tuft of yellow needles. The excess became a rivulet winding its way down the faded green of the cactus, forming into smaller drops at the bottom before dripping desultorily to the earth where they flattened on contact with the dirt, became a part of the dirt, dried and disappeared.

Spent, Faustino milked the last, residual drops of fluid from his penis. As he did so, the penis became flaccid, as soft and as pliable as his skin. He shook it a little more before stuffing it into his pants. He walked back to the truck, enjoying the hot rays of the sun on his face. He was relaxed now, peaceful, with a calmness he had not known before in his life.

He closed the door of the truck without slamming it for once. Faustino smiled all the way to the field where Buster and Casey waited.

Casey lay under the shade of the elongated tractor body. Buster sat with his back against the giant tractor tire. He was fuming. As soon as he heard the clatter of Faustino's truck entering the field, Buster stood up and adjusted his hat. In as long a stride as his short legs would permit, he went forward to meet Faustino. His ruddy face twitched, spittle foamed at the corners of his mouth and streamed down his chin.

Before Faustino could light down from the truck, Buster yelled at him. "Where in the goddamned fuck have you been?"

Faustino thought it best to put his smile away for later. By the time he was on the ground, his face was serious. "I had some trouble looking for that wrench, Mr. Buster. The toolshed is a mess. There is no light in there."

"I just bet the fucking toolshed is a fucking mess," said Buster. "I just fucking bet it is. Why the goddamned hell didn't you go in and ask my wife for a light bulb, or a flashlight, or something, huh?"

Faustino knew he was not expected to answer. He inspected the top of his boot. Buster turned to Casey.

"Did you hear that, Casey? The fucking toolshed is a fucking mess. That's what it fucking is. This fucking Mexican says my fucking tool shed is a fucking mess. He has been in the fucking mess. I'll be fucking damned. He takes three fucking hours to come back with his dick in his hand. I don't fucking see a fucking wrench in your fucking hand, Faustino."

Buster walked back to the tractor. He stretched an arm to lean against the tire and made a fist of the other hand to place on his hip. Faustino followed him, but stopped a short distance away.

Casey lay on the ground using a piece of deadwood for a pillow. His hat was draped over his face.

"You know how they are, Buster," said Casey.

"This fucker is going to say he fucking looked for the fucking wrench and couldn't fucking find it. I bet that's what he's going to fucking say. I just know it. What do you say to that, Casey?"

"I say, ask him," groaned Casey. He recognized Buster's temper.

"Where is the fucking wrench, bastard?"

"I couldn't find it, Mr. Buster."

"I knew he was going to say that, Casey. I knew he was going to fucking say that."

Buster opened the toolbox under the driver's seat on the tractor. He pulled out a long rusting wrench.

"What the fuck does this fucking look like to you, Faustino?"

"The wrench. It was there all the time?"

"Goddamned right it's the fucking wrench. It wasn't in the fucking toolbox. I had to go for it myself. Can't send a goddamned Mexican for nothing."

Buster threw the wrench back in the box and slapped the lid shut.

"While you were fucking off in the toolshed, my wife had it in the kitchen. She was trying to fix the goddamned water fucking pipes with it. It was lying right on the fucking kitchen floor by the door where she fucking threw it. You wouldn't fucking think to ask her for it, would you?"

"No, sir."

While Buster fulminated, Casey sat up and dusted his back. Lazily, he got on his feet and slapped the seat of his pants. He came up to Buster, placed his arm around Buster's shoulder in a fatherly way.

"He probably stopped to knock off a little from his señorita, Buster. What're you gettin' so riled for? You know how they are."

"If he wants to fucking fuck, let him do it on his own goddamn time, not mine." Buster's anger was easing. His voice was not as high-pitched as before.

"Can't fault a man for wanting to get laid. That's what I say." Casey strolled around to the sun side of the tractor to the water cooler. He took the tin cup from its hook and filled it with water. He poured a deep draught into his mouth, swilled it around and spit it out before drinking. Casey replaced the tin cup on its hook. He turned away from Buster and Faustino and looked toward the east, over the horizon into the past.

"You know, Buster," he said, "when yore daddy and me came out to this part of the country, one of the first things we learned about was these Mexicans. They like their fucking. Can't do without it. Now, yore daddy was a lot smarter than me and he figured it out first. He figured there ain't a damn thing a Mexican likes to do better than fuck, except maybe drink and fight."

"You and daddy figured that out, huh?" Buster was beginning to smile.

"Shore. Yore daddy was always saying the best lay he ever had was a mamacita in Gonzales. Wanted to set her up on the place here."

"Daddy used to fuck Mexicans?"

"Everybody does, Buster. You can do things to Mexicans that you can't do to your own."

"I'll be damned," said Buster.

"He shore liked that mamacita in Gonzales, yore paw did. Fucked her off and on most of his life out here. Never knew what happened to her. Man gets hard up, he'll fuck just about anything. Now, me, I can take 'em or leave 'em, you know. At my age, it don't much matter, anyhow. Not yore paw, though. Not yore paw."

"Aw, hell," said Buster. He took his hat off his head and wiped his brow. He struck his thigh with it several times. "I bet that's what this son of a mamacita bitch went and did. Jesus! I got me all this work to do and this fucking Mexican has to go home and get laid."

"Wouldn't you?" said Casey, and he started to laugh in a loud, wheezy sound. Buster, all of his anger gone, joined in, blended his squeaky laughter with Casey's. Faustino, infected by the laughter, not fully understanding its cause, but certain he was out of trouble, joined in. The three of them stood in a triangle, with the tractor inside it, laughing.

When the laughter finally died, Buster took Faustino aside. He placed his hand on Faustino's shoulder. "Casey and me are going to town. Got some business. Probably have a few beers after. I want you to go to my house. There's a grease can full of water under the sink. I ain't had time to empty it. My wife will show you what to do."

Nicholasa Mohr

To date, Nicholasa Mohr is the only U.S. Hispanic woman to have developed a long career as a creative writer for the major publishing houses. Since 1973, her books for such publishers as Dell/Dial, Harper & Row and Bantam, in both the adult and children's literature categories, have won numerous awards and outstanding reviews. Part and parcel of her work is the experience of growing up a female, Hispanic and a minority in New York City.

Nicholasa Mohr was born and raised in New York's Spanish Harlem. Educated in New York City schools, she finally escaped poverty after graduating from the Pratt Center for Contemporary Printmaking in 1969. From that date until the publication of her first book, *Nilda* (1973), Mohr developed a successful career as a graphic artist. *Nilda*, a novel that traces the life of a young Puerto Rican girl confronting prejudice while coming of age during World War II, won the Jane Addams Children's Book Award and was selected by *School Library Journal* as a Best Book of the Year. After *Nilda*'s success, Mohr was able to produce numerous stories, scripts and the following titles: *El Bronx Remembered* (1975), *In Nueva York* (1977), *Felita* (1979), *Rituals of Survival: A Woman's Portfolio* (1985), *Going Home* (1986). Selections from all of these story collections have been reprinted widely in a variety of anthologies and textbooks.

Mohr's works have been praised for depicting the life of Puerto Ricans in New York with empathy, realism and humor. In her stories for children, Mohr has been able to deal with the most serious and tragic of subjects, from the death of a loved one to incest, in a sensitive and humane way. Mohr has been able to contribute to the world of commercial publishing—where stereotypes have reigned supreme—some of the most honest and memorable depictions of Puerto Ricans in the United States. In this and in her crusade to open the doors of publishing and the literary world to Hispanics, Nicholasa Mohr is a true pioneer. The following selection, "Aunt Rosana's Rocker," is drawn from *Ritual's of Survival*, Mohr's testament to the fortitude of women in the city.

Aunt Rosana's Rocker (Zoraida)

Casto paced nervously, but softly, the full length of the small kitchen, then quietly, he tiptoed across the kitchen threshold into the living room. After going a few feet, he stopped to listen. The sounds were getting louder. Casto returned to the kitchen, switched on the light, and sat down trying to ignore what he heard. But the familiar sounds were coming directly from their bedroom where Zoraida was. They grew louder as they traveled past the tiny foyer, the living room and into the kitchen, which was the room furthest away from her.

Leaning forward, Casto stretched his hands out palms down on the kitchen table. Slowly he made two fists, squeezing tightly, and watched as his knuckles popped out tensely under his skin. He could almost feel her presence there, next to him, panting and breathing heavily. The panting developed into moans of sensual pleasure, disrupting the silence of the apartment.

"If only I could beat someone!" Casto whispered hoarsely, banging his fists against the table and upsetting the sugar bowl. The cover slipped off the bowl, landed on its side and rolled toward the edge of the table. Casto waited for it to drop to the floor, anticipating a loud crash, but the cover stopped right at the very edge and fell quietly and flatly on the table, barely making a sound.

He looked up at the electric clock on the wall over the refrigerator; it was two-thirty in the morning.

Again, Casto tried not to listen and concentrated instead on the night noises outside in the street. Traffic on the avenue had almost completely disappeared. Occasionally, a car sped by; someone's footsteps echoed against the pavement; and off at a distance, he heard a popular tune being whistled. Casto instinctively hummed along until the sound slipped away, and he then realized he was shivering. The old radiators had stopped clanking and hissing earlier; they were now ice cold. He remembered that the landlord never sent up heat after ten at night. He wished he had thought to bring a sweater or blanket with him; he was afraid of catching a cold. But he would not go back inside; instead, he opened his special section of the cupboard and searched among his countless bottles of vitamins and nutrient supplements until he found the jar of natural vitamin C tablets. He popped several tablets into his mouth and sat down, resigned to the fact that he would rather stay here, where he felt safe, even at the risk of getting a chill. This was as far away as he could get from her, without leaving the apartment.

The sounds had now become louder and more intense. Casto raised his hands and covered his ears. He shut his eyes trying not to imagine what she was doing now. But with each sound, he could clearly see her in her ecstasy. Casto recalled how he had jumped out of bed in a fright the first time it had happened. Positive that she had gone into convulsions, he had stood almost paralyzed at a safe distance looking down at her. He didn't know what to do. And, as he helplessly watched her, his stomach had suddenly turned ice-cold with fear. Zoraida seemed to be another person. She was stretched out on the bed pulling at the covers; turning, twisting her body and rocking her buttocks sensually. Her knees had been bent upward with her legs far apart and she had thrust her pelvis forward forcefully and rhythmically. Zoraida's head was pushed back and her mouth open, as she licked her lips, moaning and gasping with excitement. Casto remembered Zoraida's eyes when she had opened them for brief moments. They had been fixed on someone or something, as if beckoning; but there was no one and certainly nothing he could see in the darkness of the room. She had rolled back the pupils and only the whites of her eyes were visible. She had blinked rapidly, shutting her eyes and twitching her nose and mouth. Then, a smile had passed her lips and a stream of saliva had run down her chin, neck and chest.

Now, as he heard low moans filled with pleasure, interrupted by short painful yelps that pierced right through him, Casto could also imagine her every gesture.

Putting down his hands, Casto opened his eyes. All he could do was wait patiently, as he always did, wait for her to finish. Maybe tonight won't be a long one; Casto swallowed anxiously.

He remembered about the meeting he had arranged earlier in the evening without Zoraida's knowledge, and felt better. After work, he had gone to see his mother; then they had both gone to see Zoraida's parents. It had been difficult for him to speak about it, but he had managed somehow to tell them everything. At first they had reacted with disbelief, but after he had explained carefully and in detail what was happening, they had understood his embarrassment and his reluctance to discuss this with anyone. He told them that when it all had begun, he was positive Zoraida was reacting to a high fever and was simply dreaming, perhaps even hallucinating. But, it kept happening, and it soon developed into something that occurred frequently, almost every night.

He finally realized something or someone had taken a hold of her. He was sure she was not alone in that room and in that bed!

It was all bizarre and, unless one actually saw her, he explained, it was truly beyond belief. Why, her actions were lewd and vulgar, and if they were sexual, as it seemed, then this was not the kind of sex a decent husband and wife engage in. What was even harder for him to bear was her enjoyment. Yes, this was difficult, watching her total enjoyment of this whole disgusting business! And, to make matters more complicated, the next day, Zoraida seemed to remember nothing. In fact, during the day, she was normal again. Perhaps a bit more tired than usual, but then, who wouldn't be after such an exhausting ordeal? And, lately she had become even less talkative with him, almost silent. But, make no mistake, Casto assured them, Zoraida remained a wonderful housekeeper and devoted mother. Supper was served on time, chores were done without fuss, the apartment was immaculate, and the kids were attended to without any problems. This happened only at night, or rather early in the morning, at about two or two-thirty. He had not slept properly since this whole affair started. After all, he had to drive out to New Jersey to earn his living, and his strength and sleep were being sapped away. He had even considered sleeping on the living room couch, but he would not be driven out of his own bed. He was still a man, after all, a macho, master of his home, someone to be reckoned with, not to be pushed out!

Trying to control his anger, Casto had confessed that it had been a period of almost two months since he had normal and natural relations with his wife. He reminded them that he, as a man, had his needs, and this would surely make him ill, if it continued. Of course, he would not touch her . . . not as she was right now. After all, he reasoned, who knows what he could catch from her? As long as she was under the control of something, whatever it might be, he would keep his distance. No, Casto told them, he wanted no part of their daughter as a woman, not as long as she remained in this condition.

When her parents had asked him what Zoraida had to say about all of this, Casto had laughed, answering that she knew even less about it than he did. In fact, at one point she did not believe him and had sworn on the children's souls, claiming her innocence. But Casto had persisted and now Zoraida had finally believed him. She felt that she might be the victim of something, perhaps a phenomenon. Who knows? When Zoraida's parents and his mother suggested a consultation with Doña Digna, the spiritualist, he had quickly agreed.

Casto jumped slightly in his chair as he heard loud passionate moans and deep groans emanate from the bedroom and fill the kitchen.

"Stop it . . . stop, you bitch!" Casto clenched his teeth, spitting out the words. But he took care not to raise his voice. "Stop it! What a happy victim you are! *Puta!* Whore! Some phenomenon . . . I don't believe you and your story." But, even as he said these words, Casto knew he was not quite sure what to believe.

The first loud thump startled Casto and he braced himself and waited, anticipating what was to come. He heard the legs on their large double bed pounding the floor as the thumping became louder and faster.

Casto shuddered and folded his arms, digging his fingers into the flesh of his forearms. After a few moments, he finally heard her release, one long cry followed by several grunts, and then silence. He relaxed and sighed deeply with relief; it was all over.

"Animal . . . she's just like an animal, no better than an alley cat in heat." Casto was wet with cold perspiration. He was most frightened of this last part. "Little hypocrite!"

Casto remembered how she always urged him to hurry, be quiet, and get it over with, on account of the children. A lot she cares about him tonight! Never in all their years of marriage had she ever uttered such sounds—he shook his head—or shown any passion or much interest in doing it.

Casto looked up at the clock; it was two minutes to three. He thought about the noise, almost afraid to move, fearful that his downstairs neighbor Roberto might knock on the door any moment. He recalled how Roberto had called him aside one morning and spoken to him. "Two and three in the morning, my friend; can't you and your wife control your passions at such an ungodly hour? My God . . . such goings on! Man, and to tell you the truth, you people up there get me all worked up and horny. Then, when I touch my old lady, she won't cooperate at that time, eh?" He had poked Casto playfully and winked, "Hey, what am I gonna do? Have a heart, friend."

Casto shook his head, how humiliating and so damned condescending. They were behaving like the most common, vulgar people. Soon the whole fucking building would know! Roberto Thomas and his big mouth! Yes, and what will that sucker say to me next time? Casto trembled with anger. He wanted to rush in and shake Zoraida, wake her, beat her; he wanted to demand an explanation or else! But, he knew it wouldn't do any good. Twice he had tried. The first time, he had spoken to her the following day. The second time, he had tried to wake her up and she had only become wilder with him, almost violent, scaring him out of the bedroom. Afterwards, things had only become worse. During the day she withdrew, practically not speaking one word to him. The next few nights, she had become wilder and the ordeal lasted even longer. No, he could not confront her.

Casto realized all was quiet again. He shut off the light, then stood and slowly, with trepidation, walked through the living room and entered the small foyer leading to their bedroom. He stopped before the children's bedroom, and carefully turned the knob, partially opening the door. All three were fast asleep. He was grateful they never woke up. What could he say to them? That their mother was sick? But sick with what?

As he stood at the entrance of their bedroom, Casto squinted, scrutinizing every corner of the room before entering. The street lights seeping through the venetian blinds dimly illuminated the overcrowded bedroom. All was peaceful and quiet; nothing was disturbed or changed in any visible way. Satisfied, he walked in and looked down at Zoraida. She was fast asleep, breathing deeply and evenly, a look of serene contentment covered her face. Her long dark hair was spread over the pillow and spilled out onto the covers. Casto was struck by her radiant appearance each time it was all over. She had an air of glamour, so strange in a woman as plain as Zoraida. He realized, as he continued to stare at her, that he was frightened of Zoraida. He wanted to laugh at himself, but when Zoraida turned her head slightly, Casto found himself backing out of the room.

Casto stood at the entrance and whispered, "Zoraida, nena ... are ... are you awake?" She did not stir. Casto waited perfectly still and kept his eyes on her. After a few moments, Casto composed himself. He was sure she would remain sleeping; she had never woken up after it was all over. Slowly, he entered the room and inched his way past the bulky bureau, the triple dresser and the rocking chair near the window, finally reaching his side of the bed.

Casto rapidly made the sign of the cross before he lay down beside Zoraida. He was not very religious, he could take it or leave it; but, now, he reasoned that by crossing himself he was on God's side.

Casto glanced at the alarm clock; there were only two-and-a-half hours of sleep left before starting the long trip out to the docks of Bayonne, New Jersey. God, he was damned tired; he hardly ever got enough sleep anymore. This shit had to stop! Never mind, wait until the meeting. He remembered that they were all going to see Doña Digna, the spiritualist. That ought to change things. He smiled and felt some comfort knowing that this burden would soon be lifted. Seconds later he shut his eyes and fell fast asleep.

Everyone finished supper. Except for the children's chatter and Junior's protests about finishing his food, it had been a silent meal.

Casto got up and opened his special section of the cupboard. The children watched the familiar ritual without much interest as their father set out several jars of vitamins, two bottles of iron and liver tonic and a small plastic box containing therapeutic tablets. Casto carefully counted out and popped an assortment of twenty-four vitamin tablets into his mouth and then took several spoonfuls of tonic. He carefully examined the contents of the plastic box and decided not to take any of those tablets.

"Okay, Clarita, today you take vitamin C ... and two multivitamin supplements. You, too, Eddie and Junior, you might as well ... "

The children accepted the vitamins he gave them without resistance or fuss. They knew by now that no one could be excused from the table until Casto had finished taking and dispensing vitamins and tonic.

"Okay, kids, that's it. You can all have dessert later when your grandparents get here."

Quickly the children left.

Although Casto often suggested that Zoraida should eat properly, he had never asked her to take any of his vitamins or tonic, and she had never expressed either a desire or interest to do so.

He looked at Zoraida as she worked clearing the table and putting things away. Zoraida felt her heart pounding fiercely and she found it difficult to breathe. She wanted him to stop staring at her like that. Lately she found his staring unbearable. Zoraida's shyness had always determined her behavior in life. Ever since she could remember, any attempt that others made at intimate conversations or long discussions created feelings of constraint, developing into such anxiety that when she spoke, her voice had a tendency to fade. This was a constant problem for her; people often asked, "What was that?" or "Did you say something?" These feelings extended even into her family life. When her children asked impertinent questions, she would blush, unable to answer. Zoraida was ashamed of her own nakedness with Casto and would only undress when he was not present. When her children chanced to see her undressed at an unguarded moment, she would be distraught for several days.

It had been Casto's self-assurance and his ability to be aggressive and determined with others that had attracted her to him.

Casto looked at Zoraida as she worked. "I'll put my things back and get the coffee started for when they get here," he said. She nodded and continued swiftly and silently with her chores.

Zoraida was twenty-eight, and although she had borne four children (three living, one still-born) and had suffered several miscarriages, she was of slight build and thin, with narrow hips. She had a broad face and her smile revealed a wide space between her two front teeth. As a result, she appeared frail and childlike, much younger than her years. Whenever she was tired, dark circles formed under her eyes, contrasting against the paleness of her skin. This evening, she seemed to look even paler than ever to Casto, almost ghostlike.

Casto was, by nature, hypochondriacal and preoccupied with avoiding all sorts of diseases. He was tall and robust, with a broad frame; in fact, he was the picture of good health. He became furious when others laughed at him for taking so many vitamins and health foods. Most people ignored his pronouncements of ill health and even commented behind his back. "Casto'll live to be one hundred if he lives a day ... why, he's as fit as an ox! It's Zoraida who should take all them vitamins and then complain some. She looks like a toothpick, em una flaca! That woman has nothing to show. I wonder what Casto ever saw in her, eh?"

Yet, it was her frail and sickly appearance that had attracted him the first time he saw her. He was visiting his married sister, Purencia, when Zoraida had walked in with her friend, Anna. Anna was a beautiful, voluptuous young woman with an olive tone to her skin that glowed; and when she smiled, her white teeth and full lips made her appear radiant. Zoraida, thin and pale by contrast, looked ill. In Casto's presence, she had smiled sheepishly, blushing from time to time. Anna had flirted openly, and commented on Purencia's brother, "You didn't tell me you had such a gorgeous macho in your family. Trying to keep him a secret, girl?" But it had been Zoraida that he was immediately drawn to. Casto had been so taken with her that he had confided in a friend that very day, "She really got to me, you know? Not loud or vulgar like that other girl, who was acting like a man, making remarks about me and all. No, she was a real lady. And, she's like, well, like a little sick sparrow flirting with death and having the upper hand. Quietly stubborn, you know? Not at all submissive like it might seem to just anybody looking at Zoraida. It's more as if nobody's gonna make the sparrow healthy, but it ain't gonna die either ... like it's got the best of both worlds, see?"

Yet, in all their nine years of marriage, Zoraida had never become seriously ill. Her pregnancies and miscarriages were the only time that she had been unable to attend to her family. After the last pregnancy, in an attempt to prevent children, Casto had decided on the rhythm system, where abstinence is practiced during certain days of the month. It was, he reasoned, not only sanctioned by the Catholic Church, but there were no drugs or foreign objects put into one's body, and he did not have to be afraid of catching something nor getting sick.

Even after this recent miscarriage, Zoraida appeared to recover quickly, and with her usual amazing resilience, managed the household chores and the children all by herself. She even found time to assuage Casto's fears of sickness and prepare special foods for him.

Casto could feel his frustration building inside as he watched her. What the hell was the matter with this wife of his? Quickly he reached into his cupboard and took out some Maalox; God, the last thing he wanted was an ulcer on account of all of this.

"I think I'll coat my stomach." Casto chewed several Maalox tablets vigorously, then swallowed. "This way, I can have coffee later and it won't affect me badly." He waited for a response, but she remained silent. Casto sighed, she don't even talk to me no more . . . well, that's why I invited everybody here tonight, so they could see for themselves! He waited, staring at her, and then asked, "You got the cakes ready? I mean, you got them out of the boxes and everything?"

Zoraida nodded, not looking in his direction.

"Hey! *Coño*, I'm talking to you! Answer!"

"Yes," Zoraida whispered.

"And the cups and plates, you got them for the coffee and cake?"

"Yes," Zoraida repeated.

"I don't know, you know? It's been almost three months since Doña Digna did her job and cured you. I didn't figure you were gonna get so . . . so depressed." Zoraida continued to work silently. "Wait. Stop a minute. Why don't you answer me, eh? Will you look at me, for God's sake!"

Zoraida stopped and faced Casto with her eyes lowered.

"Look, I'm trying to talk to you, understand? Can't you talk to me?" Zoraida kept perfectly still. "Say something, will you?"

"What do you want me to say?" Zoraida spoke softly, without looking at him.

"Can't you look at me when you talk?"

Swiftly and furtively, Zoraida glanced at Casto, then lowered her eyes once more.

"*Coño*, man, what do you think I do all day out there to make a living? Play? Working my butt off in those docks in all kinds of weather . . . yeah. And for what? To come home to a woman that won't even look at me?" Casto's voice was loud and angry. He stopped, controled himself, then continued, lowering his voice. "I get up every morning before six. Every freaking morning! I risk pneumonia, rheumatism, arthritis, all kinds of sickness. Working that forklift, eight, ten hours a day, until my kidneys feel like they're gonna split out of my sides. And then, to make it worse, I gotta take orders from that stupid foreman who hates Puerto Ricans. Calling me a spic. In fact, they all hate Puerto Ricans out there. They call me spic, and they get away with it because I'm the only P.R. there, you know? Lousy Micks and Dagos! Listen, you know what they . . . ah, what's the use, I can't talk to you. Sure, why should you care? All you do is stay in a nice apartment, all warm and cozy. Damn it! I can't even have my woman like a normal man. First you had a phantom lover, right? Then, ever since Doña Digna took him away, you have that lousy chair you sit in and do your disappearing act. That's all you're good for lately. I can't even come near you. The minute I approach you like a human being for normal sex, you go and sit in that . . . that chair! I seen you fade out. Don't think I'm blind. You sit in that freaking thing, rocking away. You look . . . you . . . I don't even think you're breathing when you sit there! You should see yourself. What you look like is enough to scare anybody. Staring into space like some God damned zombie! You know what I should do with it? Throw it out, or better yet, bust that piece of crap into a thousand splinters! Yeah, that's what I ought to do. Only thing is, you'll find something else, right? Another lover, is that what you want, so you can become an animal? Because with me, let me tell you, you ain't no animal. With me you're nothing. *Mira*, you know something, I'm not taking no more of this. Never mind, when they get here they can see your whole bullshit act for themselves. Especially after I tell them . . . "

Zoraida barely heard him. The steady sound of the television program and the children's voices coming from their bedroom filled her with a pleasant feeling. How nice, she thought, all the children playing and happy. All fed and clean; yes, it's nice and peaceful.

The front doorbell rang.

"There they are." Casto had finished preparing the coffee. "I'll answer the door, you go on and get things ready."

Zoraida heard voices and trembled as she remembered Casto's threats and the fury he directed at her. Now he was going to tell them all sorts of things about her . . . untruths.

"Zoraida, where are you?" She heard her mother's voice, and then the voices of her father, mother-in-law and sister-in law.

"Mommy, Mommy," Clarita ran into the kitchen, "Nana and Granpa, and Abuelita and Titi Purencia are here. Can we have the cake now?"

"In a little while, Clarita." Zoraida followed her daughter out into the living room and greeted everybody.

"Mommy, Mommy!" Junior shouted, "Tell Eddie to stop it, he's hitting me!"

"I was not, it was Clarita!" Eddie walked over to his little brother and pushed him. Junior began to cry and Clarita ran over and smacked Eddie.

"See?" Casto shouted, "Stop it! Clarita, you get back inside." He jumped up, grabbing his daughter by an elbow and lifting her off the ground. "*Demonia*, why are you hitting him? Zoraida, can't you control these kids?" He shook Clarita forcefully and she began to whine.

"Casto," Zoraida's thin shriek whistled through the room. "Don't be rough with her, please!"

"See that, Doña Clara, your daughter can't even control her own kids no more." He turned to the children. "Now, all of you, get back inside your room and watch television; and be quiet or you go right to bed and nobody gets any cake. You hear? That means all three: Clarita, Eddie and you, too, Junior."

"Can we have the cake now?" Eddie asked.

"I'll call you when it's time. Now go on, go on, all of you." Quickly, the children left.

"Calm yourself, son." Doña Elvira, Casto's mother, walked over to him. "You know how children are, they don't know about patience or waiting; you were no angel yourself, you and your sister."

"Let's go inside and have coffee, everybody." Casto led them into the kitchen. There were six chairs set around the kitchen table. Doña Clara and her husband Don Isidro, Doña Elvira and her daughter Purencia squeezed in and sat down.

"Cut some cake for the kids and I'll bring it in to them," Casto spoke to Zoraida, who quickly began to cut up the chocolate cake and place the pieces on a plate. Everyone watched in silence. "Milk," snapped Casto. Zoraida set out three glasses of milk. Casto put everything on a tray and left.

"So, *mi hijita*, how are you?" Doña Clara asked her daughter.

"I'm okay." Zoraida sat down.

"You look pale to me, very pale. Don't she, Papa?" Doña Clara turned for a moment to Don Isidro, then continued without waiting for an answer. "You're probably not eating right. Zoraida, you have to take better care of yourself."

"All right." Casto returned and sat down with the others. "They're happy now."

"Son," Doña Elvira spoke to Casto. "You look tired, aren't you getting enough rest?"

"I'm all right, Ma. Here, everybody, have some cake and coffee."

Everyone began to help themselves.

"It's that job of his. He works so hard." Doña Elvira reached over and placed an extra large piece of chocolate cake on Casto's plate before continuing, "He should have stayed in school and become an accountant, like I wanted. Casto was so good at math, but . . . instead, he . . . "

"Pass the sugar, please," Doña Clara interrupted, "and a little bit of that rum cake, yes. Thank you."

They all ate in silence.

Doña Elvira looked at Zoraida and sighed, trying to hide her annoyance. What a sickly looking woman, *bendito*. She looks like a mouse. To think my handsome, healthy son, who could have had any girl he wanted, picked this one. Doña Elvira could hardly swallow her cake. Duped by her phony innocence is what it was! And how could he be happy and satisfied with such a woman? Look at her, she's pathetic. Now, oh yes, now, he's finding out who she really is: not the sweet innocent one, after all! Ha! First a phantom lover and now . . . who knows what! Well, we'll see how far she can go on with this, because now he's getting wise. With a sense of smug satisfaction, Doña Elvira half-smiled as she looked at her daughter-in-law, then ate her cake and drank her coffee.

Purencia saw her mother's look of contempt directed at Zoraida. She's jealous of Zoraida, Purencia smiled. Nobody was ever good enough for Casto. For her precious baby boy, well, and there you have it! Casto finally wanted Zoraida. Purencia smiled, serves Ma right. She looked at her sister-in-law who sat with her head bowed. God, she looks sicker than ever, but she never complains. She won't say nothing, even now, when he's putting her through this whole number. Poor goody-two-shoes Zoraida, she's not gonna get on Casto's case for nothing; like, why is he jiving her? I wonder what it is she's doing now? After that whole scene with Doña Digna, I thought she cured her of whatever that was. Purencia shrugged, who knows how it is with these quiet ones. They're the kind that hide the action. Maybe she's doing something nobody knows about ... well, let's just see.

Doña Clara looked at her son-in-law, Casto, with anger and a scowl on her face. *Bestia* ... brute of a man! He doesn't deserve anyone as delicate as Zoraida. She has to wait on that huge monster hand and foot. With all his stupid medicines and vitamins when he's as fit as a horse! Ungrateful man. He got an innocent girl, pure as the day she was born, that's what. Protected and brought up right by us. Never went out by herself. We always watched out who her friends were. She was guarded by us practically up until the moment she took her vows. Any man would have been proud to have her. *Canalla! Sinvergüenza!* She's clean, hardworking and obedient. Never complains. All he wants to do is humiliate her. We already went to Doña Digna, and Casto said Zoraida was cured. What now, for pity's sake? Doña Clara forced herself to turn away from Casto because the anger fomenting within her was beginning to upset her nerves.

Don Isidro sat uneasily. He wished his wife would not drag him into these things. Domestic disputes should be a private matter, he maintained emphatically, between man and wife. But, his wife's nerves were not always what they should be, and so he had to be here. He looked at his daughter and was struck by her girlish appearance. Don Isidro sighed, the mother of three children and she hasn't filled out ... she still has the body of a twelve-year-old. Well, after all, she was born premature, weighing only two pounds at birth. Don Isidro smiled, remembering what the doctors had called her. "The miracle baby," they had said. "Mr. Cuesta, your daughter is a miracle. She should not be alive." That's when he and Clara had decided to give her the middle name of Milagros. He had wanted a son, but after Zoraida's birth, his wife could bear no children, and so he had to be satisfied with what he had. Of course, he had two grandsons, but they wouldn't carry on his last name, so in a way it was not the same. Well, she's lucky to be married at all. Don Isidro nodded slightly, and Casto is a good, honest, hardworking man, totally devoted. Don't drink or gamble; he don't even look at other women. But, he too was lucky to get our Zoraida. After all, we brought her up proper and right. Catholic schools. Decent friends. Don Isidro looked around him at the silent table and felt a stiffness in his chest. He took a deep breath; what had she done? This whole business confused him. He thought Doña Digna had made the situation right once more.

"So, Casto, how are you? How's work?" Don Isidro asked.

"Pretty good. The weather gets to me, though. I have to guard against colds and sitting in that forklift gives me a sore back. But, I'm lucky to have work, the way things are going."

"You're right, they're laying off people everywhere. You read about it in the news every day."

"Zoraida, eat something," Doña Clara spoke to her daughter.

"I'm not hungry, Mami," Zoraida's voice was just above a whisper.

"Casto, you should see to it that she eats!" Doña Clara looked at her son-in-law, trying to control her annoyance. "Whatever this problem is, I'm sure part of it is that your wife never eats."

"Why should he see that she eats or not?" Doña Elvira interjected. "He has to go to work everyday to support his family ... he hasn't got time to ... "

"Wait a minute, Ma," Casto interrupted, "the problem here ain't food. That's not gonna solve what's going on."

"It seems to solve all your problems, eh?" Doña Clara looked at Casto with anger.

"Just hold on now ... wait," Don Isidro raised his hand. "Now, we are all arguing here with each other and we don't even know what the problem is. Why don't we find out what's going on?" Don Isidro turned to Castro and waited.

Everyone fell silent. Don Isidro continued, "I thought that Doña Digna's treatment worked. After all, you told us that yourself."

"It's not that no more," Casto looked around him, "it's something else now."

"What?" Doña Elvira asked.

Casto looked at Zoraida who sat with her hands folded on her lap and her eyes downcast.

"Weren't things going good for you two?" Don Isidro asked. "I mean, things were back to normal relations between you, yes?"

"Yes and no," Casto said. "Yes for a while and then ... "

"Then what?" Doña Elvira asked. "What?"

Casto looked at Zoraida. "You want to say something, Zoraida?"

She shook her head without looking at anyone.

"All right, then like usual, I gotta speak. You know that rocking chair Zoraida has? The one she brought with her when we got married?"

"You mean the one she's had ever since she was little? Why, we had that since Puerto Rico, it belonged to my Titi Rosana." Doña Clara looked perplexed. "What about the rocker?"

"Well, she just sits in it, when . . . when she shouldn't." Casto could feel the blood rushing to his face.

"What do you mean she sits in it?" Doña Clara asked. "What is she supposed to do? Stand in it?"

"I said *when she shouldn't.*"

"Shouldn't what?" Doña Clara turned to Don Isidro. "Papa, what is this man talking about?"

"Look," Casto continued, "this here chair is in the bedroom. That's where she keeps it. All right? Now when, when I . . . when we . . . " Casto hesitated, "you know what I mean. Then, instead of acting like a wife, she leaves the bed and sits in the chair. She sits and she rocks back and forth."

"Does she stay there all night?" Doña Elvira asked.

"Pretty much."

Everyone looked at Zoraida, who remained motionless without lifting her eyes. A few moments passed before Don Isidro broke the silence.

"This is a delicate subject, I don't know if it's a good thing to have this kind of discussion here, like this."

"What do you want me to do, Isidro? First she has those fits in bed driving me nuts. Then we call in Doña Digna, who decides she knows what's wrong, and puts me through a whole freakin' rigamarole of prayers and buying all kinds of crap. After all of that *pendejá*, which costs me money that I frankly don't have, then she tells me my wife is cured. Now it starts again, except in another way. Look, I'm only human, you know? And she," Casto pointed to Zoraida, "is denying me what is my right as a man and as her husband. And I don't know why she's doing this. But I do know this time you're gonna be here to know what's going on. I ain't going through this alone. No way. And get myself sick? No!"

"Just a moment, now," Doña Clara said, "you say Zoraida sits in the rocker when you . . . approach her. Does she ever sit there at other times? Or only at that time?"

"Once in a while, at other times, but always . . . always, you know, at that time!"

"*Ay . . . Dios mío!*" Doña Elvira stood up. "I don't know how my son puts up with this, if you ask me." She put her hands to her head. "Casto has the patience of a saint, any other man would do . . . do worse!"

"What do you mean, the patience of a saint?" Doña Clara glared at Doña Elvira. "And do worse what? Your son might be the whole cause of this, for all I know . . . "

"Now, wait." Don Isidro stood up. "Again, we are fighting and blaming this one or that one. This will get us nowhere. Doña Elvira, please sit down." Doña Elvira sat, and then Don Isidro sat down also. "Between a man and wife, it's best not to interfere."

"Okay then, Papa, what are we here for?" Doña Clara asked.

"To help, if we can," Purencia spoke. Everyone listened; she had not spoken a word before this. "I think that's what my brother wants. Right, Casto?"

Casto nodded, and then shrugged.

"Let Zoraida say something," Purencia continued. "She never gets a chance to say one word."

"Nobody's stopping her." Casto looked at Zoraida. "Didn't I ask her to say something? In fact, maybe she can tell us what's going on. Like, I would like to know, too, you know."

"Zoraida," Doña Clara spoke firmly to her daughter, "*mira*, you better tell us what all of this is about."

Zoraida looked up, meeting her mother's angry stare. "I don't know what Casto means about the chair."

"Do you sit in the rocker or do you not sit there, like he says?" her mother asked.

"Sometimes."

"Sometimes? What times? Is it like the way he says it is? Because, if this is so, we want to know why. Doña Digna told me, you and all of us, that there was an evil spirit in you that was turning your thoughts away from your husband, so that you could not be a wife to him. After she finished her treatment, she said the evil spirit or force was gone, and that you would go back to a normal husband-and-wife relationship. We have to accept that. She is a woman of honor that has been doing this work for many years, and that she is telling us the truth, yes?" Doña Clara took a deep breath. "But, if you feel anything is wrong, then it could be that Doña Digna did not succeed." She turned to Casto. "That's possible too, you know. These things sometimes get very complicated. I remember when the Alvarez household was having the worst kind of luck. Don Pablo had lost his job, his wife was sick, and one of their boys had an accident; all kinds of problems, remember? You remember, Papa? Well, Doña Digna had to go back, and it took her a long time to discover the exact cause and then to make things straight again." She turned to Zoraida, "*Bueno*, *mi hija*, you have to tell us what you feel, and if you are doing this to your husband, why?" Doña Clara waited for her daughter's response. "Go ahead. Answer, *por Dios!*"

"I . . . ," Zoraida cleared her throat in an effort to speak louder. "I just sit in the rocker sometimes. Because I feel relaxed there."

"Yeah!" Casto said, "Every time I go near her at night, or at two or three in the morning, she relaxes." He raised his hand and slammed the table, "God damned chair!"

"*Cálmate, mi hijito*, calm yourself." Doña Elvira put her hand over her eyes. "I don't know how long my son can put up with all of this. Now she's got an obsession with a chair. *Virgen, purísima!* Somebody has to tell me what is going on here!"

"Listen to me," Don Isidro spoke in a firm voice, "if it's the chair that bothers you, then we'll take it back home with us. Right, Mama?" He turned to Doña Clara who nodded emphatically. "There should be no objection to that, eh?"

Everyone looked at Casto, who shrugged, and then at Zoraida, who opened her mouth and shook her head, but was unable to speak.

"Very good." Don Isidro clasped his hands and smiled. "There, that ought to take care of the problems pretty much."

"Except, she might find something else," Casto said. "Who knows with her."

"Well, but we don't know that for sure, do we?" Don Isidro replied. "And in the meantime, we gotta start somewhere."

"I feel we can always call Doña Digna in again if we have to." Doña Clara poured herself a cup of coffee. "After all, she was the one that told us Zoraida was cured."

"I agree," Doña Elvira said, "and even though she don't ask for money, I know my Casto was very generous with her."

"That's right, they don't charge, but after all, one has to give these people something, or else how can they live?" agreed Doña Clara.

"Isn't the weather funny this Spring?" Doña Elvira spoke amiably. "One minute it's cold and the next it's like summer. One never knows how to dress these . . . "

They continued speaking about the weather and about television programs. Purencia spoke about her favorite movie.

"That one about the professional hit-man, who has a contract out to kill the President of England . . . no, France, I think. Anyway, remember when he goes into that woman's house and kills her? I was so scared, I loved that movie."

Everyone agreed, the best kinds of movies were mysteries and thrillers.

Zoraida half-listened to them. They were going to take away the rocker. She had always had it, ever since she could remember. When she was a little girl, her parents told her it was a part of their history. Part of Puerto Rico and her great Aunt Rosana who was very beautiful and had countless suitors. The chair was made of oak with intricate carving and delicate caning. As a little girl, Zoraida used to rub her hands against the caning and woodwork admiringly, while she rocked, dreamed and pretended to her heart's content. Lately it had become the one place where she felt she could be herself, where she could really be free.

"Bueno, we have to go. It's late."

"That's right, me too."

"Wait," Casto told them, "I'll drive you people home."

"You don't have to . . . " Don Isidro protested. "We know you are tired."

"No, I'm not. Besides, I gotta drive Ma and Purencia home, anyway."

"That's right," Purencia said, "my old man doesn't like me going out at night. It's only because of Mami that he let me. So, Casto has to take me home."

"I gotta get you the chair, wait," Casto said. "And, you don't wanna carry that all the way home. It's not very big, but still, it's a lot to lug around."

"All right, then, very good."

Everyone got up and Zoraida began to clear away the dishes.

"Let me help you," Doña Clara said as she stood up.

"Me too," Doña Elvira said, without rising.

"No, no thanks. That's all right. I can do it myself," Zoraida said. "Besides, I have to put the kids to bed and give them their milk and all."

"I don't know how she does it. Three little ones and this place is always immaculate." Doña Clara turned to Doña Elvira. "It's really too much for her, and she has no help at all."

Doña Elvira stood. "She keeps a very clean house," she said and walked out with Purencia, following after Casto and Don Isidro.

Doña Clara looked at her daughter, who worked silently and efficiently. "*Mira, mi hija*, I better talk to you." She stood close to Zoraida and began to speak in a friendly manner, keeping her voice low. "You have to humor men; you must know that by now. After all, you are no longer a little girl. All women go through this difficulty, eh? You are not the only one. Why, do you know how many times your father wants . . . well, you know, wants it? But I, that is, if I don't want to do it, well I find a way not to. But diplomatically, you know? All right, he's older now and he bothers me less; still, what I mean is, you have to learn that men are like babies and they feel rejected unless you handle the situation just right. Now, we'll take the rocker back home with us because it will make him feel better. But you must do your part too. Tell him you have a headache, or a backache, or you can even pretend to be asleep. However, once in a while you have to please him, you know. After all, he does support you and the children and he needs it to relax. What's the harm in it? It's a small sacrifice. Listen, I'll give you some good advice; make believe you are enjoying it and then get it over with real quick, eh? So, once in a while you have to, whether you like it or not; that's just the way it is for us. Okay? Do you understand?"

Zoraida turned away and, without responding, continued with her work.

"Did you hear what I just told you?" Doña Clara grabbed Zoraida's shoulder firmly, squeezing her fingers against the flesh. "You didn't even hear what I said to you!"

Zoraida pulled away and turned quickly to face her mother. She looked directly at Doña Clara. "I heard you . . . " Zoraida stopped and a smile passed her lips. "I heard every word you said, Mami."

"Oh, all right, then . . . " Doña Clara said, somewhat startled by her daughter's smile. "I only wanted to . . . "

"Mama! Come on, it's time to go," Don Isidro's voice interrupted her.

Doña Clara and Zoraida went into the living room. Casto carried the rocking chair and waited by the door. The children had come out of their room and were happily jumping about.

"Look, Mommy, Grandpa gave me a quarter," Clarita said.

"Me, too," said Eddie. "He even gave Junior one."

"All right, get to bed!" Casto shouted. "Zoraida, put them down, will you?"

Everybody said goodbye and, in a moment, Casto and the others left.

"Mommy, where is Daddy taking your chair?" Clarita asked.

"To Nana's."

"Why?"

"Because they want it now?"

"Don't you want it no more?"

"I already had it for a long time, now they need to have it for a while."

Zoraida gave the children their milk, bathed them and put them to bed. Then, she finished rapidly in the kitchen and went to bed herself. She looked over at the empty space near the window. It was gone. She wouldn't be able to sit there anymore and meet all her suitors and be beautiful. The last time . . . the last time she was dancing to a very slow number, a ballad. But she couldn't remember the words. And she was with, with . . . which one? She just couldn't remember him anymore. If she had the rocker, she could remember; it would all come back to her as soon as she sat down. In fact, she was always able to pick up exactly where she had left off the time before. She shut her eyes, deciding not to think about the rocker, about Casto, Doña

Digna or her mother. Instead, Zoraida remembered her children who were safe and asleep in their own beds. In a short while, she heard the front door open and recognized Casto's footsteps. She shut her eyes, turned over, facing away from his side of the bed. Casto found the apartment silent and dark, except for the night light.

In the bedroom, Casto looked at Zoraida, who seemed fast asleep, then at the empty space near the window where the rocker usually stood. Their bedroom seemed larger and his burden lighter. Casto sighed, feeling better. He reached over and lightly touched Zoraida; this was a safe time of the month, maybe she would wake up. He waited and, after a moment, decided to go to sleep. After all, he could always try again tomorrow.

Margarita Mondrus Engle

Margarita Mondrus Engle's writing has been concerned with the dual nature of heredity and culture. She is the daughter of a Cuban mother and had the opportunity to spend part of her childhood in Cuba. Her father is an American artist who traveled to Cuba to paint the picturesque city of her mother's birth and upbringing: Trinidad. As a journalist and writer, Engle has been able to return to Cuba during the last few years.

As noted above, Engle has led a dual career as a fiction writer and journalist whose opinion columns on topics ranging from culture and history to personal experience have been syndicated on a regular basis since 1982 to over two hundred newspapers. Her short stories have been published in *Nuestro*, *The Americas Review*, *Revista Interamericana* and various others. Engle has also published non-fiction pieces in such national magazines as *Vista*, *Hispanic*, *South American Explorer*, *Garden* and others. Many of Engle's non-fiction articles are related to plant and soil science; she is a botanist by training and profession and has worked as an irrigation specialist in Southern California up until 1990. Nevertheless, it is her fiction writing, particularly as related to Cuban and Cuban-American subjects, that is her passion, as can be seen in the following stories.

Niña

My mother was afraid it might be our last chance to visit her family in Cuba. The revolution was almost two years old, and already there was talk of an impending crisis.

At the airport in Miami she gave us three instructions.

"Never tell anyone you are tomboys."

"Why?"

"They wouldn't understand. Also, don't tell the other children about your allowance. You have more money in the bank than their fathers make in a year."

"So?"

"So, they would feel bad."

"Oh."

"And most important, don't bring animals into your grandmother's house."

"But Mom . . . "

"No animals. They don't like having animals in the house. Do you understand?"

At the airport in Havana we released the caterpillars we had hidden in our luggage.

"Just in case there are no butterflies here," my sister and I reassured each other.

We had no idea what to expect, but the island did not disappoint us. Abuelita's house was on the outer fringe of Havana, and there were animals everywhere. We put lizards in beds, and tarantulas and scorpions in the living room. The fisherman who lived across the street gave us a ripe swordfish snout to play with. When it really started to stink, my mother threw it on the roof, where it rotted quickly in the sun.

The fisherman's daughter asked me if I had money for ice cream. "Yes," I said with pride, "I have eighty dollars in the bank, which I saved all by myself."

"Dollars? Really?" I could see she didn't believe a word of it. I squirmed inside, remembering my mother's admonition.

"Well, I have something better," the girl offered. "Crabs. When my father gets home, you can have one to cook for your dinner."

She was right, of course. The crabs were better than my money. Her father came home with a truckload of them, bright orange crabs as big as cats. We put ours on a leash and led it up and down the street until it died.

My sister liked dogs better than crabs. She begged my mother for a can of dog food for my great-grandmother's mangy hound. We had to go all the way downtown, to Woolworth's, just to find dog food in cans. It cost more than a month's supply of real food, corn meal, black beans and rice.

Just to make sure there were no sins left uncommitted, I went across the street and told the fisherman's daughter I was a tomboy.

"Oh no," she said, horrified. "You're not a tomboy, don't worry. You will be fine." She fluffed her petticoats and curled a lock of hair with her fingers.

My collection of revolutionary bullets was growing. They were everywhere—in Abuelita's front yard and in the weeds where we searched for tarantulas, which we caught with wads of gum attached to strings. There were bullets in the open fields beyond the city, and in the passion vines which clung to the walls of houses.

On one of my solitary expeditions I wandered far beyond those walls, beyond the open fields, and into a mud-floored hut with a thatched roof and many inhabitants. The family greeted me as if I had some right to invade their home. The children came outside to introduce me to their mule, their chickens and the sensitive Mimosa plant which closed its leaves at the touch of a child's fingers.

One of the children was called Niña, meaning "girl." I assumed her parents had simply run out of names by the time they got around to her. In Niña's case, her name was no more unusual than her appearance. She was hardly there, just bones and eyes, and a few pale whisps of hair bleached by malnutrition.

"Doesn't she get enough to eat?" I asked my mother when I reached home.

"They say she has a hole in her stomach."

One day I was standing in the sun of the front porch, watching a black storm cloud sweep across the sky, bringing toward me its thunder and lightning, which fell only in one small corner of the sky. A motionless circle of vultures hung from the cloud, listless, with black wings barely trembling in the wind.

"Come in," my mother warned. "Don't forget your uncle who was killed by lightning, right in his own kitchen."

I ignored her. If it could happen in the kitchen, then why bother to go inside? I was just as safe outside.

Niña crept up to the porch, smiling her death's head smile, like the skull and crossbones on a bottle of medicine.

"Here," she said, offering me half of the *anon* fruit she was eating. I took it. Together we ate and stared and smiled at each other, not knowing what to say. We both knew my half of the seedy, juicy fruit was going into my body, making flesh and fat, while hers was going right out the gaping invisible hole in her stomach.

Something like a shiver passed through my shoulders.

"Someone stepped on your grave," Niña giggled.

"What do you mean?"

"They say when you shiver like that it's because someone stepped on the spot where your grave will be."

I stared at Niña's huge eyes, wondering who could have been cruel enough to inform her that she would ever have a grave.

When we trooped down the street to the bingo games at my great-grandmother's house, Niña tagged along. An endless array of uncles and cousins filed in and out, a few boasting revolutionary beards and uniforms, but most outfitted in their farmers' Sunday best, their hands brown and calloused.

Niña was quiet. She poured burnt-milk candy through the hole in her stomach, and watched. The size of her eyes made her watching feel like staring, but no one seemed to notice. Children like Niña surprised no one.

On the anniversary of the revolution, the streets filled with truckloads of bearded men on their way to the mountains to celebrate. A man with a loudspeaker walked along our street announcing the treachery of the Yanquis. I was listening inside my grandmother's house. Suddenly his voice changed.

"Let me clarify," he was saying, "that it is not the common people of the United States who we oppose, but the government which has . . . " I stopped listening. Niña was at the open door, smiling her bony smile.

"I told him," she said very quietly, "that you are from *Estados Unidos*. I didn't want him to hurt your feelings."

At the beach, my sister and I went swimming inside shark fences. We imagined the gliding fins beyond the fence. Afterwards, our mother extracted the spines of bristly sea urchins from the soles of our feet.

We visited huge caverns gleaming with stalactites. How wonderfully the Cuban Indians must have lived, I thought, with no home but a cave, nothing to eat but fruit and shellfish, nothing to do but swim and sing. "We were born a thousand years too late," I told my sister.

With a square old-fashioned camera, I took pictures of pigs, dogs, turkeys, horses and mules. Not once did it occur to me to put a friend or relative into one of my photos. I was from Los Angeles. There were more than enough people in my world, and far too few creatures. When my uncle cut sugarcane, it was the stiff, sweet cane itself which caught my eye, and the gnats clinging to his eyes. His strong arms and wizened face were just part of the landscape. When my cousins picked *mamonsillo* fruit, it was the tree I looked at, and not the boys showing off by climbing it. I thrived on the wet smell of green land after a rain, and the treasures I found crawling in red mud or dangling from the leaves of weeds and vines. I trapped lizards, netted butterflies, and once, with the help of my sister, I snared a vulture with an elaborate hand-rigged snare. Our relatives were horrified. What could one do with a vulture? It was just the way I felt about everything which mattered to them. If the goal of the revolution was to uproot happy people from their thatched havens, and deposit them in concrete high-rise apartment buildings, who needed it? Thatched huts, after all, were natural, wild, primitive. They were as good as camping. When my mother explained that the people living in the *bohíos* were tired of it, I grew sulky. Only an adult would be foolish enough to believe that any normal human being could prefer comfort to wildness, roses to weeds, radios to the chants of night-singing frogs.

I knew the hole in Niña's stomach was growing. She was disappearing, vanishing before my eyes. Her parents seemed resigned to her departure. People spoke of her as if she had never really been there. Niña was not solid. She didn't really exist.

On the day of her death, it occurred to me to ask my mother, "Why didn't they just take her to a doctor?"

"They had no money."

I went out to the front porch, abandoning the tarantula I had been about to feed. As I gazed across the open fields toward Niña's *bohío*, the reality of her death permeated the humid summer air. In my mind, I sifted through a stack of foals and ducks, caterpillars and vultures. Somewhere in that stack, I realized, there should have been an image of Niña.

Alejandro Morales

Alejandro Morales is one of the leading Chicano novelists, having published substantial novels in both Spanish and English in the United States and Mexico, and having created through them a better understanding of Mexican-American history, at least as seen from the vantage point of working-class culture. Born in Montebello, California, on October 14, 1944, Morales grew up in East Los Angeles and received his B.A. from California State University at Los Angeles. He went on to complete an M.A. (1973) and a Ph.D. (1975) in Spanish at Rutgers University in New Jersey. Today Morales is a full professor in the Spanish and Portuguese Department at the University of California-Irvine.

Morales is a recorder of the Chicano experience, basing many of his narratives on historical research, and he is also an imaginative interpreter of that experience through his creating memorable and dynamic characters and language. His first books were written in Spanish and published in Mexico, due to the lack of opportunity here in the United States. *Caras viejas y vino nuevo* (1975, translated as *Old Faces and New Wine*, 1981), examines the conflict of generations in a barrio family. *La verdad sin voz* (1979, translated as *Death of an Anglo*, 1988) is a continuation of the earlier novel, but is created against the backdrop of actual occurrences of Chicano-Anglo conflict in the town of Mathis, Texas. The novel also includes autobiographical elements in the form of a section that deals with the racism in academia that comes to a head when a Chicano professor goes up for tenure. *Reto en el paraíso* (1983, Challenge in Paradise) is based on more than one hundred years of Mexican-American history and myth, as it centers on a basic comparison of the decline of the famed Coronel family of early California and the rise of the Irish immigrant Lifford family. The novel charts the transfer of power and wealth from the native inhabitants of California to the gold- and land-hungry immigrants empowered by Manifest Destiny. *The Brick People* (1988) traces the development of two families connected with the Simons Brick Factory, one of the largest enterprises of its type in the country. Again, Morales uses the technique of comparing the lives of two families, those of the owners of the factory and those of an immigrant laborer's family. Morales' novel, *The Rag Doll Plagues* (1991), while still incorporating an historical structure, follows the development of a plague and a Spanish-Mexican doctor who is forever caught in mortal battle with this plague in three time periods and locations: colonial Mexico, contemporary Southern California and the future in a country made up of Mexico and California united together.

In all, Morales is a meticulous researcher and a creator of novelistic circumstances derived from Mexican-American history. In total, his novels have an epic sweep that are cinematic and highly literary.

Cara de Caballo

Nowhere in the recorded histories of California is there an explanation for why Doña Arcadia Bandini married Abel Stearns. Both were from prominent families, well known and respected in Southern California. But the match of these two people was considered truly a fairytale.

Don Juan Bandini's daughters were famous for their beauty, and the most beautiful of them all was the eldest, Arcadia Bandini. Don Juan, one of the most powerful and wealthy men of his time, believed he was destined to become a great leader. When the United States took over the northern Mexican territories, Don Juan supported the new government. He believed that California would prosper once the people accepted the new leadership, and he thought his support would one day be rewarded.

A small and dapper man, Don Juan was also highly intelligent and given to sarcasm when matters did not go his way. But he possessed one of the largest ranches in Southern California, lands which stretched from the Mexican frontier to the San Bernardino Mountains. At the height of his success, Don Juan was a *ranchero* whose holdings assured him a position of great respect.

Don Juan was married twice. His first wife was Doña Dolores, a lovely woman of the Estudillo family who bore him five children: three daughters, Arcadia, Isadora, and Josefa, and two sons, José María and Juanito. His second wife, Arcadia's stepmother, was Refugio, also of great beauty, from the Argüello family. Doña Refugio and Don Juan had five children: three sons, Juan de la Cruz, Alfredo and Arturo, and two daughters, Mónica and Herma. Arcadia was the oldest of all his children, and don Juan carried for her a special flame in his heart. She was born at the zenith of his power, and she buried him in 1859 a disillusioned man.

Don Juan was respected as a man of education and of generosity, even during times of personal misfortune. He made two bad investments: the financing of a store in San Diego and a hotel in San Francisco, which forced him to seek loans to cover his family's living expenses. He went to a French gambler, poet and novelist, Leon Hennique, and asked for ten thousand dollars. Hennique gladly gave him the money, but tagged on a four percent monthly interest rate. Don Juan was confident he could repay the loan in a few months with revenue from cattle sales. But an unforeseen slump in cattle sales forced Bandini to ask Hennique for an extension on the loan. The Frenchman granted the extension, but insisted on the deeds to Don Juan's homes as guarantees of payment. As the months passed, more bad luck plagued Don Juan, until he found himself trapped in an economic labyrinth from which he could see no escape. In his panic he made more impulsive decisions, causing his business affairs to decline even further.

During this period of economic crisis, the Bandini family was constantly at odds. Doña Refugio continued to plan one expensive fiesta after another, and Don Juan's sons, acting as if the money in the Bandini coffers had no end, pursued their costly gambling activities. Another kind of friction also appeared. Don Juan's sons had married Mexican women, but three of his daughters had married Anglo-American men. Don Juan became convinced that the reason for his bad luck and the disharmony in his family was due to the foreign element, the gringo influence that had entrenched itself in his family through his daughters. He was bitter that his daughters had chosen *gringos*, but what hurt most of all was the fact that he had encouraged those unions. He had supported the new government all the way, even delivering his virgin daughters to its men.

Now the Bandinis were on the verge of economic disaster. Charles R. Johnson, who had married the sixteen-year-old Mónica, offered to advise his father-in-law. Don Juan resisted, but Johnson was finally able to convince him to sign over a temporary power of attorney. Johnson then sent Don Juan and Doña Refugio to Monterey on vacation. Arcadia remained alone with the servants on the San Diego estate.

Johnson and his brother-in-law, J.C. Couts, who was married to Isadora, reflected the Anglo attitude towards Mexican men. They considered them incompetent and lazy. But J.C. Couts was, at least, a decent man, and he finally convinced Johnson to speak with Abel Stearns about a loan for Don Juan Bandini. Johnson knew Don Juan disliked Stearns because of Stearns' hostility to Mexico and Mexicans. He also knew Don Juan and Stearns had often competed for the best *vaqueros* to work their respective *ranchos*. Nevertheless, Johnson decided to ignore Don Juan's feelings, and he asked Stearns for a loan of four thousand dollars. Johnson described to Stearns the crisis the Bandini family was going through, and he told him that to save Don Juan's land was to save his life. Stearns agreed to inspect the Bandini holdings and consider the loan.

On the morning of April 28, 1851, Isadora and Mónica arrived at the Bandini estate in San Diego to inform Arcadia that Abel Stearns was to visit that afternoon. The servants were ordered to prepare a grand feast. The two sisters then lectured Arcadia for not making herself available to men, and they advised her to make herself beautiful for Abel Stearns, who just happened to be one of the richest men in the state. Arcadia listened with half an ear. The two sisters broke off their complaints when Stearns arrived with Johnson and Couts. The three women waited on the porch of the large adobe ranch home. As Stearns approached, he kept his eyes on Arcadia, not even glancing at her sisters when they were introduced. With sidelong looks of satisfaction, the two couples left Arcadia and Stearns alone on the porch.

Abel Stearns was born in Mexico in 1799 and came to California in 1829. He was fifty-one years old when he met Arcadia. He was the largest landowner in Southern California, and certainly one of the wealthiest. He was also one of the ugliest men in Southern California. Born a homely man, he was severely wounded in a quarrel over some wine. A deep cut ran through his nose and both lips, giving him a distinct speech impediment. He was called *Cara de caballo*; some people found it difficult to look at his face. This was the man who stood before Arcadia Bandini, a woman so beautiful that he could only gaze at her and whisper *gracias.*

Arcadia stared at Stearns' grotesque face. His disfigurement forced him to breathe heavily and noisily through his deformed mouth. She noticed how large his hands were, his arms ridiculously long. But as she studied his face, she saw a kindness, a promise of a good man behind the physical distortion. Stearns asked her to marry him. He spoke of his wealth and of the things he could do for her family, for her beloved father. He promised to love her forever and to make her the happiest woman in California. Arcadia made her decision. "Abel Stearns, you are the ugliest man I have ever seen. I will marry you and I will be yours to the last moment of your life." Stearns' broken lips formed a smile. He kissed her hand and went off full of excitement to explore the Bandini estate. Arcadia called for her sisters and announced her engagement. "Send for our father and mother. Tell them I am to be married upon their return. Let the people know that Arcadia Bandini will wed Abel Stearns."

And so she did. Two days after the Bandinis returned from Monterey, their most beautiful daughter was wed to the ugliest man in Southern California. At Arcadia's request, the private ceremony was held in the open plains of the Rancho Alamitos. The newlyweds spent their wedding night in a simple cabin atop a hill on Stearns' Rancho Laguna. The cabin was to become their favorite place, their escape from everyday life.

The years passed and the Stearns became even more prominent members of Southern California society. To Abel's extreme disappointment, they had no children. Arcadia was relieved, because she did not want to take the chance of passing on her husband's ugly traits to innocent children. To insure her infertility, she took special baths, ate particular herbs and drank potions prepared for her by Indians and Mexican women. To compensate for her deliberate lack of fertility, Arcadia made love to her husband as if he were Apollo himself. Abel could hardly believe his good fortune, and he lavished the same affection on his beautiful wife. They made love with such passion and so often that Abel could not understand why they did not conceive a child. There were times when he thought he had committed a grave sin by marrying such a beautiful woman, and that God was punishing him by denying him children. Arcadia's infertility preoccupied him on his business trips, but when he was with her he forgot all their problems and let himself become engulfed by the love of this beautiful woman.

Only once did Arcadia actually tell Abel she loved him. They were in their cabin on the Rancho Laguna, and she began to think about her popularity with so many men and women. She realized it was because she was married to *Cara de caballo*, because whenever she appeared on his arm at fiestas, balls or even on the sidewalks of Los Angeles or San Francisco, her beauty was instantly exaggerated. For all that attention, for the wonderful life he had given her, Arcadia loved him very much. He was seventy years old at that time, and Arcadia was as lovely as when they had married. They made love on the braided rug in front of the fireplace, and their passion was as strong as it was twenty years before.

Abel Stearns died in San Francisco in 1871. He was seventy-two. His body was returned to Arcadia in Southern California. He, of course, left his entire estate to her, making her the wealthiest woman in California. When she was fifty, Arcadia Bandini de Stearns married a handsome and prosperous young man from Rhode Island, Jonathan Hawthorn Blake. Blake never asked Arcadia her age; to his eyes she was always young and beautiful. The two of them lived contentedly in their homes in Los Angeles and San Diego. They traveled extensively to the Orient and to Europe. At the turn of the century, Arcadia was as beautiful as when she was twenty. Legend has it that she was consulting a *brujo* who prescribed a potion made from ground up brown insects. She had to drink the potion every day to conserve her beauty and her youth. Legend also has it that one day Arcadia failed to drink her potion, and the next morning her face was transformed into a *cara de caballo*. The few servants who witnessed her transformation lived only long enough to tell the story.

The Curing Woman

This is the story that Doña Marcelina Trujillo Benidorm told her friend Concepción Martínez when they met in Simons, California.

Marcelina was born into a rich family in Spain. Her highly respected parents dedicated their lives to serving the public and the Church. However, the Trujillo Benidorms never associated with the people who benefitted from their generous financial gifts. They kept company with other aristocratic families; even then, only a few other families were deemed worthy of their attention. The Trujillo Benidorms had four children—three sons and Marcelina, who was conceived by her father and one of the beautiful young servants who dedicated ten years of their lives to total obedience to the family. When Marcelina's mother was forced to leave the estate at the end of her ten-year term, she begged to take her nine-year-old daughter with her. But Mrs. Trujillo Benidorm denied the request, choosing instead to keep the child herself. She had grown to love Marcelina and, besides, the child was a reminder to her husband of his sins of infidelity. Mrs. Trujillo Benidorm also believed that Marcelina's mother could never afford to educate her daughter properly.

Both women had always loved Marcelina and both had treated her well, but, when she saw her real mother leaving the estate for the last time, Marcelina was heart-broken. She ran in tears to an upstairs window to catch a last glimpse of the woman who had given birth to her. Marcelina's mother smiled with joy and pride at the beautiful brown-eyed child framed by the ivy growing around the window. At that moment, Marcelina realized that looking into her mother's face was like looking into a mirror, that her mother had given birth to an identical twin, had in fact given birth to herself. Marcelina ran to the mirror; she looked exactly like her mother. With a cry, she rushed back to the window. Her mother was gone.

For four years, Mrs. Trujillo Benidorm gave Marcelina everything a child could want. She was well cared for and educated in an excellent school. But she never heard a word about her mother. Then one chilly, damp morning while she strolled the rocky Altean beach, a servant came to her with a crumpled piece of green paper. With the first light of the next morning, Marcelina stepped onto the road to Granada and began a journey that would eventually lead her to Simons, California.

Marcelina found her mother in the caves of the hills overlooking Alhambra. Although she had never heard her mother's name spoken aloud, on the day she approached the cave where her mother lived with her husband, Marcelina heard a voice call out, "Yerma." It was the name of Marcelina's mother/twin. Yerma walked toward her daughter, and Marcelina felt a surge of energy run through her body. Neither of them spoke. As their fingers touched, their minds were joined, and they stood smiling and looking out over the world. The clasp of their hands became a harmony, a song.

Marcelina spent seven happy years with her mother. Yerma bore no other children. Her husband, a hard-working man of the earth, damned the Trujillo Benidorms for his beautiful wife's infertility, but he accepted Marcelina as his daughter and taught her all that he knew of the earth to which he was born and to which he would one day return. Yerma dedicated her life to the study of cures. She learned from Moslem, Jewish and Christian practitioners. She mastered chants, formulas and procedures which gave her access to natural and supernatural powers. She investigated the positive and negative, good and evil, masculine and feminine forces of the cosmos. This duality she discovered and controlled in herself, and this knowledge she offered to her apprentice daughter/twin, who would one day become a *curandera*.

Marcelina learned her craft well, and one day Yerma realized she had taught Marcelina all she knew. With infinite sadness, Marcelina and her ageless mother were separated forever on this earth. The young woman made her way south to the Mediterranean port of Cádiz, where she boarded a ship bound for Veracruz on the Gulf Coast of Mexico. Marcelina was only twenty-years-old, but she was fearless and confident. She had her mother's beauty and an intelligence second to none.

The voyage to Veracruz, was invigorating, as Marcelina concentrated on the forces of the sea. Nourished by the mysteries of the Mediterranean, baptized by the sea, Marcelina knew she would grow even stronger in the New World.

In Veracruz Marcelina was met by a man called "El Gran Echbo," who introduced her to the magical, marvelous realities of the Caribbean. For several years, she cultivated the energies of this new vision of the world, adding them to her already considerable knowledge of enchantment. Towards the end of her apprenticeship with "El Gran Echbo," Marcelina met María Sabina, a saintly woman renowned for her curative powers. María Sabina communicated with the negative and positive forces of the cosmos through her knowledge of plants and animals. She spoke the language of the ancient doctors of the land—Nahuatl—which she taught to Marcelina. María Sabina traveled with her powerful pupil to Mexico City, following an ancient secret path known only to a chosen few. As the two women journeyed through thick, hot jungles, majestic mountains and treacherous swamps, Marcelina became aware of the universal duality of Ometecuhtli-

Omecihuatl. Her mind roamed through the four suns of the mandala, each passage making her stronger in the movement of the energy time-space concept of Mexican cosmology. But the journey took its toll, and Marcelina fell into a trance-like state.

When she opened her eyes, she was in María Sabina's shack in Tepito, the poorest section of Mexico City. She heard the sounds of explosions somewhere in the city. María Sabina explained that each day the city grew more dangerous and soon they would have to leave. But they would not be going together. As Marcelina stared into the other woman's cataract eyes, she saw immense sorrow. María Sabina told her to journey north, and to leave within four days. Then María Sabina was gone.

Marcelina felt a heartbreaking emptiness. For the first time in her life there was no one to guide her. She conjured up images of her lovely mother, and soon she had the strength to prepare for her journey. Marcelina left the city in the early morning of the fourth day, amidst the echoes of rifle fire.

As she proceeded north, the lands of Mexico appeared before her like a violent carnival. The Revolution continued to ravage the soil and the people. While passing through Güiseo de Abasolo, in the State of Guanajuato, she heard talk of a city in California, a fantastic city called Simons, where Mexicans lived and worked in happiness and contentment. Marcelina felt a growing conviction that she would end her journey in that city. For four months she traveled with the armies that moved ever northward, paying her way by treating the sick and wounded. The torn and bloodied bodies of the people she tended showed her the absurdity of the violent forces prevailing in the land, and she used her own powerful resources to steal many souls from death.

In tattered and bloodstained clothes, Marcelina finally penetrated the border at Ciudad Juarez/El Paso. Never losing sight of her goal, she traveled by train for three months across the vast southwest territory. When the train stopped in Simons, California, Marcelina Trujillo Benidorm stepped off, never to leave again.

* * *

Concepción Martínez and her eldest son, Delfino, walked along Vail Street towards Doña Marcelina's home. As they walked, Concepción reflected on her friendship with Marcelina, and on how their lives had intertwined since they had met in Simons years ago. Her awe of Marcelina's knowledge of the natural and supernatural had somehow never interfered with their friendship. But today was different. Today Concepción was taking her first-born to Marcelina, to the *curandera*, for treatment.

Delfino did not know if he was angry or relieved that he was finally going to see Doña Marcelina Trujillo Benidorm. She was truly his last hope. Ever since the fire consumed his home, and the terrible shock of believing it had consumed his family as well, something was wrong. All the doctors said he was well. The psychiatrist ascribed his condition to the deep shock of thinking his family was dead, but he too said there was nothing physically wrong with him. Why then was he steadily and relentlessly losing weight? He was becoming weak and delirious, even though he ate enough to satisfy two men. He was frightened by the unknown force inside him. At that moment, though, he wasn't sure which frightened him more. Doña Marcelina had always been a mystery to the townspeople, someone the children stayed away from. The fact that she was also his mother's friend did not lessen Delfino's anxiety about seeking her help.

Mother and son moved silently down Vail Street. They passed men on their way to work. On that street few women were out so early in the morning, so Concepción attracted immediate and polite attention. The men greeted the pair somberly, then moved along to their jobs. As Concepción and Delfino passed the church and came into sight of Marcelina's home across from the American Foundry, their steps slowed and stopped. A breeze came up and played in Concepción's black hair. Behind her, Delfino stared at Marcelina Trujillo Benidorm's house. He felt as if he were about to step into a photograph.

Doña Marcelina greeted them briefly. They all knew why they were there. Delfino looked at her and in an unsettling moment saw both an old woman and a beautiful young girl. The moment passed, and Doña Marcelina ushered them into an immaculate white room, empty of furniture but full of brightness. The room was large, the ceiling higher than they had expected. Evenly spaced on three of the walls were images of the Passion of Christ. In the center of the fourth wall was a door to another, smaller room. As Doña Marcelina guided Delfino through the door into the smaller room, Concepción bid her son farewell.

Delfino looked around. On the wall in front of him was a painting of a man sitting in a wheelbarrow with a woman sitting on a block in front of him. Both seemed to be praying. The painting was dark; storm clouds dominated the distant horizon. Sitting on the floor under the painting was a wheelbarrow, and in front of that was a black block. In the corner of the room was a standing cross.

Doña Marcelina asked Delfino to sit in the wheelbarrow. As he obeyed, he saw his mother watching them from the doorway. Her face was carefully devoid of emotion. Then his view was obscured by a quilted, multi-colored jacket and a black skirt as Doña Marcelina sat on the black block in front of him. With her hands lying quietly in her lap, she smiled at him reassuringly and began a litany of prayers and incantations, all the while preparing several potions. Occasionally, she made the sign of the cross before preparing yet another potion.

From the doorway, Concepción watched the *curandera* work. She noted with fascination as Doña Marcelina began her struggle to gain control of and dominate the spirit which thrived on Delfino's body and soul. As the battle evolved, Delfino took on Doña Marcelina's physical characteristics. A transformation occurred. In this way Doña Marcelina was able to explore his body and locate her enemy. Concepción stared as her son became her friend. After some time, a large grotesque form appeared on the lower back of the *curandera*. The shape grew distinctly into an octopus with powerful tentacles wrapped around Doña Marcelina's waist. The *susto* was alive, pulsating, furious at being torn from its lair. Now it clung to her. But Doña Marcelina knew how to destroy evil, and before long it disappeared. Gradually, Delfino reappeared in his own body. He was no longer tired, and his spirit felt light and free again. He realized with surprise that hours had passed since he had entered the room, but he recalled nothing of what had happened since Doña Marcelina had begun her prayers. Looking down, Delfino was startled to find he was wearing Doña Marcelina's quilted jacket. Smiling at his mother, he took off the jacket and placed it in the wheelbarrow. He never asked how he had come to be wearing it. Some time later, Doña Marcelina gave Concepción nine small pouches and instructed her to give Delfino potions for nine more days. Doña Marcelina was again herself as she walked Concepción into the large white room.

Delfino waited in the center of the room while his mother and the *curandera* conversed quietly. He looked through the doorway into the room where he had been cured. As he studied the painting on the wall, he saw to his astonishment that the composition had changed. The man had disappeared. Everything else remained the same. When he turned around to tell Concepción of his discovery, he found himself in front of his home waiting for his mother to open the door.

Elías Miguel Muñoz

While not writing about Cuba and its revolution, per se, Elías Miguel Muñoz has been an eloquent chronicler of the children who have suffered separation from their families, dislocation from their place of birth and mother culture, immigration to foreign lands and, quite often, their resilience, but at times their victimization and defeat. Like various other writers included in this anthology, Muñoz has developed a dual career as writer, creating poetry, prose and theater in both English and Spanish, and seeing them published both at home in the United States and abroad—mostly Spain, in Muñoz's case.

Born in 1954 in Cuba, Muñoz did not immigrate to the United States until 1969. His family settled in Southern California, and he attended both high school and college there. In 1984, he earned a Ph.D. in Spanish from the University of California-Irvine and embarked upon a career in academia, but by 1988 Muñoz gave it up definitively to dedicate himself to writing full-time. And Muñoz has been, indeed, very productive, publishing poetry and stories in magazines throughout the country and authoring a number of books: *Los viajes de Orlando Cachumbambé* (1984), *Crazy Love* (1988), *En estas tierras/In This Land* (1989) and *The Greatest Performance* (1991).

His most successful work to date, *The Greatest Performance*, is an intensely poetic novel of exile, which explores the personal struggles of two characters—almost mirror images in opposite sexual roles—for love and psychological integrity in their lives on the margins of family, country and sexual identity. *Publishers Weekly* considered the novel "sensitive, lyrical," and *Library Journal*, "poetically evocative." The following selection is the first chapter of *The Greatest Performance*.

Chapter One

We are in Cuba, of course. In Guantánamo, to be more precise. My parents seem happy. Papi's a public accountant. Mami, a frustrated housewife. Doesn't she look beautiful in this picture? Mami doesn't seem to age. Papi, too, looks as handsome as he does today (in spite of his black-bean potbelly); velvety hair, dark complexion, features he says he inherited from his Castilian father.

They quarrel. He plays dominoes for money, she says. And he loses and loses. She's a watchdog, he claims. She spies on him, tries to control him. They hate each other's guts, but they stay together for the children. We need to have a normal set of parents, right? A nice home, a real family. And one day we will need to be freed from the Communist tentacles.

You know how the story goes: This normal set of parents will have to leave their land to save their babies. And feeling fearful perhaps, or lonely, they will reinvent their matrimonial farce in the United States. Things will be better there, they think. They will have common goals and aspirations. He won't drink anymore. She won't be a bitch. And life will be a happily-ever-after.

But not yet. Not so easily. In a couple of years my brother Pedro is going to turn fourteen, military age. If they don't get him out before that, he'll never be able to leave. We can't take a chance waiting for our turn to enter the United States. So, fate has an unexpected voyage in store for my brother and me. Yes, I'll get to leave, too. But not to "America." We'll emigrate to Spain, thanks to a rich Spanish aunt who'll pay our way there.

Typical tale of a Cuban family of Worms, a decent home being torn apart. Rosita and Pedrito Rodríguez, two little twirps from Guantánamo who kneel by their beds every night and say their prayers are suddenly thrown into the world without their loving parents to protect them.

Our maternal grandmother, whom later in life I would baptize "La Filósofa," weeping and praying for our well-being, "May the Virgin of Charity protect you, children. May she guide your steps and keep you from danger. May she help you find your way back to us, some day." Our parents looking up at the blue Cuban sky and asking themselves, "Will we ever see our babies again?"

Later, in Garden Shore, our widow grandmother will amass a fortune from her Welfare and Social Security checks and will rent a two-bedroom apartment where she'll live by herself, free and independent, always a loving and faithful provider of *cafecito* and good old-fashioned Cuban wisdom. My parents will find assembly-line work in the aircraft industry, driven by the dream of buying a house with a garden, a swimming pool and a marble statue of the Virgin of Charity.

Yes, some dreams do come true.

* * *

Here's a picture of me at school: Rosita with her clique. The one with the curly red hair, that's Maritza. You can't see her face that well in this picture but believe me, she had the most bewitching bedroom eyes. And this is her wedding invitation. Pathetic, isn't it?

Maritza gave me little sermons about things that I couldn't and shouldn't understand: class struggle, the proletariat, Che, the capitalist pigs. She was a teacher's aide, strong in history and literature. And she spoke English. One day she'd go to the Soviet Union to study Russian, that was her plan. She wanted to read Tolstoy in the original.

She deserved her bookworm reputation, yes. But she was able to descend to my level and chitchat with me about trivialities: tube pants, miniskirts, popular music and groups like Los Bravos and Los Memes. And she translated for me the hit songs I liked that were in English, "Black is Black," "I'm a Believer," "Words."

I was a fairly good student. Good enough to have started high school a year earlier than I was supposed to. No, I wasn't a genius like Maritza; I had to study hard to get my Bs (eights and nines in the Cuban grade system).

I knew my geography from the North Pole to the South Pole. Well acquainted with the Colonization period, I knew that when Christopher Columbus set foot in Cuba one day in 1492, he uttered the famous words THIS IS INDEED THE MOST BEAUTIFUL LAND THAT HUMAN EYES HAVE EVER SEEN. I could recite by heart many of José Martí's *Versos sencillos* and name every single one of our Liberators, the men who fought for our (late) independence from the Spanish oppressors in 1898. (Too bad Martí had to be one of them).

I had read *Don Quijote*, *The Iliad* and *Romeo and Juliet*. I knew who Socrates, Aristotle, Shakespeare, Cervantes, Calderón, Marx, Lenin, Hemingway were. And I had definitely heard of the *Communist Manifesto*. I knew that Nikita was a good friend of Fidel's and that Johnson threw black people to the dogs. And I chanted, like everybody else in town (before my family decided we would emigrate) that sing-song that went, "The Worms! (Feet thumping on the floor) Let's crush the Worms!"

⋆ ⋆ ⋆

Papi told me to be tough. "Don't let anyone intimidate you, Rosita. Your trip is not a crime." But no one treated me badly at school when I announced that I had received the "exit telegram." On the contrary, the principal had watery eyes when she hugged me. She told me to continue studying and not to let myself be trapped by the American vices. She was going to miss me, she said. And my classmates stared at me with puppy-dog eyes, as if I were traveling to a death camp and they were saying goodbye to me forever.

My only wish (I remember this clearly) was to stand in the middle of the school, right next to the flag, and to embrace Maritza, kissing her curly red hair and her lips. Telling her in front of the whole world that I loved her.

We walked to the park, I remember. And there we sat, in silence at first, then like two chatty parrots. And when it started to get dark, like two lovers saying *Adiós*, knowing they'd never see each other again.

My secret, impossible dream: that Maritza would come with me to the North, that she would abandon her communist family and escape to a land where dreams became reality. We would be free there. We'd go to school together and one day we'd buy a house at the beach and there we'd make our happy "nest."

I wrote to her a lot from California. I tried not to make a big deal of my brand new typewriter, my camera, my tape recorder, my color TV set, my family's car and the abundance of food. I told her of the music that was popular, Elvis, The Fifth Dimension, The Mamas and the Papas. I'd cut pictures of celebrities from the magazines and I'd send them to her.

There was little in my letters about Garden Shore, where we lived, about the gringos and about my classes. All of that seemed unreal, uninteresting, a boring tale not worthy of telling. Her letters, the few that I got, were literary jewels. In the last one I received, and which I didn't answer, she sent me this wedding invitation . . .

Pathetic, isn't it?

Seeing her name printed over a red heart, on that cheap cream-colored paper and next to the name of a man, MARITZA GARCIA & DAVID PEREZ, I felt for the first time that Cuba was vanishing from my life.

* * *

Look at this picture. See that cute guy there, in the back, behind Maritza? He's the one. My buddy. In my childhood story you have become that kid, Marito. Or rather, he has become you. And I can no longer remember his real name.

You live next door. We share a stereotypical biography: macho-father, puppet-mother. The Works. We help and comfort each other. You have a secret life similar to mine; we're accomplices. Best friends. But our friendship doesn't have a chance. My father has forbidden me to hang out with you because you're obvious, Marito. Blatantly obvious.

The first time you came to visit, my father didn't even greet you. Remember? And then when you left, his disgusting orders: "I never ever want to see you with that boy again! Can't you tell he's a *pájaro*?"

Pájaro. Bird. One of the words Cubans used in those days (still today?) to denigrate a gay man. What were some of the other ones? Ah yes, Duck, Butterfly, Inverted One, Sick One, Broken One, Little Mary, Addict, Pervert.

"I don't want to see you with that boy again, is that clear? Don't even speak to him!"

One day they started to pick up all the long-haired men, women in miniskirts or hot pants, the whores, the ducks and the dykes (*Las Tortilleras*). Helterskelter, chopped off the ground as if they were sugar cane. And you, my neighbor friend, were one of the first to fall. Or did you escape The Raid? Were you as lucky as me? No. I remember hearing the news at school, from Maritza: "They got Mario. For being queer."

Even Julito Martínez, the macho dude who played the lead in the country's most popular TV serial, *Zorro*!, had fallen. And two of the singers who formed one of my favorite pop groups, Los Memes, were gone, too. "What's going on?" I asked Maritza, seeking comfort, some sort of affirmation in her wisdom. "Those people are sick, Rosita," she responded. "And their sickness is contagious."

How much pain we would've saved each other had we been there together, at the genesis, for real. How much strength we would've found in our friendship, Mario.

Truth is, I grew up alone in my lair, just like you.

No. It didn't happen overnight. I remember feeling attracted to women since I was a baby. When I was seven I used to play doctor with a neighbor girl. She'd hug me and I'd touch her "sick" tummy and she'd touch the "bebé" I had between my legs and it felt so good. We closed our eyes and kissed each other on the mouth, kisses of tight and bumbling lips. We played house and I was the husband. And we had children.

My fantasies started early. In them I was usually a handsome knight in love with a princess. Or a tough militia man who carried two guns, one hanging from each hip. A virile and feared lieutenant (for some reason I never wanted to be a captain). Oh yes, and I drove a jeep. Everyone respected me and loved me. Especially the women. And I always managed to get the lady of my dreams.

I begged God to help me. Damn how I prayed! I'd kneel during Mass and I'd tell Jesus Christ and the Virgin of Charity: "Look, here, please, you guys, pretty please, you've got to save my body from temptation and my soul from eternal damnation. Tell you what, so that everything goes fast and easy, I'll close my eyes and I'll think real hard that I'm a normal girl and that I like boys. Then I'll open my eyes, I'll look at the statue of Christ on the cross and—Wham!—Rosita Rodríguez has been cured! She's a new person! Is that a deal?"

But there were no miracles for me.

Papi and Mami did nothing but argue and insult each other and walk like zombies all over the house. He was drunk most of the time. She'd do whatever she could do not to break down. How could they possibly help me? And then there was my brother, Pedro, too much of a typical *machito* to understand how I was feeling, or for me to trust him.

Mami did try to teach me the Cuban birds and bees. Was she worried, perhaps, about my Tomboy look, my disdain for domestic activities, my total apathy toward the opposite sex? She was determined, I could tell, to drive out of me all traces of masculinity, to force me to be fragile, tender, womanly.

Lucky for me there were no beatings and no broken jaws, as I know there were in other homes. From my sinful hideaway I listened (I imagine now that I listened) to your cries. Things were much worse for you, because you had been born a man. Your crime deserved no forgiveness and no mercy.

Blows and kicks for you, The Butterfly. For me, advice: "Your behavior must be ... calmer, Rosita. You should lower your voice when you talk. You shouldn't be out there hunting birds and climbing trees. You should play house with your dolls and not play war games with the boys. You must help me more around the house, and stay home more. You should start wearing skirts. And you should follow my advice . . . "

Your mother threw a fork at you one day. She was having lunch and you kept pestering her. What irked her about you that morning? What were you bugging her about? I know, you wanted her to tell you why she cried some times at night, "Does he hurt you, Mima? Does he hurt you? Is that why you cry? Why do you put up with him, Mima? Why do we put up with him?"

So she threw the fork at you. She didn't mean for it to hurt you; it was just an impulse, wasn't it? The fork punctured your arm, hanging there like a dead limb. The next day she started to direct traffic in the neighborhood. Would you say she went crazy? You got ten stitches and then you couldn't move your arm for a long time. Did seeing you hurting like that provoke her insanity? Was it remorse?

At the crack of dawn she'd put on your father's baseball cap and she'd hang a whistle from her neck. And there she went, stopping every car or pedestrian that passed in front of the house, blowing her whistle and giving bizarre orders, "Show me your identity. You can't go on unless you show me your identity." And people just cracked up in her face.

"What do I have to do to show you my identity?"

"Anything that would prove who you are."

The person (in most cases a man) would then make a gesture, sticking out his tongue or farting. "Very well," she'd respond, feeling accomplished, "you can go on, but carefully, don't forget that we are in the War Zone."

The fantasy ended abruptly one day, weeks later, when your father found out that a man had opened his fly to show your mother his enormous identity. Your Pipo nearly killed the guy. But why didn't he stop her from making a fool of herself from the very beginning? Why did he wait?

Did he want to laugh at her, too?

The school sent out a van to pick us up and take us home. You and I rode together the whole way, because we were in the same grade, and we were neighbors. I'm sure all the kids thought you and I were an item. Little did they know.

Why am I remembering this, Marito? Is it because . . . there was something peculiar about you? Something I need to remember? Yes, you didn't like to go to the bathroom at school. How you managed to hold it all until you got home is beyond me, but you did. Until that afternoon, when we were sitting in the back and . . . there was that nauseating smell. "What is this?!" asked the driver when he saw you getting out of the van. "This kid took a shit in his pants!" Everyone laughed and called you Shit Head and Dirty Asshole (or whatever the Cuban equivalents were, all of them having to do with the word *Mierda*).

You didn't go to the restroom at school because the prospect of exposing yourself in front of the other boys horrified you. (The toilet stalls didn't have doors.) But why? Was it because the ogre you had for a father punished you by making you take off all your clothes and then had you sit in the living room, stark naked? Was that the reason? Did you associate your nudity with punishment and pain?

I saw you there once, on the floor, in the middle of the living room, covering your parts and begging me with your eyes to end your torture, to leave perhaps, or bring you a blanket.

I'm sure I saw you naked once.

* * *

True, in most of my fantasies I was a man. But then there were those few occasions when I felt totally fem. When I would become *LA MUJER*.

My idol and role model for that fantasy was Rosita Fornés, the glamorous television queen, the greatest *artista*, the one and only Cuban star. Rosita was blonde and sexy and she sang heart-rending songs. She could dance and crack jokes and she had the body of a goddess.

It occurred to me during one of those fem fantasies that I should do Rosita Fornés' variety show in my backyard. Why not. I mean, wasn't it like destiny, like a mysterious fate that we both had the same name? (I asked Mami once if I had been named after the famous TV star, since Papi liked her so much and she was so famous and beautiful and maybe they wanted me to be famous like her some day. But Mima said absolutely not, that I had been named after Rosa María Fernanda Lucrecia Virginia, my great-grandmother on my father's side. *Coño*!) I could get some of my friends involved in the show, give them parts and songs to sing and funny things to say. And we could invite all the neighbors and charge money.

This artistic enterprise, I was sure, would be more profitable and far more successful than the lemonade sale, when there were so many lemons falling from the tree in our backyard that we didn't know what to do with them. "Make lemonade and sell it," Papi suggested. And I did. And I made enough money to buy three *Vanidades* and two *Bohemias*, all of them including lyrics of popular songs. But the ROSITA SHOW would top the lemonade sale; it would make neighborhood history. Or so I thought.

"Sing all you want," said Mami. "Sing Rosita's songs and do her dances. But no smooching. Understand?" What was she talking about? Rosita never kissed anybody in her TV show, or at least not that I'd noticed. And besides, did I have a tainted reputation? Quite the opposite, I was clean! But Mami's advice backfired. Yes, she put an idea in my head and in my heart, a wonderful idea for the show. We'd make it a love story, just like one of those Mexican movies that they showed on TV every day, where people talked about *El Amor* all the time, unrequited love, drunken love, betrayed love, sublime love. *El Amor*!

"And one more thing," Mami went on, "make sure you include Pedrito in your show. Just because he's little doesn't mean he doesn't have a right to have fun." My brother would eventually find his way into a thrillingly fun experience of his own. His wild awakening would come much later, in Spain. But that's another story.

We rehearsed outside, in the backyard, and Mami would spy on us through the kitchen window. We'd notice the tip of her nose, supervising, who knows if bored or fascinated, the rehearsal for our great melodrama, CARNIVAL QUEEN.

I'd play the female lead, of course. And you, Mario, would be my beloved and broken-hearted boyfriend Amor. You were a short and whitish boy, with light brown hair and unusually fine features. Perfect for the part of leading man. What I liked about you the most were your hands: impeccably white fingers, rosy nails; your dove hands, Amor.

Dressed in pink with a fur coat I am La Rosa, a delicate, ephemeral and desirable flower. I sing a song and then a fat old man gives me jewels and I accept them. Why not, all he wants from me is that I let him admire my beauty. Besides, the fatso's right: those jewels make me look radiant, more gorgeous than I am already.

We live in a village and it's Carnival time. I meet him one night, while I stroll through the plaza, watching the masquerading crowds. His name is

Mario but I will call him Amor. We'll become sweethearts and he'll take me to his home, to meet his parents.

I walk in looking humble and average, wearing a simple summer dress, no jewelry and no fur coat. And his folks greet me. I am a decent girl and they are so pleased that their boy has met me, because I go to Mass on a weekly basis. The sign of the cross and God bless you my child.

But then. Oh then. Amor finds out that I have a secret life, that I am the Carnival Queen. (How could I have possibly volunteered to play such a total fem?) He discovers me one night, half-naked, dancing my butt off on a majestic float.

Another dress, another song.

He cries because I'm not the decent girl he thought I was. I catch his glance full of sadness and rage. He runs, I jump off the float and run after him. I must tell him the truth! (I didn't know what that truth was, but I knew I had to explain it to him.) He runs to the pier and there he stops, and there I see him. He's thinking of jumping in; he's going to take his life! I scream, "No, Amor! Don't do it! Wait! You must listen to me, I am not who you think I am!" (But I really was, know what I mean?) Then there's a wave, a tidal wave that swells up and swallows him in one gulp. Amor! My love!

Another dress and the last song, *From the moment the day is born, to the moment when the sun dies, Amor, my love, I think of you. Amor, my love, you live in my heart . . .*

"How about a happy ending?" you asked. And you were right, Marito. We couldn't just leave the story hanging there with such a revolting, unoriginal *Fin.* So you came up with a great idea:

I'd go back to my glamorous float to dance my pain away and then one night, many years later, you'd show up. I'd see you smiling down below, in the crowd, still in love with me. You'd embrace me, and now we're both dancing on this magical float. And the float stops and the people gather around us. They listen to your story:

"A pirate ship picked me up and saved me from the sharks. I became a pirate and I sailed around the globe. I burned many houses and I stole many treasures. But then I repented from all those crimes and I came back searching for my Rosita. And now that we have found each other, I will no longer be a pirate. And she will no longer be The Carnival Queen, but only the Queen of my Heart. The End."

One evening, after our daily rehearsal, you brought me a plate of *mer-*

cocha, that wonderful gooey stuff that Cuban mothers made from cooked sugar and cinnamon. "Here," you said, "my mother just made this . . . for you." And right then and there you asked me timidly if you could give me a kiss, just a little kiss, you said. And I responded, "Of course, Marito, but not on the mouth, okay? Because that's for older people and, besides, I don't like to kiss boys." And you said, "Fantastic, Rosita, because I don't like to kiss girls but I'd love to kiss you, because you're my sister." And so you gave me this breathy kiss on the cheek and then I saw you blushing.

You shared your secret with me that evening. And I shared mine with you. You told me that you didn't like playing the handsome Amor, that who you really wanted to play was the Carnival Queen. I told you that if you ever played the Queen, some day, I'd play the leading man for you. Because deep down inside I didn't want to be her, that who I really wanted to be was Amor. And so you said, "Why do we have to wait? Why can't we do the show for ourselves, being the person that we want to be?" And we performed for each other, didn't we? And we fulfilled our wish.

The next day we announced to the "cast" that our show had been cancelled. The reason we gave our disillusioned friends was that the rehearsals were taking up too much of our time and we weren't doing our homework or studying enough. The real reason? You and I had already had our spectacular debut.

⋆ ⋆ ⋆

Here's a picture of me at the farm, which the Communists called "La Cooperativa." And that's my clique again. Don't I look like I'm having the time of my life?

Papi and Mami made such a fuss about my having to go work at La Cooperativa. Unfortunate little angel who never had to lift a finger in her entire life, having to go break her back and soil her hands, working for the Bearded Serpent. Baby Rosita was going to be cleaning out furrows of sweet potato and cutting sugar cane for forty days! What an insult, what a slap in the face for my family.

But I loved the country. We had to work, yes, but not much; and we got slim and good-humored and playful. The saddest girls seemed to bloom at La Cooperativa.

We bathed together in a large hut that was ironically and properly named *Los Buenos Baños*, The Good Baths. My legs wobbled every time I went in there, I won't deny that. Tits tits tits. A room full of tits. But later, alone, I thought of someone special. Always about Maritza.

I know you didn't do anything "bad," you swear on it. But you were tempted. Oh how you were tempted! I imagine that the worst, the very worst torture you went through was the Cocks' Parade, *El Desfile de las Pingas*. How were you able to resist the temptation when you saw those giant *chorizos* willing, available, anxious and wasted? All those boys comparing each other, boasting about the shapes and sizes of their powerful erections; exploring each other to see who had the biggest, the thickest, the circumcised ones, the ones with more foreskin. Competing with each other by squirting their "milk" the longest distance. Or by breaking through a watermelon and parading around the barracks with the fruit hanging from their sex. Let's see who can hold it up the longest!

The most difficult test was the one you endured with Paquito, wasn't it? Paquito, the barber's son, had a habit of offering you tidbits of wisdom for survival: "Never be a tattletale. Never. Be anything you want except a tattletale. Be a cocksucker, a ball-licker, a Duck, a Little Mary. Bend down and spread your cheeks, but don't be a tattletale. No one here's gonna treat you bad for being a queer. But if you're a tattletale you'll get killed, we'll cut you up with a machete." Minutes later he opened his fly and displayed a long and dark and wrinkled pecker. "Suck it, I won't tell anyone. I'm not a tattletale."

You said no, trembling inside, resisting the temptation like a true hero. "Suck it, I know you want to," the barber's son insisted. But you didn't.

You didn't dare.

Maritza and I had a reunion at La Cooperativa. It was kind of magical, if you can believe that. She had been distant and aloof at school. Afraid of me, maybe. Afraid of being picked up or contracting my contagious "illness"?

She smiled at me again when we got to the country. And we ended up talking a lot about music. Our latest idol was Armando Manzanero, the Mexican singer-songwriter. He had a hideously romantic voice, an unbearably touching falsetto. And his words, oh his words! He sang of rainstorms and lonely crowds and forsaken lovers and adoring lovers and forever-ever-lovers.

I knew every one of Manzanero's songs. I could imitate his high-pitched voice, the exact modulation of his notes, the violin part, the piano solos. Inevitably, I ended up serenading Maritza whenever I had the opportunity. One morning, much to my surprise, she asked me if I would sing for her in private, "Where no one can hear you. Sing only to me." My mouth dropped.

I suggested we go to the plantain field after dawn. And we did. And as soon as we were out of sight I kissed her. Then we walked holding hands, laughing, discussing her favorite books (*War and Peace*, *Don Quijote*), my favorite movies (*Fantomas*, *Jotavich*), talking about us, about being friends forever. And about my singing. She said I had a pretty voice, that I should try to sing professionally. But I couldn't, I said, I wouldn't want to sing anymore if she were not around to hear me.

We were far from the barracks when I asked her to sit down, to lean against the trunk of a tree and relax, close her eyes and just let herself dream. Softly I said, "We're alone. And I'm going to serenade you." And then I saw that from behind the tree appeared this woman, this woman who sang, entranced, *We are sweethearts*, who whispered, *because we feel this love, sublime and profound*. She hummed, she sang, *This love that makes us proud*. She cried, *This love so weary of goodbyes*. She pleaded, *Come hear, come hear my sweetheart's lullaby*.

Judith Ortiz Cofer

Judith Ortiz was born in Puerto Rico in 1952 into a family that was destined to move back and forth between Puerto Rico and Paterson, New Jersey. Her father, Jesús Ortiz Lugo was a Navy man, first assigned to the Brooklyn Navy Yard and then other points around the world. In Puerto Rico, the young Judith attended San José Catholic School in San Germán, and in Paterson she went to public schools at first, and then to Saint Joseph's Catholic School. In 1968, after her father had retired from the Navy with a nervous breakdown, the family moved to Augusta, Georgia, where she attended high school and graduated from Augusta College. She later earned an M.A. degree in English at Florida Atlantic University. She was also awarded a scholarship to do graduate work at Oxford University by the English-Speaking Union of America. Included among many other awards were fellowships from the Florida Arts Council (1980), the Bread Loaf Writers Conference (1981) and the National Endowment for the Arts (1989).

While teaching English in south Florida colleges, Ortiz Cofer began writing poetry, and her works were soon appearing in such magazines as the *New Mexico Humanities Review*, *Kansas Quarterly*, *Prairie Schooner*, *Revista Chicano-Riqueña*, *Southern Humanities Review*, *Southern Poetry Review* and elsewhere. Her collections of poetry include four chapbooks—*Latin Women Pray* (1980), *Among the Ancestors* (1981), *The Native Dancer* (1981), *Peregrina* (1986)—and two books: *Reaching for the Mainland* (1987) and *Terms of Survival* (1987). Judith Ortiz Cofer is a respected fiction and non-fiction writer, as well. Her book of autobiographical essays, *Silent Dancing: A Remembrance of a Puerto Rican Childhood* (1990), won a citation from PEN and was chosen a Best Book for the Teen Years by the New York Public Library. Her novel, *The Line of the Sun* (1990), is based on her family's gradual immigration to the United States, and chronicles the years from the Depression to the 1960's. In her prose writing, as well as in her poetry, Ortiz Cofer reflects her struggle as a writer to create a history for herself out of the cultural ambiguity of a childhood spent traveling back and forth between the United States and Puerto Rico. In *Silent Dancing*, she explores from a feminist perspective her relationship with her father, mother and grandmother, while also considering the different expectations for the males and females in Anglo-American and Hispanic cultures.

Silent Dancing

We have a home movie of this party. Several times my mother and I have watched it together, and I have asked questions about the silent revellers coming in and out of focus. It is grainy and of short duration but a great visual aid to my first memory of life in Paterson at that time. And it is in color—the only complete scene in color I can recall from those years.

We lived in Puerto Rico until my brother was born in 1954. Soon after, because of economic pressures on our growing family, my father joined the United States Navy. He was assigned to duty on a ship in Brooklyn Yard, New York City—a place of cement and steel that was to be his home base in the States until his retirement more than twenty years later.

He left the Island first, tracking down his uncle who lived with his family across the Hudson River, in Paterson, New Jersey. There he found a tiny apartment in a huge apartment building that had once housed Jewish families and was just being transformed into a tenement by Puerto Ricans overflowing from New York City. In 1955 he sent for us. My mother was only twenty years old, I was not quite three, and my brother was a toddler when we arrived at *El Building*, as the place had been christened by its new residents.

My memories of life in Paterson during those first few years are in shades of gray. Maybe I was too young to absorb vivid colors and details, or to discriminate between the slate blue of the winter sky and the darker hues of the snow-bearing clouds, but the single color washes over the whole period. The building we lived in was gray, the streets were gray with slush the first few months of my life there, the coat my father had bought for me was dark in color and too big. It sat heavily on my thin frame.

I do remember the way the heater pipes banged and rattled, startling all of us out of sleep until we got so used to the sound that we automatically either shut it out or raised our voices above the racket. The hiss from the valve punctuated my sleep, which has always been fitful, like an non-human presence in the room—the dragon sleeping at the entrance of my childhood. But the pipes were a connection to all the other lives being lived around us. Having come from a house made for a single family back in Puerto Rico—my mother's extended-family home—it was curious to know that strangers lived under our floor and above our heads, and that the heater pipe went through everyone's apartments. (My first spanking in Paterson came as a result of playing tunes on the pipes in my room to see if there would be an answer). My mother was as new to this concept of bee hive life as I was, but had been given strict orders by my father to keep the doors locked, the noise down, ourselves to ourselves.

It seems that Father had learned some painful lessons about prejudice while searching for an apartment in Paterson. Not until years later did I hear how much resistance he had encountered with landlords who were panicking at the influx of Latinos into a neighborhood that had been Jewish for a couple of generations. But it was the American phenomenon of ethnic turnover that was changing the urban core of Paterson, and the human flood could not be held back with an accusing finger.

"You Cuban?" the man had asked my father, pointing a finger at his name tag on the Navy uniform—even though my father had the fair skin and light brown hair of his northern Spanish family background and our name is as common in Puerto Rico as Johnson is in the U.S.

"No," my father had answered looking past the finger into his adversary's angry eyes, "I'm Puerto Rican."

"Same shit." And the door closed. My father could have passed for European, but we couldn't. My brother and I both have our mother's black hair and olive skin, and so we lived in *El Building* and visited our great uncle and his fair children on the next block. It was their private joke that they were the German branch of the family. Not many years later that area too would be mainly Puerto Rican. It was as if the heart of the city map were being gradually colored in brown—*café-con-leche* brown. Our color.

The movie opens with a sweep of the living room. It is "typical" immigrant Puerto Rican decor for the time: the sofa and chairs are square and hard-looking, upholstered in bright colors (blue and yellow in this instance, and covered in the transparent plastic) that furniture salesmen then were adept at making women buy. The linoleum on the floor is light blue, and if it was subjected to the spike heels as it was in most places, there were dime-sized indentations all over it that cannot be seen in this movie. The room is full of people dressed in mainly two colors: dark suits for the men, red dresses for the women. I have asked my mother why most of the women are in red that night, and she shrugs, "I don't remember. Just a coincidence." She doesn't have my obsession for assigning symbolism to everything.

The three women in red sitting on the couch are my mother, my eighteen-year-old cousin, and her brother's girlfriend. The "novia" is just up from the Island, which is apparent in her body language. She sits up formally, and her dress is carefully pulled over her knees. She is a pretty girl but her posture makes her look insecure, lost in her full-skirted red dress which she has carefully tucked around her to make room for my gorgeous cousin, her future sister-in-law. My cousin has grown up in Paterson and is in her last year of high school. She doesn't have a trace of what Puerto Ricans call "la mancha"(literally, the stain: the mark of the new immigrant—something about the posture, the voice, or the humble demeanor making it obvious to everyone that that person has just arrived on the mainland; has not yet acquired the polished look of the city dweller). My cousin is wearing a tight red-sequined cocktail dress. Her brown hair has been lightened with peroxide around the bangs, and she is holding a cigarette very expertly between her fingers, bringing it up to her mouth in a sensuous arc of her arm to her as she talks animatedly with my mother, who has come up to sit between the two women, both only a few years younger than herself. My mother is somewhere halfway between the poles they represent in our culture.

It became my father's obsession to get out of the barrio, and thus we were never permitted to form bonds with the place or with the people who lived there. Yet the building was a comfort to my mother, who never got over yearning for *la isla*. She felt surrounded by her language: the walls were thin, and voices speaking and arguing in Spanish could be heard all day. *Salsas* blasted out of radios turned on early in the morning and left on for company. Women seemed to cook rice and beans perpetually—the strong aroma of red kidney beans boiling permeated the hallways.

Though Father preferred that we do our grocery shopping at the supermarket when he came home on weekend leaves, my mother insisted that she could cook only with products whose labels she could read, and so, during the week, I accompanied her and my little brother to *La Bodega*—a hole-in-the-wall grocery store across the street from *El Building*. There we squeezed down three narrow aisles jammed with various products. Goya and Libby's—those were the trademarks trusted by her Mamá, and so my mother bought cans of Goya beans, soups and condiments. She bought little cans of Libby's fruit juices for us. And she bought Colgate toothpaste and Palmolive soap. (The final *e* is pronounced in both those products in Spanish, and for many years I believed that they were manufactured on the Island. I remember my surprise at first hearing a commercial on television for the toothpaste in which Colgate rhymed with "ate.")

We would linger at *La Bodega*, for it was there that mother breathed best, taking in the familiar aromas of the foods she knew from Mamá's kitchen, and it was also there that she got to speak to the other women of *El Building* without violating outright Father's dictates against fraternizing with our neighbors.

But he did his best to make our "assimilation" painless. I can still see him carrying a Christmas tree up several flights of stairs to our apartment, leaving a trail of aromatic pine. He carried it formally, as if it were a flag in a parade. We were the only ones in *El Building* that I knew of who got presents on both Christmas Day and on *Día de Reyes*, the day when the Three Kings brought gifts to Christ and to Hispanic children.

Our greatest luxury in *El Building* was having our own television set. It must have been a result of Father's guilty feelings over the isolation he had imposed on us, but we were one of the first families in the barrio to have one. My brother quickly became an avid watcher of Captain Kangaroo and Jungle Jim. I loved all the family series, and by the time I started first grade in school, I could have drawn a map of Middle America as exemplified by the lives of characters in "Father Knows Best," "The Donna Reed Show," "Leave It to Beaver," "My Three Sons," and (my favorite) "Bachelor Father," where John Forsythe treated his adopted teenage daughter like a princess because he was rich and had a Chinese houseboy to do everything for him. Compared to our neighbors in *El Building*, we were rich. My father's Navy check provided us with financial security and a standard of life that the factory workers envied. The only thing his money could not buy us was a place to live away from the barrio—his greatest wish and Mother's greatest fear.

In the home movie the men are shown next, sitting around a card table set up in one corner of the living room, playing dominoes. The clack of the ivory pieces is a sound familiar. I heard it in many houses on the Island and in many apartments in Paterson. In "Leave It To Beaver," the Cleavers played bridge in every other episode; in my childhood, the men started every social occasion with a hotly debated round of dominoes: the women would sit around and watch, but they never participated in the games.

Here and there you can see a small child. Children were always brought to parties and, whenever they got sleepy, put to bed in the host's bedrooms. Babysitting was a concept unrecognized by the Puerto Rican women I knew: a responsible mother did not leave her children with any stranger. And in a culture where children are not considered intrusive, there is no need to leave the children at home. We went where our mother went.

Of my pre-school years I have only impressions: the sharp bite of the wind in December as we walked with our parents towards the brightly lit stores downtown, how I felt like a stuffed doll in my heavy coat, boots and mittens; how good it was to walk into the five-and-dime and sit at the counter drinking hot chocolate.

On Saturdays our whole family would walk downtown to shop at the big department stores on Broadway. Mother bought all our clothes at Penny's and Sears, and she liked to buy her dresses at the women's specialty shops like Lerner's and Diana's. At some point we would go into Woolworth's and sit at the soda fountain to eat.

We never ran into other Latinos at these stores or eating out, and it became clear to me only years later that the women from *El Building* shopped mainly at other places—stores owned either by other Puerto Ricans, or by Jewish merchants who had philosophically accepted our presence in the city and decided to make us their good customers, if not neighbors and friends. These establishments were located not downtown, but in the blocks around our street, and they were referred to generically as *La Tienda*, *El Bazar*, *La Bodega*, *La Botánica*. Everyone knew what was meant. These were the stores where your face did not turn a clerk to stone, where your money was as green as anyone else's.

On New Year's Eve we were dressed up like child models in the Sears catalogue—my brother in a miniature man's suit and bow tie, and I in a black patent leather shoes and a frilly dress with several layers of crinolines underneath. My mother wore a bright red dress that night, I remember, and spike heels; her long black hair hung to her waist. Father, who usually wore his Navy uniform during his short visits home, had put on a dark civilian suit for the occasion: we had been invited to his uncle's house for a big celebration. Everyone was excited because my mother's brother, Hernán—a bachelor who could indulge himself in such luxuries—had bought a movie camera which he would be trying out that night.

Even the home movie cannot fill in the sensory details such a gathering left imprinted on a child's brain. The thick sweetness of women's perfume mixing with the ever-present smells of food cooking in the kitchen: meat and plantain *pasteles*, the ubiquitous rice dish made special with pigeon peas—*gandules*—and seasoned with the precious *sofrito* sent up from the island by somebody's mother or smuggled in by a recent traveler. *Sofrito* was one of the items that women hoarded, since it was hardly ever in stock at La Bodega. It was the flavor of Puerto Rico.

The men drank Palo Viejo rum and some of the younger ones got weepy. The first time I saw a grown man cry was at a New Year's Eve party. He had been reminded of his mother by the smells in the kitchen. But what I remember most were the boiled *pasteles*—the plantain or yucca rectangles stuffed with corned beef or other meats, olives, and many other savory ingredients, all wrapped in banana leaves. Everyone had to fish one out with a fork. There was always a "trick" pastel—one without stuffing—and whoever got that one was the "New Year's Fool."

There was also the music. Long-playing albums were treated like precious china in these homes. Mexican recordings were popular, but the songs that brought tears to my mother's eyes were sung by the melancholic Daniel Santos, whose life as a drug addict was the stuff of legend. Felipe Rodríguez was a particular favorite of couples. He sang about faithless women and broken-hearted men. There is a snatch of a lyric that has stuck in my mind like a needle on a worn groove: "De piedra ha de ser mi cama, de piedra la cabecera ... la mujer que a mi me quiera ... ha de quererme de veras. Ay, Ay, corazón, ¿por qué no amas ... ?" I must have heard it a thousand times since the idea of a bed made of stone, and its connection to love, first troubled me with its disturbing images.

The five-minute home movie ends with people dancing in a circle. The creative filmmaker must have asked them to do that so that they could file past him. It is both comical and sad to watch silent dancing. Since there is no justification for the absurd movements that music provides for some of us, people appear frantic, their faces embarrassingly intense. It's as if you were watching sex. Yet for years, I've had dreams in the form of this home movie. In a recurring scene, familiar faces push themselves forward into my mind's eye, plastering their features into distorted close-ups. And I'm asking them: "Who is she? Who is the woman I don't recognize? Is she an aunt? Somebody's wife? Tell me who she is. Tell me who these people are."

"No, see the beauty mark on her cheek as big as a hill on the lunar landscape of her face—well, that runs in the family. The women on your father's side of the family wrinkle early; it's the price they pay for that fair skin. The young girl with the green stain on her wedding dress is *La Novia*—just up from the island. See, she lowers her eyes as she approaches the camera like she's supposed to. Decent girls never look you directly in the face. *Humilde*, humble, a girl should express humility in all her actions. She will make a good wife for your cousin. He should consider himself lucky to have met her only weeks after she arrived here. If he married her quickly, she will make him a good Puerto Rican-style wife; but if he waits too long, she will be corrupted by the city, just like your cousin there."

"She means me. I do what I want. This is not some primitive island I live on. Do they expect me to wear a black *mantilla* on my head and go to mass every day? Not me. I'm an American woman, and I will do as I please. I can type faster than anyone in my senior class at Central High, and I'm going to be a secretary to a lawyer when I graduate. I can pass for an American girl anywhere—I've tried it—at least for Italian, anyway. I never speak Spanish in public. I hate these parties, but I wanted the dress. I look better than any of these *humildes* here. My life is going to be different. I have an American boyfriend. He is older and has a car. My parents don't know it, but I sneak out of the house late at night sometimes to be with him. If I marry him, even my name will be American. I hate rice and beans. It's what makes these women fat."

"Your *prima* is pregnant by that man she's been sneaking around with. Would I lie to you? I'm your great uncle's common-law wife—the one he abandoned on the island to marry your cousin's mother. I was not invited to this party, but I came anyway. I came to tell you that story about your cousin that you've always wanted to hear. Remember that comment your mother made to a neighbor that has always haunted you? The only thing you heard was your cousin's name and then you saw your mother pick up your doll from the couch and say: 'It was as big as this doll when they flushed it down the toilet.' This image has bothered you for years, hasn't it? You had nightmares about babies being flushed down the toilet, and you wondered why anyone would do such a horrible thing. You didn't dare ask your mother about it. She would only tell you that you had not heard her right and yell at you for listening to adult conversations. But later, when you were old enough to know about abortions, you suspected. I am here to tell you that you were right. Your cousin was growing an *Americanito* in her belly when this movie was made. Soon after she put something long and pointy into her pretty self, thinking maybe she could get rid of the problem before breakfast and still make it to her first class at the high school. Well, *Niña*, her screams could be heard downtown. Your aunt, her Mamá, who had been a midwife on the Island, managed to pull the little thing out. Yes, they probably flushed it down the toilet, what else could they do with it—give it a Christian burial in a little white casket with blue bows and ribbons? Nobody wanted that baby—least of all the father, a teacher at her school with a house in West Paterson that he was filling with real children, and a wife who was a natural blond.

"Girl, the scandal sent your uncle back to the bottle. And guess where your cousin ended up? Irony of ironies. She was sent to a village in Puerto Rico to live with a relative on her mother's side: a place so far away from civilization that you have to ride a mule to reach it. A real change in scenery. She found a man there. Women like that cannot live without male company. But believe me, the men in Puerto Rico know how to put a saddle on a woman like her. *La Gringa*, they call her. Ha, ha, ha. *La Gringa* is what she always wanted to be . . . "

The old woman's mouth becomes a cavernous black hole I fall into. And as I fall, I can feel the reverberations of her laughter. I hear the echoes of her last mocking words: *¡La Gringa, La Gringa!* And the conga line keeps moving silently past me. There is no music in my dream for the dancers.

When Odysseus visits Hades asking to see the spirit of his mother, he makes an offering of sacrificial blood, but since all of the souls crave an audience with the living, he has to listen to many of them before he can ask questions. I, too, have to hear the dead and the forgotten speak in my dream. Those who are still part of my life remain silent, going around and around in their dance. The others keep pressing their faces forward to say things about the past.

My father's uncle is last in line. He is dying of alcoholism, shrunken and shriveled like a monkey, his face is a mass of wrinkles and broken arteries. As he comes closer, I realize that in his features I can see my whole family. If you were to stretch that rubbery flesh, you could find my father's face, and deep within *that* face—mine. I don't want to look into those eyes ringed in purple. In a few years he will retreat into silence, and take a long, long time to die. *Move back, Tío*, I tell him. *I don't want to hear what you have to say. Give the dancers room to move, soon it will be midnight. Who is the New Year's Fool this time?*

Estela Portillo Trambley

Estela Portillo Trambley is one of the first women writers to successfully publish prose in the early male-dominated stages of the Chicano literary movement. Born in El Paso, Texas, on January 16, 1936, she was raised and educated in El Paso, where she attended high school and the University of Texas at El Paso for her B.A. (1957) and her M.A. (1977). After graduation from college, she became a high school English teacher and administrator. Since 1979, she has been affiliated with the Department of Special Services of the El Paso Public Schools. From 1970 to 1975, she served as dramatist in residence at El Paso Community College.

Estela Portillo Trambley was the first woman to win the national award for Chicano literature, Premio Quinto Sol, in 1973 for her collection of short stories and novela, *Rain of Scorpions and Other Writings*, which was published in 1975. Besides publishing stories and plays in magazines and anthologies, Portillo Trambley has published a collection of plays, *Sor Juana and Other Plays* (1981) and a novel, *Trini* (1983). In both her prose and drama, Portillo Trambley develops strong women who resist the social roles that have been predetermined for them because of their sex. In her fiction, women command center stage and achieve a level of self-determination and control over social and cultural circumstances. The culmination of her pursuit of strong women is represented in her exploration of the life of the eighteenth-century poet and essayist, Sor Juan Inés de la Cruz, in her play, "Sor Juana." The protagonist of her novel, *Trini*, is a fictional character who struggles against poverty and adversity to make her way in life; she eventually leaves Mexico and crosses the border without papers to find the power over her own life for which she has been searching. "La Jonfontayn" is a humorous addition to Portillo's gallery of feminine portraits. It was first published in *Revista Chicano-Riqueña* (now *The Americas Review*) in 1982.

La Jonfontayn

Alicia was forty-two and worked hard at keeping her weight down. Not hard enough really, and it was very frustrating for her never to quite succeed. She wanted to be pencil-thin like a movie star. She would leaf through movie magazines, imagining herself in the place of the immaculately made-up beauties that stared back at her. But in essence she was a realist and was very much aware of the inevitable body changes as years passed. She often studied her face and body in the mirror, not without fears. The fantasy of glamour and beauty was getting harder and harder to maintain. Getting old was no easy task. Why didn't someone invent some magic pill . . . ?

Sitting naked, defenseless, in a bathtub brimming with pink bubbles, she slid down into the water to make the usual check. She felt for flabbiness along the thighs, her underarms for the suspicious cottage cheese called tired, loose fat. Suddenly she felt the sting of soap in her eye. Carefully she cupped water in her hand to rinse it out. Damn it! Part of her eyelashes were floating in the water. It would take close to an hour to paste new ones on again. Probably Delia's fault. Her girl was getting sloppy. Mamie was a new face at the beauty parlor, anxious to please the regular customers. Maybe she would ask for Mamie next time. No dollar tip for Delia after this. The soapy warmth of her body was almost mesmerizing. In her bubbly pink realm Alicia was immortal, a nymph, sweet-smelling, seductive, capable of anything.

Heck! She had to get out if she had to paste the damned eyelashes on. She stood up, bubbles dripping merrily off her nice, plump body. She had to hurry to be in time for her blind date. She giggled in mindless joy. A blind date! She could hardly believe that she had agreed to a blind date. Agreed? She smiled with great satisfaction and murmured to herself, "You insisted on nothing else, my girl. You wanted him served on a platter and that's the way you're getting him."

Rico was her yard boy, and at Katita's wedding she had seen Rico's uncle, Buti, from afar. Such a ridiculous name for such a gorgeous hunk of man. From that moment on she had been obsessed with the thought of owning him. It was her way, to possess her men. That way she could stay on top, teach them the art of making her happy. "Oh, I have such a capacity for love!" she told herself. Humming a love song, she stepped out of the bathtub and wrapped a towel around her body gracefully, assuming the pose of a queen. A middle-aged queen, the mirror on the bathroom door told her.

There are mirrors and there are mirrors, she gloomily observed. She sucked in her stomach, watching her posture. But the extra pounds were still here and there. Time had taken away the solid firmness of youth and replaced it with extra flesh. She turned away from the mirror, summarizing life under her breath, "Shit!"

The next instant she was smiles again, thinking of the long-waist bra that would smooth out her midriff and give her an extra curve. Then there was the green chiffon on her bed, the type of dress that Loretta Young would wear. She visualized herself in the green chiffon, floating towards Buti with outstretched hand. There would be the inevitable twinkle of admiration in his eye. In her bedroom, she glanced at the clock on her dresser. It was late. With rapid, expert movements, she took out creams, lipstick, eye shadow, rouge, brushes from her cosmetic drawer. She wrapped a towel around her head and had just opened the moisture cream when she remembered the eyelashes. Did she really need them? She remembered Lana Turner with her head on Clark Gable's shoulder, her eyelashes sweeping against her cheeks. Max Factor's finest, Alicia was sure of that.

Hell! She rummaged hurriedly around the bottom drawer until she found a plaster container with the words Max Factor emblazoned on the cover. Anything Lana did, she could do better. She took out a bottle of glue, then carefully blotted the excess cream from her eyes and began the operation.

"Hey, slow down!" yelled Rico as Buti made a turn on two wheels.

Rico turned around to check the load on the back of the pick-up. They were returning from Raton where at the Ranger Station they had gotten permits to pick *piñones* in the Capitan Mountains. Buti had presented the rangers with a letter from Don Rafael Avina giving him permission to pick *piñón* from his private lands. Buti had also signed a contract with the Borderfield Company to deliver the *piñones* at the railroad yards in Ancho, New Mexico, where the nuts would be shipped along with cedar wood to Salt Lake City—his first profitable business venture since he had arrived in the United States. He had a check from Borderfield in his pocket. He was well on his way to becoming what he always wanted to be—a businessman. From there—a capitalist—why not? Everything was possible in the United States of America. He even had enough *piñones* left to sell to small *tienditas* around Valverde, and a special box of the best *piñones* for his blind date, the richest woman in Valverde. Things were coming up money every which way. He had had qualms about letting Rico talk him into the blind date until Rico started listing all the property owned by Alicia Flores—two blocks of *presidios*, ten acres of good river land, an office building. That made him ecstatic. Imagine him dating a pretty widow who owned an office building! There was no question about it—he was about to meet the only woman in the world whom he would consider marrying. By all means, she could have him. It was about time he settled down.

All that boozing and all those women were getting to be too much for him. What he needed was the love and affection of one good wealthy woman. Yes, ever since he had met Don Rafael things had gone for the better. Only six months before, he had even considered going on welfare. Poker winnings had not been enough, and his Antique Shop was not doing very well. He had resorted to odd jobs around Valverde, a new low for Buti. Then, he met Don Rafael at El Dedo Gordo in Juarez.

At the Fat Finger everybody knew Buti. That's where he did the important things in his life—play poker, start fights, pick up girls and, most important of all, drink until all hours of the morning. It was his home away from home. His feet on native soil and mariachi music floating through his being—that was happiness. One early dawn when only Elote, the bartender, and Buti were left at the Fat Finger—they were killing off a bottle of tequila before starting for home—who stumbles in but this little fat man with a pink head, drunker than a skunk. He fell face down on the floor soon enough. Buti helped him up, dusted him off and led him to the table where Elote had already passed out.

"You sit right there. I'll get us another bottle." Buti wove his way between tables and made it to the bar. The little man just sat staring into space until Buti nudged him with a new bottle of tequila.

"Where am I?" the little man asked, clearing his throat.

"In the land of the brave . . . " Buti responded with some pride.

"Where's that?"

"The Fat Finger, of course."

The friendship was cemented over the bottle of tequila. The little man had been a good ear. Focusing on the pink head, with tears in his eyes, Buti had unloaded all his woes on the little fat man. Buti recounted how he had tried so hard to become a capitalist in the land of plenty to no avail. He tried to look the little fat man in the eye, asking, "Are you a capitalist?"

"Yes," assured the little man with a thick tongue. "I am that."

"See what I mean? Everybody who goes to the United States becomes a capitalist. Now—look at me. Great mind, good body, what's wrong with me?"

"What you need is luck," advised the little man with some wisdom, as he reeled off his chair. Buti helped him up again and shook his head. "That's easier said than done. I know the principles of good business—contacts, capital and a shrewd mind. But where in the hell do I get the contacts and the capital?"

"Me," assured the little fat man without hesitation. "Me, Don Rafael Aviña will help you. I'm a millionaire."

"That's what they all say." Buti eyed him with some suspicion.

"Don't I look like a millionaire?" demanded the little man starting to hiccup. The spasmodic closure of the glottis caused his eyes to cross. Buti looked at him, still with some suspicion, but decided that he looked eccentric enough to be a millionaire. "Okay, how're you going to help me?"

"First, you must help me," said Don Rafael between hiccups, "find my car."

"Where did you park it?"

"I don't know. You see, I have no sense of direction," confessed Don Rafael, leaning heavily on Buti. "It's a green Cadillac."

That did it. A man who owned a Cadillac did not talk from the wrong side of his mouth. "Can you give me a hint?"

Don Rafael had gone to sleep on his shoulder. Now is the time to be resourceful, Buti told himself. How many green Cadillacs can be parked in the radius of six blocks? Don Rafael could not have wandered off farther than that on his short little legs. It would be a cinch, once he sobered up Don Rafael, enough for him to walk on his own speed.

It took six cups of coffee, but Don Rafael was able to hold on to Buti all the way to Mariscal, where Buti spotted a lone green Cadillac parked in front of Sylvia's Place, the best whorehouse in Juarez.

"Hey, Don Rafael," Buti had to shake the little man from his stupor, "is that the car?"

Don Rafael squinted, leaning forward, then back against Buti. "Is it a green Cadillac?"

"A green Cadillac."

"That's my car." Don Rafael began to feel around for the keys. "Can't find my keys." Buti helped him look through all his pockets, but no keys.

"You could have left them in the ignition."

"That would be dumb." Don Rafael kept on searching until Buti pushed him toward the car to look. Sure enough, the keys were in the ignition.

"There are your keys and your car." Buti gestured with a flourish.

"Then, let's go home."

"Your home?" queried Buti.

"Why not? You can be my guest for as long as you like—if you can stand my sister . . . "

"What's wrong with your sister?"

"Everything—Does everything right, prays all the time, and is still a virgin at fifty."

"I see what you mean. You can drop me off at my place in Valverde."

They drove off, and it was not until they were crossing the immigration bridge that they heard the police sirens. A police car with a red flashing light cut right across the green Cadillac. In no time, three policemen had pulled Buti and Don Rafael roughly out of the car.

"What is the meaning of this?" demanded Don Rafael, sobering up in a hurry.

"You're under arrest," informed a menacing looking policeman.

"What are you talking about?" Buti asked angrily, shaking himself free from another policeman's hold.

"You stole that car," accused the first policeman.

Don Rafael was indignant. "You're crazy. That's my car!"

"That's the mayor's car. He reported it stolen."

"The mayor's car?" Buti was dumbfounded. He would never believe little fat men with pink heads again.

"I have a green Cadillac," sputtered Don Rafael. "I demand to see my lawyers."

"Tomorrow you can call your lawyer. Tonight you go to jail," the third policeman informed them with great stoicism. All of Don Rafael's screaming did no good. They wouldn't even look at his credentials. So they spent a night in jail. Buti diplomatically offered Don Rafael his coat when he saw the little man shivering with cold, and even let him pillow his pink head on his shoulder to sleep. Buti had decided there was more than one green Cadillac, in the world, and that Don Rafael threw his weight around enough to be rich. Don Rafael snuggled close to Buti and snored all night.

They were allowed to leave the next morning after Don Rafael made a phone call and three lawyers showed up to threaten the government of Mexico with a lawsuit for false arrest. Outside the jail stood Don Rafael's green Cadillac from heaven knows where.

On the way home, Don Rafael gave Buti a written permit to pick *piñón* on his property for free, thus Buti could count on a clear profit. Don Rafael wrung his hand in goodbye, making him promise he would come up to Ratón to visit him and his sister, which Buti promised to do. Yes, Buti promised himself, he would soon go to Ratón for a social visit to thank Don Rafael for the *piñón*. He was well on his way to becoming a capitalist . . .

"Hey, Buti," called out Rico, "you just passed your house."

Buti backed the pick-up next to a two-room shack he had built on the edge of his sister's one acre of land. The two room house sported a red roof and a huge sign over the door that read, "Antiques." After the roof and the sign, he had built himself an inside toilet, of which he was very proud. That had been six years before when he had come from Chihuahua to live with his sister and to make a fortune. He had fallen into the antique business by chance. One day he had found an old victrola in an empty lot. That was the beginning of a huge collection of outlandish discards—old car horns, cupie dolls, wagon wheels, a stuffed moose head, an old church altar. At one time, he had lugged home a rusty, huge commercial scale he claimed would be a priceless antique someday. The day he brought home the old, broken merry-go-round that boasted one headless horse painted blue, his sister, Trini, was driven to distraction. She accused him of turning her place into an eyesore and ordered he get rid of all the junk.

"Junk!" exclaimed Buti with great hurt in his voice, "Why, all these antiques will be worth thousands in a few years."

Rico had to agree with his mother—the place was an eyesore. After parking the pick-up, Rico reminded Buti about his date with Alicia that night.

"Put on a clean shirt and shave, okay, Buti?"

"*Baboso*, who you think you're talking to?"

"She's a nice lady, don't blow it," Rico reminded him.

"Sure, she is. I'm going to marry her," Buti informed his nephew who stared at him incredulously.

"She's not the marrying kind, Tío," Rico warned him.

"She's a widow, ain't she? She gave in once."

"That's cause she was sixteen," explained Rico.

"How old was he?" Buti inquired.

"Seventy and very rich."

"Smart girl. Never married again, eh? What for?"

"She's had lovers. Two of them."

"Smart girl. What were they like?"

Rico wrinkled his brow trying to remember. "The first one was her gardener. She took him because she claimed he looked like Humphrey Bogart."

"Humf . . . what?"

"Don't you ever watch the late, late show? He was a movie star."

"What happened to him?"

"Humphrey Bogart? He died . . . "

"No, stupid, the gardener."

"He died, too. Fell off the roof, fixing the television antenna."

Buti wanted all the facts. "What about the second lover?"

"He had a cleft on his chin like Kirk Douglas," Rico remembered.

"Another movie star? What's this thing with movie stars?"

"That's just the way she is." Then Rico added reassuringly, "But don't worry, Tío. She says you are the image of Clark Gable."

* * *

After the dog races, Buti took Alicia to Serafín's. It had become their favorite hangout. For one thing, the orchestra at Serafín's specialized in *cumbias*, and Buti was at his best dancing *cumbias*. No woman could resist him then. He could tell that Alicia was passionately in love with him by the way she clung to him and batted those ridiculous lashes. As he held her sweet-smelling plump body against him and expertly did a turn on the floor, she hissed in his ear, "Well, are you going to move in?"

"Haven't changed my mind," he informed her in a cool, collected voice.

"Oh, you're infuriating!" She turned away from him, making her way back to the table. He noticed that the sway of her hips was defiant. Tonight could be the night. She plumped down on the table. "I've had it with you, Buti."

"What do you mean?" He tried to look perplexed.

"Stop playing cat and mouse."

"Am I supposed to be the mouse?" His voice was slightly sarcastic. "I've never been a mouse."

"Let's put our cards on the table." Her voice sounded ominous.

"Okay by me."

"Well then, don't give me that jazz about you loving me too much to live with me in sin. Sin, indeed. When I hear about all those girls you run around with . . . "

"Used to run around with," corrected Buti, looking into her eyes seductively. "I only want you. You are the world to me. Oh, how I want to make love to you. It tortures me to think about it. But I must be strong."

"There you go again. Come home with me tonight and you can make love to me all you want to." It was her stubborn voice.

"Don't say those things, my love. I would never sully our love by just jumping into bed with you." Buti was proud of the fake sincerity in his voice. "Our love is sacred. It must be sanctified by marriage."

"Marriage be damned!" Alicia hit her fists on the table. She was really angry now. He could tell. She accused him. "You just want my money."

"You're not the only girl with money. But you are the only woman I could ever love." Buti was beginning to believe it himself.

"You liar! All the girls you've had have been penniless, submissive, ignorant wetbacks from across the river." Her anger was becoming vicious now.

"Wait a minute!" Buti was not playing a game any more. He looked at the woman across the table, knowing that she was a romantic little fool, passionate, sensuous, selfish, stubborn, domineering and full of fire. The kind of woman he would want to spend the rest of his life with. Nevertheless, he took affront. "What am I? I'm penniless—not quite, but almost. You could say I'm a wetback from across the river. And you, in your mindless way, want me to submit. Stop throwing stones. We seem to have the same likes!"

She looked at him with her mouth open. She had sensed the sincerity in his voice. She could tell this was not a game anymore. She knew she had been ambushed, but she would not give in.

"If you love me, and I believe you do, you'll come live with me, or . . . ," there was a finality in her voice, "I simply will not see you again."

"I will not be another scalp on your belt." There was finality in his voice, too.

* * *

"Hell!" Alicia slammed the half-full can of beer against the porch railing. She hated the smell of honeysuckle, the full moon and the heavy sense of Spring. She hated everything tonight. And look at her—this was her sixth can of beer—thousands of calories going straight to her waistline. She hated herself most of all. Buti was through with her. He must be, if what Rico had told her was true. He had come over to help her plant some rose bushes and she had casually asked him how Buti was doing these days. According to Rico, he spent a lot of time up in Ratón, New Mexico, visiting his friend, Don Rafael Aviña and his unmarried sister.

"Is she rich?" Alicia asked nonchalantly.

"Very rich," Rico answered in innocence, setting up the young rose bushes against the fence.

She didn't ask much more, but knowing Buti, she could put two and two together. He had found himself a greener pasture and a new playmate. He loves me. I know he loves me, but I've lost him forever. She couldn't stand it anymore—the moon, the smell of honeysuckle. She went back into the house and turned on the late, late show on television. She threw a shawl over her shoulders and huddled in a corner of the sofa. She sighed deeply, her breast heaving under the thin negligee.

She recognized the actress on the screen. It was Joan Fontaine with the usual sweet, feminine smile and delicate gestures. She always looked so vulnerable, so helpless. Clark Gable came on the screen. Oh, no—why him? Even his dimples were like Buti's! Damn it all. She wanted to see the movie. They had had some kind of quarrel and Joan Fontaine had come to Clark to ask forgiveness, to say she was wrong. Joan's soft beautiful eyes seemed to say—you can do what you wish with me. You are my master . . . Alicia began to sniffle, then the tears flowed, especially when she saw big strong powerful Clark become a bowl of jelly. All that feminine submissiveness had won out. Joan Fontaine had won the battle without lifting a finger. Hell, I'm no Joan Fontaine. But Clark was smiling on the screen, and Alicia couldn't stand it any longer. She turned off the set and went out into the night wearing only a negligee, a shawl and slippers. She didn't care who saw her. She was walking—no, running—towards Buti's shack almost a mile away. The princess leaving her castle to go to the stable. It was her movie now, her scenario. She was Joan Fontaine running towards the man she loved, Clark Gable. It mustn't be too late. She would throw herself at his feet—offer him all she had. She suddenly realized the night was perfect for all this!

The lights were on. She knocked at the door, one hand against her breast, her eyes wide, beseeching . . . in the manner of Joan Fontaine.

"What the hell . . . " Buti stood in the doorway, a hero half sandwich in his hand.

"May I come in?" There was a soft dignity in her voice. Buti took a bite of his sandwich and stared at her somewhat speechless. She walked past him into the room, and when she heard the door close, she turned around dramatically with outstretched arms. "Darling . . . "

"You're drunk . . . " Buti guessed.

"I only had five beers," she protested hotly, then caught herself. "No, my love, I'm here for a very good reason . . . " Again, the Fontaine mystique.

Buti took another bite from the sandwich and chewed nervously.

"Don't you understand?" She lifted her chin and smiled sweetly as she had seen Joan Fontaine do hundreds of times. Buti shook his head unbelievingly. She began to pace the floor gracefully, her voice measured, almost pleading. "I've come to tell you that I was wrong. I want to be forgiven. How could I have doubted you. I'm so ashamed—so ashamed." Words straight from the movie.

Buti finished off the sandwich, then scratched his head. Alicia approached him, her hand posed in the air, gently falling against his cheek. "Do you understand what I'm saying?"

"Hell no. I think you've gone bananas . . . "

She held back her disappointment with strained courage. "You're not helping much, you know . . . " Then she bit her lip, thinking that Joan Fontaine would never have made an unkind judgment like that. She looked into his eyes with a faint, sweetly twisted smile, then leaned her head against his shoulder. She was getting to him. There was worry in his voice.

"Are you feeling okay?"

She began to cry in a very unlike Joan Fontaine way. "Why can't you be more like him?"

"Like who?"

"Like Clark Gable, you lout!" She almost shouted it, regretfully.

Buti's eyes began to shine. She was beginning to sound like the Alicia he knew and loved. "Why should I be like some dumb old movie star?"

"Don't you see . . . " she held her breath out of desperation. "It's life . . . "

"The late, late show?" He finally caught on—the dame on television.

"You were watching it, too!" She accused him, not without surprise.

"Had nothing else to do. They're stupid, you know . . . "

"What!" Her dark eyes blazed with anger.

"Those old gushy movies . . . " He gestured their uselessness.

"That proves to me what a brute you are, you insensitive animal!" She kicked his shin.

"Well, the woman, she was kind of nice . . . "

"Joan Fontaine . . . "

"Jonfontayn?"

"That's her name. You're not going to marry her, are you?" There was real concern in her voice.

"Jonfontayn?" He could not keep up with her madness.

"No—that woman up in Ratón."

"Berta Aviña?" The whole scene came into focus. Buti sighed in relief.

"Rico told me she is very rich."

"Very rich."

"Is she slender and frail and soft-spoken like . . . "

"Jonfontayn?" Buti silently congratulated himself on his subtle play.

"Yes . . . "

Buti thought of Berta Aviña, the square skinny body, the tight lipped smile. He lied. "Oh, yes. Berta is the spitting image of Jonfontayn."

"I knew it. I knew it . . . " Alicia threw herself into his arms. "Please please, marry me. Oh, I love you so, you beast!"

"Not tonight, baby. We have better things to do . . . " He pulled her roughly against him, first giving her a Clark Gable smile, then he kissed her for a long, long time. Still, relying on his dimples, he picked her up, not without effort, and headed for the bed. She tried to push him away, protesting, "Oh, we can't . . . we mustn't . . . not before we're married."

He stopped in his tracks, not believing his ears. "What?"

"Well, that's—that's what she would say . . . " Alicia smiled meekly, batting the Max Factor lashes.

"Who?"

"Joan Fontaine, silly . . . "

"Frankly, my dear, I don't give a damn."

He threw her on the bed.

Tomás Rivera

Tomás Rivera (1935–1984) is one of the most beloved figures in Chicano literature. Besides authoring a pioneering novel, *... y no se lo tragó la tierra / ... And the Earth Did Not Devour Him*, and other important shorter works, Rivera was a tireless organizer and popularizer of the Chicano literary movement. Through numerous speeches, essays and formal presentations, as well as through collaborations in small magazines and correspondence with writers around the country, he proclaimed the need for a literature of the Chicano people, he outlined the parameters of such a literature and he offered encouragement and publishing opportunities to younger writers.

Rivera was born and raised in Crystal City, Texas, as the son of Mexican immigrants who became seasonal farmworkers in the migrant stream to the Midwest. Despite the disruptions of migrant labor, Rivera was able to finish high school and, with his parents' encouragement, only work the fields in the summer months in order to attend college. After continuing his education and earning his Ph.D. in Romance Languages and Literature at the University of Oklahoma in 1969, his rise in academia was meteoric: just ten years later he was appointed chancellor of the University of California at Riverside. He had held this position for five years when he died of a sudden heart attack in 1984.

Rivera's most important contribution as a writer has been his novel, *... y no se lo tragó la tierra*. The inter-related stories that made up the novel are tied together by the central character who is trying to remember and understand his experiences and those of his family. As such, the novel takes on two levels: the first, in which the adolescent searches for his identity in society and the universe and, the second, an ordering of the Chicano experience and the social and psychological forces that condition it.

"First Communion" is one of the central triad of narratives in *... y no se lo tragó la tierra*. After the adolescent protagonist has confronted God, the Devil and fatalism from within the context of folklore, family and religion, in "First Communion" the adolescent remembers the events leading up to his initiation into the body of the Catholic faithful and into adult society.

"Las Salamandras / The Salamanders," written in Spanish and later re-written in English by Rivera, is one of his most touchingly poetic and profound explorations of the heart of darkness. Like much of *... y no se lo tragó la tierra*, "The Salamanders" is inspired in the migrant labor experience. The story explores alienation and dislocation in the concrete experience of a family looking for work and in the metaphysical struggle with death symbolized by the killing of the salamanders.

First Communion

The priest always held First Communion during mid-spring. I'll always remember that day in my life. I remember what I was wearing and I remember my godfather and the pastries and chocolate that we had after mass, but I also remember what I saw at the cleaners that was next to the church. I think it all happened because I left so early for church. It's that I hadn't been able to sleep the night before, trying to remember all of my sins, and worse yet, trying to arrive at an exact number. Furthermore, since Mother had placed a picture of hell at the head of the bed and since the walls of the room were papered with images of the devil and since I wanted salvation from all evil, that was all I could think of.

> "Remember, children, very quiet, very very quiet. You have learned your prayers well, and now you know which are the mortal sins and which are the venial sins, now you know what sacrilege is, now you know that you are God's children, but you can also be children of the devil. When you go to confession you must tell all of your sins, you must try to remember all of the sins you have committed. Because if you forget one and receive Holy Communion, then that would be a sacrilege and if you commit sacrilege, you will go to hell. God knows all. You cannot lie to God. You can lie to me and to the priest, but God knows everything; so if your soul is not pure of sin, then you should not receive Holy Communion. That would be a sacrilege. So everyone confess all of your sins. Recall all of your sins. Wouldn't you be ashamed if you received Holy Communion and then later remembered a sin that you had forgotten to confess? Now, let's see, let us practice confessing our sins. Who would like to start off? Let us begin with the sins that we commit with our hands when we touch our bodies. Who would like to start?"

The nun liked for us to talk about the sins of the flesh. The real truth was that we practiced a lot telling our sins, but the real truth was that I didn't understand a lot of things. What did scare me was the idea of going to hell because some months earlier I had fallen against a small basin filled with hot coals which we used as a heater in the little room where we slept. I had burned my calf. I could well imagine how it might be to burn in hell forever. That was all that I understood. So I spent that night, the eve of my First Communion, going over all the sins I had committed. But what was real hard was coming up with the exact number like the nun wanted us to. It must have been dawn by the time I finally satisfied my conscience. I had committed one hundred and fifty sins, but I was going to admit to two hundred.

"If I say one hundred and fifty and I've forgotten some, that would be bad. I'll just say two hundred and that way even if I forget lots of them I won't commit any kind of sacrilege. Yes, I have committed two hundred sins ... Father, I have come to confess my sins ... How many? ... Two hundred ... of all kinds ... The Commandments? Against all of the Ten Commandments ... This way there will be no sacrilege. It's better this way. By confessing more sins you'll be purer."

I remember I got up much earlier that morning than Mother had expected. My godfather would be waiting for me at the church and I didn't want to be even one second late.

"Hurry, Mother, get my pants ready, I thought you already ironed them last night."

"It's just that I couldn't see anymore last night. My eyesight is failing me now and that's why I had to leave them for this morning. But tell me, what's your hurry now? It's still very early. Confession isn't until eight o'clock and it's only six. Your godfather won't be there until eight."

"I know, but I couldn't sleep. Hurry, Mother, I want to leave now."

"And what are you going to do there so early?"

"Well, I want to leave because I'm afraid I'll forget the sins I have to confess to the priest. I can think better at the church."

"All right, I'll be through in just a minute. Believe me, as long as I can see I'm able to do a lot."

I headed for church repeating my sins and reciting the Holy Sacraments. The morning was already bright and clear but there weren't many people out in the street yet. The morning was cool. When I got to the church I found that it was closed. I think the priest might have overslept or was very busy. That was why I walked around the church and passed by the cleaners that was next to the church. The sound of loud laughter and moans surprised me because I didn't expect anybody to be in there. I thought it might be a dog but then it sounded like people again and that's why I peeked in through the little window in the door. They didn't see me but I saw them. They were naked and embracing each other, lying on some shirts and dresses on the floor. I don't know why but I couldn't move away from the window. Then they saw me and tried to cover themselves, and they yelled at me to get out of there. The woman's hair looked all messed up and she looked like she was sick. And me, to tell the truth, I got scared and ran to the church but I couldn't get my mind off of what I had seen. I realized then that maybe those were the sins that we committed with our hands. But I couldn't forget the sight of that woman and that man lying on the floor. When my friends started arriving I was going to tell them but then I thought it would be better to tell them after communion. More and more I was feeling like I was the one who had committed a sin of the flesh.

> "There's nothing I can do now. But I can't tell the others 'cause they'll sin like me. I better not go to communion. Better that I don't go to confession. I can't, now that I know, I can't. But what will Mom and Dad say if I don't go to communion? And my godfather, I can't leave him there waiting. I have to confess what I saw. I feel like going back. Maybe they're still there on the floor. No choice, I'm gonna have to lie. What if I forget it between now and confession? Maybe I didn't see anything? And if I hadn't seen anything?"

I remember that when I went in to confess and the priest asked for my sins, all I told him was two hundred and of all kinds. I did not confess the sin of the flesh. On returning to the house with my godfather, everything seemed changed, like I was and yet wasn't in the same place. Everything seemed smaller and less important. When I saw my Dad and my Mother, I imagined them on the floor. I started seeing all of the grown-ups naked and their faces even looked distorted, and I could even hear them laughing and moaning, even though they weren't even laughing. Then I started imagining the priest and the nun on the floor. I couldn't hardly eat any of the sweet bread or drink the chocolate. As soon as I finished, I recall running out of the house. It felt like I couldn't breathe.

> "So, what's the matter with him? Such manners!"
>
> "Ah, *compadre*, let him be. You don't have to be concerned on my account. I have my own. These young ones, all they can think about is playing. Let him have a good time, it's the day of his First Communion."

> "Sure, *compadre*, I'm not saying they shouldn't play. But they have to learn to be more courteous. They have to show more respect toward adults, their elders, and all the more for their godfather."
>
> "No, well, that's true."

I remember I headed toward the thicket. I picked up some rocks and threw them at the cactus. Then I broke some bottles. I climbed a tree and stayed there for a long time until I got tired of thinking. I kept remembering the scene at the cleaners, and there, alone, I even liked recalling it. I even forgot that I had lied to the priest. And then I felt the same as I once had when I had heard a missionary speak about the grace of God. I felt like knowing more about everything. And then it occurred to me that maybe everything was the same.

Translated by Evangelina Vigil-Piñón

The Salamanders

What I remember most about that night is the darkness, the mud and the slime of the salamanders. But I should start from the beginning so you can understand all of this, and how, upon feeling this, I understood something that I still have with me. But I don't have this with me only as something I remember, but as something that I still feel.

It all began because it had been raining for three weeks and we had no work. We began to gather our things and made ready to leave. We had been with that farmer in Minnesota waiting for the rain to stop but it never did. Then he came and told us that the best thing for us to do was to leave his shacks because, after all, the beets had begun to rot away already. We understood, my father and I, that he was in fact afraid of us. He was afraid that we would begin to steal from him or perhaps that one of us would get sick, and then he would have to take the responsibility because we had no money. We told him we had no money, neither did we have anything to eat and no way of making it all the way back to Texas. We had enough money, perhaps, to buy gasoline to get as far south as Oklahoma. He just told us that he was very sorry, but he wanted us to leave. So we began to pick up our things. We were leaving when he softened up somewhat and gave us two tents, full of spider webs, that he had in the loft in one of his barns. He also gave us a lamp and some kerosene. He told my dad that, if we went by way of Crystal Lake in northern Iowa, perhaps we would find work among the farmers and perhaps it had not been raining there so much and the beets had not rotted away. And we left.

In my father's eyes and in my mother's eyes, I saw something original and pure that I had never seen before. It was a sad type of love, it seemed. We barely talked as we went riding over the gravel roads. The rain seemed to talk for us. A few miles before reaching Crystal Lake, we began to get remorseful. The rain that continued to fall kept on telling us monotonously that we would surely not find work there. And so it was. At every farm that we came to, the farmers would only shake their heads from inside the house. They would not even open the door to tell us there was no work. It was when they shook their heads in this way that I began to feel that I was not part of my father and my mother. The only thing in my mind that existed was the following farm.

The first day we were in the little town of Crystal Lake everything went bad. Going through a puddle, the car's wiring got wet and my father drained the battery trying to get the car started. Finally, a garage did us the favor of recharging the battery. We asked for work in various parts of that little town, but then they got the police after us. My father explained that we were only looking for work, but the policeman told us that he did not want any gypsies in town and told us to leave. The money was almost gone, but we had to leave. We left at twilight and we stopped the car some three miles from town and there we saw the night fall.

The rain would come and go. Seated in the car near the ditch, we spoke little. We were tired. We were hungry. We were alone. We sensed that we were totally alone. In my father's eyes and in my mother's eyes, I saw something original. That day we had hardly eaten anything in order to have money left for the following day. My father looked sadder, weakened. He believed we would find no work, and we stayed seated in the car waiting for the following day. Almost no cars passed by on that gravel road during the night. At dawn I awoke and everybody was asleep, and I could see their bodies and their faces. I could see the bodies of my mother and my father and my brothers and sisters, and they were silent. They were faces and bodies made of wax. They reminded me of my grandfather's face the day we buried him. But I didn't get as afraid as that day when I found him inside the truck, dead. I guess it was because I knew they were not dead and that they were alive. Finally, the day came completely.

That day we looked for work all day, and we didn't find any work. We slept at the edge of the ditch and again I awoke in the early morning hours. Again I saw my people asleep. And that morning I felt somewhat afraid, not because they looked as if they were dead, but because I began to feel again that I no longer belonged to them.

The following day we looked for work all day again, and nothing. We slept at the edge of the ditch. Again I awoke in the morning, and again I saw my people asleep. But that morning, the third one, I felt like leaving them because I truly felt that I was no longer a part of them.

On that day, by noon, the rain stopped and the sun came out and we were filled with hope. Two hours later we found a farmer that had some beets which, according to him, probably had not been spoiled by the rain. But he had no houses or anything to live in. He showed us the acres of beets which were still under water, and he told us that, if we cared to wait until the water went down to see if the beets had not rotted, and if they had not, he would pay us a large bonus per acre that we helped him cultivate. But he didn't have any houses, he told us. We told him we had some tents with us, and, if he would let us, we would set them up in his yard. But he didn't want that. We noticed that he was afraid of us. The only thing that we wanted was to be near the drinking water, which was necessary, and also we were so tired of sleeping seated in the car, and, of course, we wanted to be under the light that he had in his yard. But he did not want us, and he told us, if we wanted to work there, we had to put our tents at the foot of the field and wait there for the water to go down. And so we placed our tents at the foot of the field and we began to wait. At nightfall we lit up the lamp in one of the tents, and then we decided for all of us to sleep in one tent only. I remember that we all felt so comfortable being able to stretch our legs, our arms, and falling asleep was easy. The thing that I remember so clearly that night was what awakened me. I felt what I thought was the hand of one of my little brothers, and then I heard my own screaming. I pulled his hand away, and, when I awoke, I found myself holding a salamander. Then I screamed and I saw that we were all covered with salamanders that had come out from the flooded fields. And all of us continued screaming and throwing salamanders off our bodies. With the light of the lamp, we began to kill them. At first we felt nauseated because, when we stepped on them, they would ooze milk. It seemed they were invading us, that they were invading the tent as if they wanted to reclaim the foot of the field. I don't know why we killed so many salamanders that night. The easiest thing to do would have been to climb quickly into our car. Now that I remember, I think that we also felt the desire to recover and to reclaim the foot of the field. I do remember that we began to look for more salamanders to kill. We wanted to find more to kill more. I remember that I liked to take the lamp, to seek them out, to kill them very slowly. It may be that I was angry at them for having frightened me. Then I began to feel that I was becoming part of my father and my mother and my brothers and sisters again.

What I remember most about that night was the darkness, the mud and the slime of the salamanders, and how hard they would get when I tried to squeeze the life out of them. What I have with me still is what I saw and felt when I killed the last one, and I guess that is why I remember the night of the salamanders. I caught one and examined it very carefully under the lamp. Then I looked at its eyes for a long time before I killed it. What I saw and what I felt is something I still have with me, something that is very pure—original death.

Floyd Salas

Floyd Salas is the author of three critically acclaimed novels and an autobiography. Raised in Colorado and California in a family that traces both its maternal and paternal ancestry to the original seventeenth-century Spanish colonizers of Florida and the Southwest, Salas and his older brother entered the world of boxing and petty crime as one of the few avenues open to them for economic survival during the Depression and World War II. Salas later received a university education and creative writing fellowships that opened up a new career for him, while his brother went on to one penitentiary after another and one drug treatment program after another. But, never truly far from the underworld and the destruction of drugs, Salas based his first novels on the drug, pachuco and prison cultures.

His first novel, *Tattoo the Wicked Cross* (1967), about a boy who becomes a killer in a reform school, won the Joseph Henry Award and was called "the best first novel published in ten years" by the *Saturday Review of Literature*. *What Now My Love* (1970) follows the flight of three hippies after they get involved in the shooting of a policeman during a drug raid. *Lay My Body on the Line* (1978) examines the uprisings at San Francisco State University in the late 1960's through the eyes of an activist teacher and former boxer.

His latest work, *Buffalo Nickel* (1992), is an autobiography that reads like a novel. It chronicles his dramatic coming-of-age in the conflicting shadows of two older brothers: one a drug addict and petty criminal, the other an intellectual prodigy. Through intense, passionate prose, Salas takes us through the seedy bars, boxing rings and jails of his youth as he searches for his own true identity amid the tragedy that envelopes his family. *Kirkus Reviews* called *Buffalo Nickel* a "piercing and eloquent coming-of-age story (. . .) Beautifully written, gritty, and deeply human."

The following are two chapters from *Buffalo Nickel*.

Chapter 1
of *Buffalo Nickel*

His big plaster leg took up the whole back seat and he held his crutches next to him. He was eleven and I was almost two. We were taking my brother Al home from the hospital, where he had been put after jumping headfirst off a thirty-foot water tower. I stared at him. He was a spectacular sight to me.

It was the deep depression of 1933. We lived in a mining town called Brighton and my father was lucky to have a job. He had a job because he was a hard worker, the best, a deputy sheriff's son who grew up on a ranch and knew how to get things done, like blow coal out of the tunnel walls with dynamite, so other men could load it.

I remember that tower. My oldest brother, Eddy, who was thirteen and an intellectual prodigy, swung me around by an arm and a leg up there and scared the hell out of me. I caught my breath, got dizzy and nauseated and saw a damp, dark spot on the earth beneath the water spout under the tower.

When Eddy came to bring Al home to get a spanking for selling one of Dad's rabbits for a big jar of marbles, Al jumped headfirst from the tower. That's my first memory of my brother Al. It has set the tone for the rest of his life, as I see it: tragic, but with a stubborn streak of survival in it that has denied defeat.

Oh, he was fun, though. He took me to my first movie when I was three. It was in a red brick building across the dirt alley from our yard in the small town of Lafayette, Colorado. He took me right down to the first row, where we sat looking up. I remember being astounded by the size of the big cowboys in front of me. And somebody behind us was shining a big flashlight down on them. I kept looking back and forth from it to the spinning wheels of the stagecoach. It astounded me. I couldn't figure it out. It was real and not real, another spectacular sight.

Next, I remember this little suburb in Denver called Elyria, where my father worked in a packing plant. Al took me to a house where somebody stuck a rake under a front porch and pulled out little warm puppies. Then, he taught me to shoot little green buds off a tree like spit wads. I was still three then. Then, I remember him when I was four and we lived in a red brick, two-story building on Curtis Street in Denver. We lived on the bottom floor.

My birth broke my mother's rheumatic heart, it is said. She had my little sister three years later, so she had to sleep in the afternoons or she'd die. I remember her lying down in the bedroom. I had nothing to do and would wander around the house.

One day, I was rummaging around and I found the black suit with short pants and white silken shirt that my mother used to dress me in when we went somewhere. I liked it and put it on. Since I was dressed, I decided to go for a walk. I wandered a block down to Curtis Park, which was a big park with a swimming pool. I stayed there all afternoon, had all kinds of fun. I remember playing with these bigger boys who carried me and another little boy on their shoulders so we could wrestle and try to throw each other down. We were the arms, they were the legs. It was great fun.

Then I wandered to the other side of the park, where a woman in an alley told another woman I was the brother of Al Salas. He must have been thirteen at the time. I went back to the park and it must have gotten very late, almost dark already. Al appeared. He said he had been sent to find me and that I was going to get a beating when I got home. I can still see him lying down in the grass next to me: dark, wavy hair, strong-boned face, telling me very seriously that I better put a book under the back seat of my short pants so the whipping wouldn't hurt so much. I took him very seriously, but the book was too big and didn't fit. I did need it, though, because the next thing I knew, I was running around in a circle in the kitchen, hollering, while my mother held onto one of my hands and switched me. Even then my brother knew how to lighten the punishment you got for being too free.

Al put the first pair of boxing gloves on me then. Some cute little blond kid who lived next door was in the kitchen with me. So he taught the both of us how to box, or, rather, he put the gloves on us and had us slug it out on the linoleum floor. And we punched and punched at each other, getting all sweaty and red-faced. I remember it as a rainy day. That's why we didn't go outside. He kept stopping us and pouring hot water on the gloves so we could hit harder. It made the gloves heavier and they splat more when we hit each other. I didn't know then how many fights he was going to get me into during the years to come.

He taught me to tie my shoes, sort of. I don't know how old I was, but I didn't go to school, not even kindergarten, so I had to be four or five. We were living on Welton Street. Our house was pretty and bigger than the previous one, more lighted, too. It must have been cold outside, because we were inside again, and again he was watching me and my little sister. I kept going up to him to get my shoe tied. It kept coming undone. I watched him as he did it. He was getting tired of tying it. I knew he was annoyed. But a little while later, it came untied again. So I sat down and tied it myself. I never asked him or anyone to tie my shoes again. He taught me that without even trying. Before it was over, he'd teach me a lot of things without trying, some good, some bad.

He protected me, too. I had a little dog by the name of Trixie, a little terrier. She was very pretty, black with perfect markings. She had a natural white collar around her neck, white feet, a white star on the back of her head, white tip at her tail and a white throat. She started barking one day at some Mexican kids about ten or twelve years old who had come into the backyard and grabbed my bicycle. When she threatened them, one of them hit her in the nose with a Vaseline jar. She started yelping and ran back to the house across the big back yard. I yelled, "They hurt Trixie!"

Al ran out of the house and, with all the neighborhood kids, chased those guys down to the ballpark on the next block, where Al tackled the guy who had hit Trixie. He then held him down and let me hit him in the face for hurting my dog. I leaned over the big kid, who stared at me with wide eyes, and touched him with my little fist. Then, satisfied, my brother let him up. The kid ran off across the baseball field and never came back to our neighborhood. My brother was a hero to me that day, as he would be on many other days.

The next thing I remember is my father taking me to a boxing match somewhere in Denver. As a small child, things seemed to suddenly materialize before me. There I was sitting next to my father watching the Golden Gloves. I was astounded again. Another spectacular sight. I saw a great big brown man get into the ring. Heavy flesh filled him out, rounding him off. He had black hair and black, narrow eyes. He was fighting a pink man who had hair on his chest. The bell rang and they ran out at each other. There was a big thud and the pink man flew backwards and landed on the mat. Everybody yelled and some stood up, then some man on the other side of my father said, "Who's that? He knocked him out." Another man, in a white jacket with a bony face, who was selling beer said, "He's an Indian!" Suddenly the cowboy movies I'd seen came to strange life again. Another spectacular sight. But that wasn't all. Then they brought out Albert, my brother.

I saw him go into the ring and stand opposite some kid with light brown hair who was built husky, like him. I got worried. He looked tough. Then, the bell rang and they ran at each other. My brother hit him, but got hit back. I jumped up on my seat and, standing on it, started swinging my arms like I was fighting, shouting, "Come on, Albert! Hit him, Albert! Hit him!"

He needed all my help, I could see. I forgot all about the people around me and threw all the punches I could, shouting all the time for him, shouting so much my father told the man on the other side of him, "That's his brother! That's his brother!" He said it a couple more times to other people who turned to look at me. Little kid, five years old, standing on a wooden seat, throwing punches for his brother. It paid off, though. When it was over, they raised my brother's hand. I was really happy. He had won.

I found out that he would fight again at the end of the week. I couldn't wait to go see him again. For some reason, however, we didn't. But the very next morning after the second fight, as soon as I woke up, I went into my brother's room and touched him, my eyes wide, my mouth open.

"Did you win?" I asked.

He shook his head and said, "No," then he laid back down, his wavy hair dark against the white pillow, his handsome face looking sad.

I was disappointed and lowered my eyes and shut my mouth and walked out. I was going to be disappointed in him a lot, too.

I did well in school. I could read before I even went to kindergarten. I remember my father reading the funny papers about a little kid my age riding down a snow slope on a sled, screaming, "Eeeeee eeeeeeeeee!" all the way across the page. My father made the sound and followed it with his finger. Picture and sound and letter came together and made words for the first time for me. The corner grocer's name was Freeeee-man. I could see that "e" in the word. I read it out after that. So, when I went to school, I could already do that part.

One night, when I was six, I went out into the back yard with Albert to get a pail of coal for the stove. I don't remember why I went with him. Maybe because my mother didn't trust him out alone. Maybe she wasn't home and he was supposed to stay with me. But when we were out by the coal shed, he suddenly said, "Do you want to go to the Epworth Gym with me?"

"Yes," I answered right away, thinking of another spectacular sight.

So, off we went on his new bicycle. My father bought it new for Al because he had stolen one and gotten in trouble over it. It had cost a lot of money for those depression days of 1937: sixty-five dollars. You could buy a decent car for that, then. He sold all the fancy parts off it, a piece at a time, until it was stripped bare, without fenders even. That disappointed me, too, because it had been so pretty. But off we went across town to the Epworth Gym, which was near Curtis Park, where we used to live and where I had so much fun the day I went for a walk.

We got there and Al took me inside. I remember playing around a while, even though I didn't know anybody. But then it came to be seven o'clock and all the little guys had to go home and the man put me out. I told him my brother was inside and that I had to wait for my brother. It got cold and the man kept telling me to go away. I kept saying I had to wait for my brother. But Al didn't come out. I waited there for two hours before he did. I remember how worried I was that he might run off without me. It was nippy, too, and I got bored, besides.

Al finally came out with all the big boys at closing time. The next thing I knew, he said to this other big kid about his age, "My brother can whip yours!" I looked up at this tall, skinny kid who had come out with the big boys. He was at least a head taller than I was.

They made a circle around us in the dark, with just the glow of streetlights shining on the residential street. "Fight!" Albert told me. I turned to face the tall kid, who immediately smashed me in the nose. Blood spurted out of it and stars filled my head. He almost knocked me down, and then he hit me a few more times. Albert stopped the fight, and tried to wipe the blood off my face.

Finally, when the blood stopped, Al said, "Here!" and gave me a buffalo head nickel. I took it, thanked him and got on the bike again. I was a little guy even for six and I fit handily on the handle bar in front of him. He pumped down the dark streets for a long time. I remember how cold it was and that my nose kept dribbling blood. I liked my brother, though. He had finally come outside at closing time, had stopped the fight, and had given me a nickel.

But when we were almost home, he told me not to tell my mother that we had gone to the Epworth Gym or that I had been in a fight.

"Okay," I said.

"Good," he said, then asked me, "Floyd, could you give me that nickel back? I need it."

"Sure." I handed it over to him.

He'd do that a lot to me, also, before it was over.

Al sure was fun, though. He'd take me with him when he had to go get a gallon of fresh milk from the dairy for our Sunday breakfast of pork chops and eggs. That was fun, walking hand in hand with him to pick up the big gallon glass jug with the thick yellow cream caked at the top. We'd stop and take a sip before we got home, and he'd say not to say anything. I didn't.

Maybe I thought he owed me something for the nickel, or maybe I was just naturally a predator. I remember my older sister Dorothy, who was seven years older than I and two younger than Albert, giving my little sister Annabelle and me dinner. She told us that she was saving a small bowl of preserved plums for Albert far up on a pantry shelf. I don't know. Maybe she thought I was a thief, or maybe she just wanted to get them out of sight and out of mind. In any case, I later sneaked into the kitchen and, using a chair, climbed up into the pantry and took down the bowl of plums. I can still see them, pale purple, swimming around in the juice. I ate them down. I was a sloppy crook, though, because the next thing I knew, Al, my fifteen-year-old boxer brother, was home. And Dorothy, who was a good housekeeper and baby-sitter, was showing him the empty plate. Al was right on me.

"Stole my plums, huh?" he said, and slapped me right across the face.

I yelled and started crying as I felt the blood gush out of my nose again. But he didn't try to comfort me this time, and neither did my pretty sister, Dorothy. I was a crook and, feeling sorry for myself, went into my bedroom, where I stood at the back window that overlooked the backyard and cried for myself, for the sting and the hurt. I dabbed at the blood with my mother's lace curtains. Then I got bawled out for that when she came home.

I told her, feeling full of self-pity, "Albert hit me!"

She said, "You shouldn't have wiped your nose on the curtains, anyway!" She knew I was a thief and didn't feel sorry for me either. That hurt a lot, too. Maybe that's why I never became a thief.

Albert did, though. I sensed it was about him when I came home from school and saw Mom walking back and forth in the kitchen. Her green eyes were all wet and pink as she walked back and forth from the table to the stove while cooking dinner. Her cheeks were pink, too, but they often were, because she had high blood pressure, and her skin would get so pink and white, it was almost transparent. This and the heat of the stove could make them burn. But next to her eyes, her cheeks looked worse, now. She sniffled every once in a while and I looked up at her. But she avoided my eyes when she turned back from the table and stepped toward the stove.

I was drawing on my chalkboard, which was located right next to the warm stove, with the colored chalks my father had gotten me. I didn't want her to hurt, but she kept me out of her world and I didn't say anything. I was well trained. Yet, I knew it was about Albert. He didn't come home that night. Often, he wouldn't be around for days at a time. The world was still a wonder to me. I didn't question its turning. My mother took care of all that. My life was well ordered and I never asked when Albert disappeared or where my father was when he left somewhere for months at a time. She and he kept the worries of the world away from their children as much as possible. She kept a six-year-old child out now.

Soon after that, we took a Sunday drive to the town of Golden, some thirty miles away from Denver. Again, nothing was said to my little sister or me. But we saw Al there in a blue dungaree uniform, sitting with a hundred other boys out on the lawn, talking to their families in front of a big yellow building. I remember my mother making sure that she gave him a carton of cigarettes. Then, later, all the boys lined up and took down the flag, and we got in our '31 Model-A Ford and drove back through the settling darkness to Denver. I told my father all about how the Indians lived on the plains of Colorado, which I had learned in school, where I had gotten an unbroken string of A's. I never asked where Al was. I wasn't told and I didn't question.

But I knew he was locked up, though it didn't look like those reform schools for dead-end kids I had seen in the movies.

The next thing I remember, it was summer. I was eight years old and skipping the last half of the third grade to enter the fourth. I was taken to a ranch near Pueblo, Colorado, called "Pinyon" for the pinyon-nut trees. My grandfather and grandmother lived with their sons in an old, long bunkhouse with only one separate room for them. The house was on land, I heard, that my grandfather had owned before his brother had lost it. His brother had been a college graduate who was county auditor and had power of attorney. He had gotten syphilis of the brain, went crazy and lost the family fortune to his cheating bank partner just before he died in 1927. This was twelve years later in '39. Now, my grandfather worked with his sons as a picking crew on other men's land. I didn't know this. I thought it was my grandfather's ranch and that all the horses were his.

I was surprised to see Al there, with his head shaved bald. It didn't take me long after my mother and father went back to Denver to learn that Al had escaped from Golden Reform School. I found this out because he stole my grandfather's new car for a joyride and wrecked it. Al was always pulling some kind of trick. I liked him, but I must have had some reservations already, because my Uncle Willy saw how much I liked my little dog, Trixie, and, smiling, asked, "Floyd, who do you like the most, Albert or Trixie?"

I looked up into his soft, gray eyes, then at Al, who looked away. "Trixie!" I said, and Uncle Willy burst out laughing.

Chapter 9
of *Buffalo Nickel*

My heart started pounding at the sight of the crowd, the roar of voices bouncing off the walls as I stepped into the hotel ballroom in Santa Clara for the smoker bout. To me, it was like walking into the Roman Coliseum. Puffs of smoke floated in clouds over the bald heads, the gray hair, the pink, puffy faces and pot bellies, the eyes that were all looking at me!

I was in a new, shiny blue and silver Judson Pacific Murphy boxing robe with a silver sash. I was going to fight in front of a real fight audience for the first time. Al had decided I should box amateur with Babe Figuera's Judson Pacific Murphy iron foundry team, because I had gone to Alameda High School with half of them. Babe wanted me on the team, which was all right. But it also meant that I was going to have to keep boxing Ortega forever. I was afraid he was going to break my nose again tonight.

When we got close to the ring, which was set right on the floor in the middle of the ballroom and padded with mats, I could see Curly Upshaw and Roy, his older brother, a highclass pimp, too, with one of Curly's blond whores sitting on the other side of the ring. Al T. was there, too, in his dark tea-timers. They gave me some support, but their presence also put pressure on me, because I knew I had to fight good for them. I was worried I'd look bad.

I could see them all watching me walk up. They made me feel so shy, I ducked my head and started shadowboxing like a welterweight amateur main eventer I'd seen kayo some guy in Vallejo. Babe had said, "That's the way you should fight, Floyd." Babe astounded me because the guy was so good and so tough. He even looked tough with hair on his chest and beard stubble. I never dreamed Babe would think I could fight like that. So, right now I copied the guy, the way he shuffled down to the ring. I tried to fall into it, get inside myself and keep the self-consciousness and fear off. I did not want to see all the eyes staring at me.

I shuffled forward on the balls of my feet, sanding the floor with the leather soles of my boxing shoes, my heels barely touching, hands flickering with subtle feints, barely suggesting punches, the twist of a wrist and turn of a shoulder for a hook, the knuckle point of my fist twice for two fast jabs. I teetered my head and rocked my shoulders to slip a punch and began to feel good. I slipped inside myself, safe from the crowd for the moment.

But I was still scared. I still saw everybody looking at me, still knew they were there. I tried to concentrate on the feeling in my body, and it helped. I floated toward the ring, less a victim now. I could win this fight. I could beat Johnny, even if it was my very first amateur fight ever. I had beaten him in the gym only last week, and afterwards lots of guys had told me how good I looked against him, in front of him. Even Jack Mendonca's fighters said so. I could beat Johnny, I told myself, and squeezed my fists into tight balls in the twelve-ounce gloves. I gritted my teeth and set my jaw. I was going to win! I was determined to win!

I stopped shadowboxing and got scared again when I reached the ring and all eyes turned on me. I stepped through the ropes onto the mats set on the floor and into the bright lights all alone, tense, self-conscious. I walked in a blur to the neutral corner to sand my shoes in the resin box, then back to my corner, where Al untied my belt and slipped my robe off.

Now, I felt naked. The referee was beckoning me. Up close, he was a red-faced man with lines in his cheeks. Johnny stepped up. Babe Figuera, his eyes looking steel-rimmed in his glasses, was behind him, rubbing his shoulders.

With the bright lights shining down on us, Johnny looked like a tiny Atlas, like a miniature body builder at five-three, a hundred twelve pounds. He smiled stiffly at me. At nineteen, there was a toughness in the tight lines of his face from having to work so hard as a migrant farmworker when he was a child. He was supposed to be half Apache and had won every tournament he'd ever entered for two straight years, from boys club bouts to the Golden Gloves.

I could hear the announcer calling Johnny the Golden Gloves champion of California and then announcing my name and weight. But when the referee started mumbling instructions, all I could hear was my heart thudding against my chest: bu-bump! bu-bump! bu-bump!

When we got back to the corner, Al said, "He's going to try and get even with you for the whipping you gave him last week. So keep moving and keep fighting. Don't wait for him to pick his shots. Go get him. Beat 'im to the punch. Keep the pressure on him. He's not used to that."

He jammed my mouthpiece into my mouth and pushed me around to face Johnny at the sound of the bell. I froze with fright for a second when I saw him charging at me. But I caught my breath and danced away along the ropes, fast, running to get time to think. I skipped completely out of the corner and around to the other side of the ring, where I had a safe distance between us and I could see Johnny for the first time, really. Then, when I saw him chugging after me like a little locomotive, I knew I could hit him with a jab right away. All I had to do was beat him. Now I was thinking. Now I could fight. I wasn't afraid. It was just a fight. I'd been in lots of fights.

I was in another world when I skipped out under the bright lights on the balls of my feet to meet Johnny, my body sizzling as if the mats under my shoes were white hot, skimming over them toward him like a water mosquito. My hands were up and I peeked over the gloves in front of my face, my chin tucked into my left shoulder, my arms like two fence posts in front of my face and body, elbows covering my belly. I was pale from working in the library all the time, but my shoulders were thick and muscular, and muscles rippled on my belly. My thighs were slim but muscular and popped out like turkey legs, knots of muscles above the knees. My calves were slim and muscular, too, with ridges of muscles outlining them.

I started firing with a jab as soon as I got in range to keep him off. But I was forced to jump back when Johnny charged with a flurry of hooks, overhand rights and lefts, grunting as he punched. He drove me around the ring, going all out to get me, trying to knock me out just as Al said he would. Johnny "The Killer" Ortega.

But I suddenly stopped and counterpunched with a quick one-two, left-right, and danced out again as Johnny charged in again. He was still throwing hooks with both hands, barely grazing me, only the slightest turn of my head making the punches slide off instead of connecting full force. And as soon as he paused after missing a couple, I leaped back in again with two jabs, pop-pop, then one-two, left-right, and leaped out again as the crowd started shouting.

Johnny chased me, kept coming and trapped me against the ropes, where he threw a barrage at me and caught me on the sides of the head. He kept punching, forcing me to fall inside the hooks and cover up, take the punches on the arms and shoulders and gloves as much as I could. I felt the sting of them on my face, my forehead, my cheekbone, but none were solid.

I could hear Johnny grunting with the swings, feel his weight pressing against me, leaning on me, keeping me trapped against the ropes. I shifted to my left and when Johnny pressed harder, I quickly shifted to my right and shoved Johnny by the left shoulder to his right, spinning out of the way and sending him sprawling over the second rope.

I heard the crowd cry out with approval as I danced back until Johnny was facing me again. Then I went in again, pop-popping with my left, and I shifted back a step to make the countering left miss and shifted back in with a left-right, one-two. I wasn't thinking of what I was doing. I was just doing what I'd been trained to do, what I knew I could do, anything to keep the fear away.

When Johnny charged, I waited and popped him with another jab, but I caught one to the nose myself. It stung. I danced away, then back in with another jab, then back out again, out and in, again and again and again, jabbing, jabbing, jabbing, crossing with my right every time Johnny charged, stopping the charge, punching back every time Johnny punched, even when dancing back, throwing a flurry of punches as I backed up, short lefts and rights, all of them crosses, pumping them straight out in front of me, "Bam-bam-bam-bam-bam!" inside Johnny's hooks, catching the hooks to the forehead and temples, not letting any one punch get me in the face and landing every punch I threw square in Johnny's face until he finally backed off. Then I waited, facing him until I heard Al shout, "Go get'im!" and I leaped in again.

But Johnny caught me with a right hook that stunned me. For just one second my sight blurred and Johnny fuzzed out of focus, and my head went "Bzzzzzzz." I caught another punch square in the face, and I grabbed Johnny's arms, tied him up and felt myself being pushed back against the ropes.

I could hear the excited voices of the crowd and knew I was hurt and in trouble. I held on desperately until my sight cleared and I heard Al shout, "Move! Move!" And I shoved Johnny back and danced away just as the bell rang.

Johnny walked away. When I got to my corner and sat down, I could see him on the other side of the ring, sitting on his stool. I met his heavy-lidded eyes with my own just for a moment. His eyes looked strangely at me. There was a question in them, the quizzical way he studied me that showed he was surprised, that he respected me for giving him, the Gloves Champ, such a battle in my very first fight. But there was no fear in his eyes. Ortega feared no one.

I was clear-headed now, but the rest of the fight was a blur for me. I started jabbing and connecting again, then let go with a sharp right when he started to come in and caught him right on the jaw. I heard the whole hall shout and saw Johnny stagger back, then just stand there staring at me with his arms down, mouth open, looking surprised.

I stared at him. His eyes were glazed. Yet, I just stood there, as surprised as he was. We stared at each other. Suddenly, I heard Al shout, "Go get him. He's all yours!"

And the whole crowd cheered as I leaped in as Al told me, but Babe yelled, too: "Hands up, Johnny!" and Johnny ducked his head down when I jumped in and started hooking over his head with both hands. We slugged it out there on the ropes. I could feel his punches but they didn't hurt me. And I could feel my gloves thudding against his face and body. I could hear shouts. My face was hot and my body was pouring sweat, moving like magic, without strain or fatigue, full of wind and endurance, punching, punching, punching, with all thought of fear and anxiety long gone. Everything was pure intuition, automatic. My whole body was behind and in every punch with fluid, effortless motion, without thought or feeling, firing punch after punch after punch. It was thrilling.

Suddenly, the fight was over. There had been another round but I didn't even remember fighting it. I could hear the crowd shouting and cheering and clapping while the referee grabbed both Johnny's and my arms and turned us in a circle, calling it a draw. It was a draw. Al was in the ring, grinning, taking my mouthpiece out and throwing my robe over my shoulders. I felt a great sense of jubilation, with nervous skirmishes of fluctuating sound beating on my exposed, sweating face like quick blasts of wind. I couldn't think of anything to say. I couldn't speak. I just stepped through the ropes and down the aisle as if I were tip-toeing on air.

Virgil Suárez

Born in Cuba in 1962 and raised in the United States since 1970, Suárez is the holder of an MFA in Creative Writing (1987) from Louisiana State University, where he studied with Vance Bourjaily. He is currently an instructor of creative writing at his alma mater. Although educated in the United States since the age of eight, Suárez has been preoccupied with the themes of immigration and acclimatization to life and culture in the United States.

Suárez is the author of three successful books and numerous stories published in literary magazines. He is also an active book reviewer for newspapers around the country. His first novel, *Latin Jazz* (1989), chronicles the experiences of a Cuban immigrant family in Los Angeles by adopting the narrative perspectives of each of the family members. New York's *Newsday* hailed the novel as, "a striking debut. A well crafted and sensitive novel. An engrossing, honest book by a writer who cares deeply about preserving ties within the family unit and, by extension, within the Hispanic community and America. Suárez is marvelous." His second novel, *The Cutter* (1991), deals with the desperate attempts of a young sugar-cane cutter to leave Cuba and join his family in the United States. *Publishers Weekly* stated that "Suárez's powerful novel about one individual's response to the abuses and arbitrariness of totalitarianism shows us how ordinary people can be driven to take extraordinary risks."

Suárez's most recent book is a collection of his short fiction, *Welcome to the Oasis* (1992)—from which the selection for this present anthology is drawn—which portrays a new generation of young Hispanics who struggle to integrate themselves into an Americanized culture while maintaining pieces of their heritage. *Kirkus Reviews* has baptized Suárez as a leading spokesperson for his Cuban-American generation: *Welcome to the Oasis* is "a tightly controlled but affecting exploration of fundamental tensions in a community for whom Suárez is becoming an eloquent and promising voice."

A Perfect Hotspot

This idea of selling ice cream during the summer seems ridiculous, pointless. I'd much rather be close to water. The waves. Where I can hear them tumble in and then roll out, and see the tiny bubbles left behind on the sand pop one by one. Or feel the undercurrents warm this time of year. Swimming. Watching the girls in bikinis with sand stuck to the backs of their thighs walk up and down the boardwalk. At this time of the morning, the surfers are out riding the waves.

Instead, I'm inside an ice cream truck with my father, selling, cruising the streets. The pumps suck oil out of the ground rapidly with the creaking sounds of iron biting iron in a fenced lot at the end of the street. They look like giant rocking horses. Father turns at the corner, then, suddenly, he points to another ice cream truck.

"There's the competition," he says. "If the economy doesn't improve soon, these streets'll be full of them."

He's smoking, and the smoke floats back my way and chokes me. I can't stand it. Some of the guys on the swim team smoke. I don't understand how they can smoke and do their best when it's time for competition. I wouldn't smoke. To do so would be like cheating myself out of winning.

All morning he's been instructing me on how to sell ice cream.

"Tonio," he says now, "come empty your pockets."

I walk to the front of the truck, stick my hands deep into my pockets and grab a handful of coins—what we've made in change all morning. The coins fall, overlap and multiply against the sides of the grease-smudged, change box. I turn my pockets inside-out until the last coin falls. He picks out the pieces of lint and paper from the coins.

When he begins to explain the truck's quirks, "the little problems," as he calls the water leaks, burning oil, and dirty carburetor, I return to the back of the truck and sit down on top of the wood counter next to the window.

"Be always on the lookout for babies," father says. "The ones in pampers. They pop out of nowhere. Check your mirrors all the time."

A CAUTION CHILDREN cardboard sign hangs from the rearview mirror. Running over children is a deep fear that seems to haunt him.

All I need, I keep reminding myself, is to pass the CPR course, get certified, and look for a job as a beach lifeguard.

"Stop!" a kid screams, slamming the screen door of his house open. He runs to the grassy part next to the sidewalk. Father stops the truck. The kid's hand comes up over the edge of the window with a dollar bill forked between his little fingers.

"What do you want?" I say.

"A Froze Toe," he says, jumping up and down, dirt rings visible on his neck. He wets the corners of his mouth with his cherry, Kool-aid-stained tongue. I reach inside the freezer and bring out a bar. On its wrapper is the picture of an orange foot with a blue bubble gum ball on the big toe.

"See what else he wants," father says. "Make sure they always leave the dollar."

The kid takes his ice cream, and he smiles.

"What else?" I ask him.

He shrugs his shoulders, shakes his head, and bites the wrapper off. The piece of paper falls on the grass. I give him his change; he walks back to his house.

"Should always make sure they leave all the money they bring," father says. "They get it to spend it. That's the only way you'll make a profit. Don't steal their money, but exchange it for merchandise." His ears stick out from underneath his L.A. Dodgers cap. The short hair on the back of his head stands out.

I grin up at the rearview mirror, but he isn't looking.

"Want to split a Pepsi, Tonio?" he says.

"I'm not thirsty."

"Get me some water then."

The cold mist inside the freezer crawls up my hand. After he drinks and returns the bottle, I place it back with the ice cream.

"Close the freezer," he says, "before all the cold gets out and they melt."

If the cold were out I'd be at the natatorium doing laps.

* * *

On another street, a group of kids jumps and skips around a short man. The smallest of the kids hangs from the man's thigh. The man signals my father to stop, then walks up to the window. The kids scream excitedly.

"Want this one, daddy," one of the girls says.

"This one!" a boy says.

The smallest kid jumps, pointing his finger at the display my father has made with all the toys and candies.

"No, Jose," the man says, taking the kid by the wrist. "No candy."

The kid turns to look up at his father, not fully understanding, and then looks at me. His little lips tremble.

"Give me six Popsicles," the man says.

"I don't want no Pop—"

"Popsicles or nothing. I don't have money to buy you what you want."

"A Blue Ghost. I want a Blue Ghost."

"No, I said."

The smallest kid cries.

"Be quiet, Jose, or I'm going to tell the man to go away."

I put the six Popsicles on the counter.

"How much?" the man asks. The skin around his eyes is a darker brown than that of his nose and cheeks.

"A dollar-fifty," I say.

He digs inside his pockets and produces two wrinkled green balls which he throws on the counter. The two dollar bills roll. I unfold the bills, smooth them, and give them to father, who returns the man his change through the front window.

The man gives each kid a Popsicle, then walks away with his hands in his pockets. Jose, still crying, grabs his as he follows his father back to their house.

"He doesn't want to spend his beer money," father says, driving away from the curb.

After that, we have no more customers for hours. Ever since he brought the truck home two years ago, father has changed. Ice creams have become his world. According to father, appearance and cleanliness isn't important as long as the truck passes the Health Department inspection in order to obtain the sales license. The inside of the truck is a mess: paint flakes off, rust hides between crevices, the freezer lids hold layer upon layer of dirt and melted ice cream. Here I'll have to spend the rest of my summer, I think, among the strewn Doritos, Munchos, and the rest of the merchandise.

The outside of the truck had been painted by father's friend, Gaspar, before mother died. I remember how Gaspar drank beer after beer while he painted the crown over the K in KING OF ICE CREAM and assured mother, who never missed one of my swim meets and who always encouraged me to become the best swimmer I could be, that I was going to make it all right in the end.

Father lives this way, I know, out of loneliness. He misses mother as much as I do.

I count the passing of time by how many ice creams I sell. It isn't anything like swimming laps. Doing laps involves the idea of setting and breaking new limits.

"How much do you think we have?" my father asks. The visor of his cap tilts upward.

"I don't know." I hate the metallic smell money leaves on my fingers.

"Any idea?"

"No."

"A couple of months on your own and you'll be able to guess approximately how much you make."

A couple of months, I think, and I'll be back in high school. Captain of the varsity swim team. A customer waits down the street.

"Make the kill fast," father says.

A barefooted woman holding a child to her breast comes to the window. She has dirty fingernails, short and uneven, as if she bites them all the time. Make the kill fast, I think.

Ice creams on the counter, I tell her, "Two dollars."

She removes the money out of her brassiere and hands it to me, then she walks away. She has yellow blisters on the back of each heel.

After that, he begins to tell me the story of the wild dog. When he was a kid, a wild bitch came down from the hills and started killing my grandfather's chickens. "Seeing the scattered feathers," father says, "made your grandfather so angry I thought his face would burst because it'd turned so red."

"Anyway," he continues, "the wild dog kept on killing chickens."

Not only my grandfather's, but other farmers' as well. The other farmers were scared because they thought the wild dog was a witch. One morning, my grandfather got my father out of bed early and took him up to the hills behind the house with a jar of poison. A farmer had found the bitch's litter. My grandfather left my father in charge of anointing the poison all over the puppies fur so that when the mother came back, if he hadn't shot it by then, she'd die the minute she licked her young. My father didn't want to do it, but my grandfather left him in command while he went after the wild dog to shoot it. The dog disappeared and the puppies licked each other to death.

When he finishes telling me the story, father looks at the rearview mirror and grins, then he drives on. He turns up the volume in the music box and now *Raindrops Keep Falling On My Head* blares out of the speakers. The old people'll complain, he says, because the loud music hurts their eardrums, but the louder the music, the more people'll hear it, and more ice creams'll get sold.

Farther ahead, another kid stops us. The kid has his tongue out. His eyes seem to be too small for his big face. Though he seems old, he still drools. He claps his small hands quickly.

"Does he have money?" father asks.

"Can't see."

The kid walks over to the truck and hangs from the edge of the window.

"Get him away from the truck," father says, then to the kid, "Hey, move away!"

"Come on," I tell the kid, "you might fall and hurt yourself."

"Wan icleam," the kid says.

"We'll be back in a little while," father tells him.

"Wan icleam!" He doesn't let go. "Wan icleam!"

"Move back!" father shouts. "Tonio, get him away from the truck."

I try to unstick the kid's pudgy fingers from the metal edge of the window, but he won't let go. His saliva falls on my hands.

"Wan icleam!"

I reach over to one of the shelves to get a penny candy for him so that I can bait him into letting go, but father catches me.

"Don't you dare," he says.

He opens the door and comes around the back to the kid, pulling him away from the truck to the sidewalk where he sets the kid down, and returns.

"Can't give your merchandise away," he says. "You can't make a profit that way, Tonio."

The kid runs after us shouting, waving his arms. I grab a handful of candies and throw them out the window to the sidewalk, where they fall on the grass and scatter.

* * *

The sun sets slowly, and, descending, it spreads Popsicle orange on the sky. Darkness creeps on the other side of the city.

If I don't get a job as a lifeguard, I think, then I'm going to travel southeast and visit the islands.

"How are the ice creams doing?" father asks. "Are they softening?"

I check by squeezing a bar and say, "I think we should call it a day."

"Tonio," he says. He turns off the music, makes a left turn to the main street, and heads home. "Why didn't you help me with that kid? You could have moved him. What will happen when you're here by yourself?"

"Couldn't do it."

"Here," he says, giving me the change box. "Take it inside when we get home."

"I'll get it when we get there."

He puts the blue box back down on top of the stand he built over the motor. Cars speed by. The air smells heavy with exhaust and chemical fumes. In the distance, columns of smoke rise from factory smokestacks.

He turns into the driveway, drives the truck all the way to the front of the garage, and parks underneath the long branches of the avocado tree.

"Take the box inside," he says, turning off the motor. He steps down from the truck and connects the freezer to the extension cord coming out of the kitchen window.

I want to tell him that I won't come out tomorrow.

"Come on, Tonio. Bring the box in."

"You do it," I say.

"What's the matter, son?"

"I'd rather you do it."

"Like you'd rather throw all my merchandise out of the window," he says, growing red in the face. "I saw you."

He walks toward me, and I sense another argument coming. Father stops in front of me and gives me a wry smile. "Dreamers like you," he says, "learn the hard way."

He turns around, picks up the change box, and says, "I'm putting the truck up for sale. From now on you're on your own, you hear. I'm not forcing you to do something you don't want to."

I don't like the expressionless look on his face when usually, whenever he got angry at me, his face would get red and sweaty.

He unlocks the kitchen door and enters the house.

I jump out of the truck, lock the door, and walk around our clapboard house to the patio. Any moment now, I think, father'll start slamming doors inside and throwing things around. He'll curse. I lean against the wall and feel the glass of the window behind me when it starts to tremble.

Sabine Ulibarrí

Short-story writer, poet and essayist Sabine Ulibarrí has had one of the longest and most productive literary careers in Chicano literature. He is a well-known and highly respected chronicler of the way things once were in his beloved New Mexico. Born on September 21, 1919, in the small village of Tierra Amarilla, New Mexico, he was raised on a ranch by his parents, both of whom were college graduates. Besides learning the ways of rural life and the rugged countryside, Ulibarrí also experienced first-hand the folk culture of the area, which not only included the full repository of oral literature, but also connected him strongly to the language and oral literature of Spain and the Spanish-speaking Americas. His early love for the Spanish language and Hispanic literature took Ulibarrí to college and eventually to a Ph.D. in Spanish. Over the years he taught at every level, from elementary school to graduate school, except during World War II when he flew thirty-five combat missions as an Air Force gunner. Today he is an emeritus professor of the University of New Mexico, where he spent most of his academic career as a student and professor.

Ulibarrí has published two books of poems, *Al cielo se sube a pie* (1966, *You Reach Heaven on Foot*) and *Amor y Ecuador* (1966, *Love and Ecuador*), and the following collections of short stories in bilingual format: *Tierra Amarilla: Stories of New Mexico / Tierra Amarilla: Cuentos de Nuevo México* (1971, previously published in Ecuador in Spanish only in 1966), *Mi abuela fumaba puros y otros cuentos de Tierra Amarilla / My Grandma Smoked Cigars and Other Stories of Tierra Amarilla* (1977), *Primeros encuentros / First Encounters* (1982), *El gobernador Glu Glu* (1988, *Governor Glu Glu*) and *El Cóndor and Other Stories* (1989).

In all of his work, Sabine Ulibarrí preserves a style, narrative technique and language that owes much of its style and technique to oral storytelling. Through his works he has been able to capture the ethos and the spirit of rural New Mexico before the coming of the Anglo. His works memorialize myths and legends and such distinctive characters of the past as cowboys, sheriffs, folk healers, penitents and just the common everyday folk. Quite often writing two versions of the same story, in English and Spanish, in all of modern Chicano literature his works are among the most direct and accessible to broad audiences. The following selection, "Amena Karanova," is from *El Cóndor and Other Stories*.

Amena Karanova

The plane crashed at the Albuquerque airport. Fortunately, there were no deaths nor serious injuries. Ambulances showed up and took the passengers to the hospital.

Amena Karanova found herself at St. Joseph's Hospital with her secretary, Datil Vivanca. Datil had a few bruises on her forehead and a few superficial cuts on her right arm. Miraculously, Amena escaped without a scratch. Both of them were shaken up, but otherwise they were perfectly fine.

Before anyone saw Amena, one looked at her eyes. They were magnetic. They hypnotized and immobilized you. They were immense green eyes with flakes of gold. A fiery green, an incendiary gold. Something wild, something untamed. They lurked inside deep wells, set apart and in darkness. From there they fired flashes and sparks like a vigilant panther from the shadows of her cave.

When you could tear yourself away from her eyes, you became aware of the whiteness of her skin, the whiteness of alabaster, transparent and luminous from within, with a something, an echo, of the green of the olive. Down the sides of her face, upon the pillow, fell cascades of black and wavy hair, the black of ebony with glimmers of the green of the olive.

Her neck was somewhat long, elegant, and had the grace and lightness of the palm tree. Farther down, her full and subtle breasts rejected all disguises and insisted on being recognized, even under the loose and baggy hospital gown.

Her profile, like everything about her, was exquisite and delicate. A high, broad and clear forehead. A long, fine and pointed nose. Full, ripe and flowering lips. A tiny, daring and sharp chin.

When you walked away, you took with you the majestic and imposing image of a glowing green woman. An arrogant and aristocratic woman of a statuesque and classical beauty. You imagined that there was passion and violence, tenderness and compassion in her. You left convinced that she carried a great sorrow, that she concealed a deep mystery, without knowing how or why that woman frightened you. You were certain that menace and danger came with her.

Datil was pretty. As fresh and lusty as an apple. She had sparks in her eyes and cherries on her lips. Her flesh and contours were full and round, attractive in every way, but already pointing towards plumpness.

The two women must have been about twenty-eight-years old. Now they were chatting animatedly in a foreign language.

"Datil, did you notice the light in this place? I've never seen such luminosity. I have the impression that it is pouring into my eyes, and even into my pores, and setting me on fire inside. I didn't see the sun, but it must be fierce. The skies are high and vast, of a blue never seen before. What a ceiling! Since we don't have to go anywhere, and we're in no hurry, we're staying here a few days. This very day we rent a car and travel around and see the place."

That's the way it was. They went to Santa Fe and Taos. They visited the villages and the Indian pueblos. Everything, absolutely everything fascinated Amena. It was as if she had discovered a new world. Her spirit and her body, crushed before, were now vibrating with a vitality already forgotten.

The light, the sky and the landscape, the silence of the desert, the solitude of the mountains filled every void in her desires, filled the emptiness of her spirit. They brought back the joy and the peace she had lost. She was ecstatic, intoxicated. She sang, laughed and shouted. The land and the mountains answered her. She felt at home.

The human landscape enchanted her too. The whole range of human pigmentation, from the darkest to the lightest, and everything in between. The courtesy she ran into everywhere reminded her of the gentleness of her own people back home. She felt a mysterious affinity with the gracious people of New Mexico, as if she had known and loved them always. She felt at home.

There's more. Those adobe houses, mud-plastered by hand, with the traces of fingers on the walls, vigas, lattice ceilings, fireplaces in the corners and strings of chile hanging outside. Those houses, a harmonious blend of Indian and Spanish architecture, that become part of the landscape with grace and dignity, also gave Amena a feeling of serenity, to such an extent that at a given moment she told Datil, "Stop the car. I want a house just like that one." She felt more and more at home.

Datil could not be happier. Her mistress had lost interest in her life months ago. This trip was a flight from an unbearable life and reality. To see her now madly on fire, laughing and singing again, was for Datil a reason for rejoicing. She had given up on her.

The return trip was silent and pensive for Amena. Datil didn't say anything either. She knew her mistress very well. Later, in the hotel, the silence and the far-off look of the lady continued. Hazy thoughts and nebulous feelings were taking shape, falling into place, forming a personal and implacable logic.

Suddenly she sat up in bed, her face resolute, her eyes steady. She had made up her mind.

"Here I stay. Here I want to live and die. Here I'll marry. My son will be born here."

Her voice was passionate, but controlled. Datil kept silent. She was used to the wild and sudden impulses of her mistress. She accepted whatever she wished.

It was necessary to go to the bank. Amena and Datil showed up at the Central Bank. Funds from European banks had to be transferred. They were shown into the office of the vice-president, Petronilo Armijo.

As they entered, Amena stopped abruptly and stared intensely at the banker who had risen from his chair. She fixed him with a look that was a lance, a green look with flakes of burning gold. They both remained staring at each other for a long while, their eyes locked, in a pulsating vital silence. He, a slave. She, a queen.

In this dense and throbbing silence, she, transfigured, kept saying to herself, "This is the one! This one is going to be the father of my son!" He, fascinated, kept saying to himself, "This one has to be the most beautiful woman in the whole world!"

Suddenly she turned off the ray, and cut off the electric current. Petronilo felt loose and foggy, as if he were made of rags. Amena came forward in the most natural way and offered him her hand.

"Sr. Armijo, I have been told that you can help me with my financial affairs. I am Amena Karanova."

Petronilo, still shaking and not quite sure of himself, stammered: "Have a seat, señora, I am entirely at your service."

They spent some two hours making the necessary arrangements. The appropriate contracts were made out and signed. Amena knew how to put Petronilo at ease, how to make him relax, restraining her powerful personality, suppressing her potent will. She made him think that she was a vulnerable woman placing her destiny in his manly hands. He considered himself her protector. Her fortune could not help but impress him greatly. Suddenly: "Sr. Armijo, I beg another favor of you. I want to buy some property in this city and build a house. Since I don't know anyone, and since I don't know about those things, I need a person I can trust to take me by the hand. I'll pay you whatever you say."

"Sra. Karanova, say no more. I'll be delighted to serve you in any way I can. A fee for my services is out of the question."

They agreed that on the following day he would pick her up at the hotel at ten o'clock in the morning. She gave him her hand and an almost imperceptible squeeze. He was not sure. And she fired the green look that burns with flakes of flaming gold. The look appeared and disappeared instantaneously, almost as if it had never existed. She left, a conqueror. He remained, conquered. She knew what it was all about. He didn't know anything.

Petronilo did not know what he was doing for the rest of that day. That night he could not sleep. He was totally bewitched. He could not see anything but the face and the eyes of Amena. He could not hear anything but the musical voice of the most charming woman in the world. At ten o'clock on the dot he showed up at the hotel.

"I think we are friends, Petronilo. Call me Amena, please."

This is the way the strange and incredible relationship between one from here and one from there began. That day they covered all the outlying areas of the city without any luck. They stopped for lunch. That night they also had dinner together. He was becoming more and more sure of himself. She drew him out with tricks, jokes and witticisms. Her laughter, her eyes, now playful, caressed, awakened and cheered his body and soul.

From then on they could be seen together everywhere: restaurants, nightclubs, church, out in the country. Always smiling, always happy. Petronilo no longer walked on the ground, he walked on feathers and foam. His family and friends began to suspect a wedding was in the offing.

They finally found the property, just what Amena wanted. She bought it and launched the operation. Petronilo found her an architect who sketched what she told him.

In the meantime, the indoctrination and education of Petronilo went on at a pace marked by Amena. She taught him how to be a man first, and how to be a lover later. At the right moment, determined by Amena, naturally, Petronilo declared his passionate love, and later, his marriage proposal. She accepted both declarations and said yes with due demureness. He was astounded at the courage he did not know he had.

Amena continued to be a mystery to everyone, including Petronilo. She was gracious, generous and affectionate to everyone. But there was something, an enigmatic secret that never came out. This added to her attractiveness, created a certain mysticism that surrounded her, elevated her to high and inaccessible clouds. This was without ever seeing the green look with flakes of flaming gold. She only used that look when she wanted to cut or kill.

Amena told Petronilo the story of her life, but not all. She told him that she came from a distant and exotic land, that she had been the most famous star of the Wagnerian opera on three continents, that she had amassed a great fortune. She told him that the excitement, the coming and going, the constant movement of the life of fame and art had exhausted her. That she had run away in search of peace and tranquility. That was what she was doing when the plane crashed and she had found here what she was seeking, what she needed. That she would never go back.

Petronilo was blinded and astonished as he examined the albums and posters of Amena. She appeared there in the garments of the great characters she portrayed in Wagner's operas in the grand theaters of the world. She appeared in photographs with kings, presidents, generals, the grandees of the world. He read the clippings of the world press praising the artistic triumphs of "La Karanova," suggesting possible love affairs with one or another mandarin of fortune.

Petronilo saw all of this and felt misgivings and jealousy because he had not shared in this scintillating life with her. Then, after thinking it over, when he remembered that he was a humble banker in a humble bank, a nobody, and that now he was the master of the most beautiful and most seductive lady in the world, then he swallowed and gave thanks to God.

What Amena did not tell Petronilo was about Damian. Damian had been "La Karanova's" lover and fiance. They had loved each other and planned to marry. They danced, laughed, sang and said sweet things in the most select and sensual corners of the old and the new world. The press and television recorded, with every detail, their mad and joyous dance, their happy song of love. Those pictures and those clippings were not in the albums.

Damian was rich, handsome and arrogant. He was a sportsman. He drove racing cars on the most famous tracks in the world. Amena went with him to his races. He went with her to her theatrical performances. Everything was as soft and sweet as a pink dream, a robe of silk.

When the two of them were at the peak, on the very threshold of illusion, Damian killed himself in an automobile accident. When this happened, the sun went out for Amena and so did the moon and the stars. The horizons disappeared. The future became black. Amena found herself bewildered and lost in a night without end, in infinite space, without landmarks and without lights. Without a will to live, without a will to die.

Datil took her by the hand and out of the theater, out of the world she knew. She watched over her as over a child. Amena let it happen, as a child. They traveled around the world, no destination in mind, fleeing from the terror, fleeing from the night without end.

That was how they came to Albuquerque. The crash perhaps shook Amena in such a way that she came out of her withdrawal. Perhaps it was the high skies and the fierce light of New Mexico that lit up the dark night of Amena. She came to and became aware of herself. Here, her desperate need to have a son was born.

The construction of her house was on its way. Amena and Petronilo went to Mexico to get the materials. Tiles, obsidian for the floors, carved wood, potted plants, fountains, wrought iron and many more decorations. Everything chosen with the utmost care. Large crates started to come in from overseas: furniture, statues, paintings, fine silks. Amena stayed on top of it all. She did not miss a single detail. The house and its decoration was a passion, an obsession.

The house was taking shape. On the outside, it was a traditional New Mexican house: adobe, vigas, strings of chile, *portales*, fireplaces. Inside it was a palace of the Middle East: patios, fountains, arches, porches, gardens. Flowers and more flowers. Amena had brought seeds from her native land. Exotic plants and flowers appeared in her gardens, never before seen, strange and sensual perfumes. What attracted everyone's attention were the black roses with flashes of green and an intoxicating aroma. The gardens and orchards spread out in every direction. To enter the house was to leave the world of every day and to enter the Arabian Nights. It was as if Amena had not built a house. She had created an inheritance, a life not yet born, a life to be lived.

The wedding of Amena and Petronilo took place in the new house on the 25th of September. The Archbishop himself married them. All the distinguished New Mexicans were there. Some came for friendship, many for curiosity. The fame of the house and the lady echoed throughout the area. The mystery of Amena intrigued everyone. They said she was Russian, Arabian, Jewish, Gypsy, Hungarian. Nobody knew for certain and she was not telling.

Amena could not have been more gracious and more charming. She did not fire the magic look a single time. Everyone felt singled out to receive her courtesy and warm affection. She sang for the first time since her tragedy, several arias, accompanied by a symphony orchestra. The New Mexicans had never seen or heard anything like it. It was something out of the dream world, something unforgettable. She won them over, she made them hers, for herself and for her son, who had not been born yet. Petronilo felt himself master and king of the republic.

The married life of the newlyweds could not have been more pleasant. Amena was the most fervent lover and the most generous wife that Petronilo could have imagined, even in his wildest fantasies. In love, happy and satisfied, his life was a dream come true.

The social life of the Armijos was strictly upper crust. The most important people competed among themselves to socialize with them. The presence of Amena at any party lit it up with incandescence. Petronilo's business affairs flourished. He was sought out by the most important business men. Amena made him look good.

Everything was as smooth as silk. Nevertheless, one could tell that Amena was not entirely happy, not entirely satisfied. Petronilo would surprise her in states of deep contemplation, her eyes vague and distant. She spent long hours with Datil in secret and mysterious conversations. It was as if she were giving her instructions, preparing her for something.

Datil got married about that time, at Amena's suggestion, to the robust foreman of the hacienda. The newlyweds moved into a small house, built precisely for them. Everything was taking place according to a plan.

Amena had an altar with a big bowl constructed in one of the patios. It had small statues of strange figures. No one had been able to figure out its purpose.

"Petronilo, tonight you are going to see something you've never seen. You won't be able to understand what you see. I beg you not to ask me about it now or later. It is something I have to do alone, something you cannot share with me. I want you to have faith in me."

"What is it all about, my love? You know that whatever you ask of me I shall give you."

"It's a religious ceremony. My religion and yours are different. Mine will appear strange and incomprehensible to you."

"Tell me what you want me to do."

"Tonight, the first night of the full moon, I have to offer prayers and devotion to my gods. I don't want to hide anything from you. You may watch from the balcony."

"So be it. I don't understand. I only know that I love you so much that your wishes are mine."

That night when it got dark and the full moon came out, Datil lit a fire in the bowl on the altar. The flames rose high and reached higher. She then decorated the altar with black roses, and on the altar cloth set out incense and other jars with mysterious powders and liquids.

When her preparations were finished, she withdrew into the shadows. The flames teased the waves of moonlight with moving lights and shadows. The black roses filled the air with an intoxicating scent. Out of the shadows came the slow and rhythmic boom of a primitive drum. It was as if time had stopped with a breathless suspense ready to produce a miracle.

Suddenly Amena appeared, tall, slender, dressed in white tulle, a statue of living marble. She walked to the altar. Her steps were slow, deliberate. She walked like a goddess, a hypnotized goddess. Gesticulating, as if in a trance, she lighted the incense, sprinkled water on the black roses, shook powder on the fire. The flames waved voluptuously and took on a garnished hue. The incense let out a green smoke full of sensual insinuations. The roses opened their black blouses. Amena postrated herself at the foot of the altar, her body straight, her arms stretched out, a black rose in each hand. Her feet bare. She seemed to be crucified face down on an invisible cross.

Suddenly, brusquely, she stood up on tip toes. She raised her face and her arms to the moon. The drum came alive. It sighed, it sobbed. Tremulous waves rose from her naked heels to her naked neck. Ecstatic exaltation. Hypnosis. The flames dancing madly. The light, the smells and the colors floating magically.

The drum accelerated its rhythmic beats. It became feverish and violent. The marble statue came alive. It danced. Danced like an angel, like a spirit, like an illusion. It seemed to float, wave its mantle of white tulle floating like wings of transparent mist around the altar of fire and incense, around the altar of unknown gods.

The drum stopped. Amena stopped. She raised her eyes to the eyes of the smiling moon. Her voice rose to the very lap of her moon mistress. Her sonorous song of magic words never heard rose in tremors to rest in pain at the feet of the pleasant moon. At times it whispered. One moment it sang, the next it weeped. Then it stopped. From joyous rebellion it passed to submissive sorrow, over and over again.

Suddenly, nothing. She remained motionless for a long time. Slowly, she bowed her head, let it fall on her chest. Her arms limp at her sides. Her tense body relaxed. The arrogant marble goddess became a humble rag doll. Slowly she disappeared in the shadows.

Petronilo had seen everything from the balcony in a state of tremendous agitation, without beginning to understand what he was seeing. It was a sight outside of time, out of this world. The miracle, the magic and the mystery were beyond the reach of his understanding. It seemed that he was not himself, and she was someone else.

When it was all over, he remained on the balcony for a long while. Then he walked for a long time through the orchard. The rays of the moon through the velvety lace of the trees sketching luminous green stains on the ground.

He could not find a key to the mystery. The woman he had seen was not his wife and never would be. She was a spirit—free and unconquerable. A spirit that challenged men and gods. How small and insignificant he felt!

He had a vague notion that what he had seen was a primitive and prehistoric ceremony. That perhaps it was a pagan ritual of fertility. A prayer to the gods. A ritual offering. Was it divine or Satanic adoration? There was, he was sure, something more, something completely in the dark, and for that reason much more frightening. It could be a childish whim arising from her volatile and violent nature. Or, perhaps, a throwback, a nostalgia, to her theatrical life, her artistic temperament.

He resolved nothing. He returned home in total confusion. He came back scared. He did not know how he was going to face Amena. He did not know if Amena was going to reject him.

He entered his bedroom silently and depressed. Amena was already in her pajamas and in bed, as if nothing had happened.

"You took so long I was about to go out and look for you. Come to bed."

Petronilo went to bed without a word. Amena received him with open arms and every affection. She was so amorous, so tender and generous to him that he almost forgot what he had seen. Then, she fell asleep peacefully, and he lay awake very much disturbed.

Life went on good and rich. Petronilo kept his anxieties and concerns to himself. Amena offered him sufficient comfort with her love. The fact is, he had nothing to complain about. The next night of the full moon he refused to watch his wife's ritual performance; he went on a business trip.

Although everything was going well, it could be seen in Amena, and also in Datil, that a sense of urgency was upon them, nervously busy as two ants at a task that only they understood.

Amena had a large room built. The builders made only the shell of the salon. But only she and Datil would do all of the interior work. Petronilo's protests came to naught. Amena was fervently determined that she would do all the work with her own hands.

The purpose of the apartment soon became evident. It was a studio for a painter. It had large windows facing the western horizon that flooded the room with light and color. Draw drapes filled it with mystery and solitude. It had a blackboard and an easel, ready to use. There was a New Mexican fireplace in the corner. An easy chair and a couch of Moroccan leather. A select library of sketching and technique books, collections of copies of the most famous paintings of the world. Everything necessary for a painter, who had not yet been born.

Amena wrote continuously. She filled three notebooks. One for her son for when he could read. One for her husband for when he wanted to read. One for Datil that she had to read. All this writing was projected into an imprecise future. She set down in these notebooks only what could be put into words. She had other ways to communicate the ineffable. Something harmful happens to concepts and illusions when they are put into words. They come out, damaged, distorted and incomplete.

Halfway through their labors it became evident that both women were pregnant. It was noticed then that the two women were working desperately to finish their task, as if their job were of extreme importance. They worked and talked in their strange native language.

Amena got it into her head to plaster and whitewash the mud walls herself, with her tender, naked hands. The task was rough and difficult, and she dedicated herself to it as if her life depended on it. Involved, affectionately, as if the brush of her fingers on the mud were caresses, she converted the walls into canvasses with strange drawings, into manuscripts of mysterious messages. The marks of her fingers on the mud sketched odd designs and rare arabesques. She did the same thing with the woodwork. She carved on it mystic scriptures with a sharp and obedient knife. It was as if she were saying there what she could not say in the notebooks.

At last the studio was finished. The two women were exhausted, but happy. Amena had a look of supreme satisfaction on her face. She could be heard humming about the house, sometimes singing in a low voice. She spent every moment possible with Petronilo. She fixed his favorite dishes herself. She spoiled him in the most uninhibited way. The moment of truth was approaching.

All of this, her open and sensual satisfaction, her exaggerated affection, the fatigue she could not hide, had Petronilo quite worried. Something was out of joint. He could not figure out what. When he asked her, when he tried to talk about it, Amena laughed and told him not to worry.

The day came, the two women gave birth on the same day. Amena's son was born alive. Amena died. Datil's son was born dead. Datil lived. A mother and a son died. A son and a mother lived. It was as if all this had been expected, as if it had all been programmed. Who knows?

Amena's death was a fatal blow to Petronilo. He was crushed. He would never recover. Amena had been an illusion, a blessing, for him. She had elevated him to heights of happiness he had never known. His life with her had been a fantasy. He remembered and relived every shared moment between sobs and joys. He roamed about the house like a sleepwalker. He wandered through the gardens like a lost soul. He could not accept living without her. He sought no consolation.

The child, baptized Damian, was a jewel, a smile of God, cheerful and good-natured. From the very beginning Datil was crazy about him. She rocked and swung him, danced with him, sang to him. The little one responded with trills and smiles, later with bursts of laughter. Damian was a son to Datil, the son she gained after having lost him. Petronilo said and did all the things expected of a new father, but without excessive enthusiasm. He was burdened with sorrow. The child did not look very much like him, or like Amena. He did not have green eyes.

Damian was growing up in his large painter's salon with its large windows open to the lovely sunsets of Albuquerque. Surrounded by beautiful paintings. Hearing his mother's voice in the wonderful songs that had made her famous on the records Datil played for him. The cheerful fireplace and the smell of piñon and cedar. Datil's love above all else. All of this beauty told little Damian things that he did not understand but that he absorbed night and day.

Damian became so attached to his apartment that it was only there that he felt at ease, only there he felt secure. When they took him into the house or out in the garden, he was all right for a while, then he cried. Datil realized what was wrong and took him back to his favorite nest. The tears disappeared and the laughter returned. When he first began to talk, one day at the table Damian began to cry and shout, "My pillow!" Datil ran and brought him a pillow. The child rejected it and continued crying, "My pillow!" Datil had to take him to his room. As they came to his door the child stopped crying and said, "My pillow, my pillow!" with so much feeling and so much satisfaction that everyone knew that "my pillow" meant "my room." From then on that apartment had that name. Who knows why children name things the way they do?

Datil dedicated her life and her soul to little Damian. She taught him his mother's language, the songs and dances of her country. She started him out in drawing when he was very little, drawing animals, trees, houses for him. Providing him with pictures to color. Reading him illustrated stories, later tracing the pictures. The education of the child, disguised as fun and bursting with affection, began very early. Datil was his dedicated and disciplined teacher.

Petronilo was affectionate but somewhat distant. They liked each other, but did not seek each other very much. When Damian reached the age of six, his father tried to draw closer. They chatted, went on camping and fishing trips, played sports. Sometimes they would watch a football game on television and talk about it. Petronilo would take his son to visit his New Mexican relatives. They treated Damian like a prince. The boy was charming. He gave speeches, recited, sang, danced. And he did it well. By that time his drawings and watercolors were beginning to attract attention. It was obvious that Damian had talent. He always took each one of his uncles an original. Father and son were friends in spite of not understanding each other very well.

Damian had a normal childhood, and also a normal adolescence. It was normal in that he went to school like all the rest of the children, and he was one of them. He participated in sports, parties and escapades with them. He was very popular with the girls, and he lost his innocence at the right moment, with honors and without shame.

So far, normal. But there was a certain something in Damian that set him off from the rest. He had mysterious substances and essences within him that he himself did not manage to understand and that commanded his thoughts and attention, substances and essences that frequently determined his behavior or released his fantasies. He did things without knowing why, that always turned out well. It was as if an inner voice told him where to go. He was a good son, a good student, a good friend. This everyone could see. What they could also see was that he was different in an unexplainable way.

His manner of being imposed solitude upon him. He pursued solitude avidly, sometimes desperately. He would disappear unexpectedly from a party. He would not show up at another. He went by himself into the fields or into the streets. His favorite refuge, naturally, was "my pillow." The attachment he had as a child for the apartment his mother had built for him had not diminished, it had grown instead. He spent long hours there, sometimes days.

He spent his time painting, reading, writing or contemplating the glorious sunsets of his open horizon. There he read and reread the pages of the manuscript his mother had left him and that Datil was giving him according to the calendar marked by her. The most intriguing part was the fascination, the obsession, with which he contemplated the walls of his "pillow." His eyes examined the traces of his mother's fingers on the clay over and over again. Many times he ran his own fingers over those traces with tender affection and deep emotion. He was convinced there was a hidden message in those designs and arabesques. In the background the magic voice of La Karanova. The sensual aroma of the incense of black roses in the air.

We cannot know if Damian ever deciphered the designs on the clay or the writings on the woodwork. He never said. Perhaps because there were no words to say it; the message was ineffable, something his mother herself could not say but found a way to communicate with her son in her way. What we do know is that Damian began to change. He stopped being the cheerful young man he once was and slowly became serious and formal.

When he entered the university he was already a young man apart, more solitary than ever, more than a little melancholy. He had become a romantic type—from another time, another place. Always friendly and courteous when it was necessary, otherwise shy and taciturn. Now he painted with a passion: nocturnal scenes, strange and bizarre subjects, dark figures, flaming labyrinths. His canvasses began to appear in the good galleries. The voice of La Karanova could be heard in the background. Thick was the incense in the air.

One day he read in one of his mother's letters: "I want you to do my portrait. I want Father Nasario to see it." Damian did not sleep that night. The images of his mother flashed through his head, one after another, in a giddy procession. Every image was different, a living representation of a woman full of life, complex and mysterious, a woman of many whims, many facets, many moods.

Sometime in the early dawn, when the fire in the fireplace had turned to ashes, the swift parade began to slow down. A thousand images began to come together, began to blend. Only one remained, containing the elements of all of them. Static and ecstatic. Damian's fantasy came to rest. He was left in a near stupor, contemplating the image he had brought back from a past that was not his own, in complete and submissive adoration. He fell asleep because he was exhausted. He fell asleep murmuring softly: "My Amena."

The following day he told the family that he was going to paint his mother's portrait, and that he did not want anyone to enter "my pillow" until the painting was finished. Datil tried to provide him with photographs of Amena as an artist, as a bride, as a wife. Damian told her that he did not need them. Petronilo thought that this was strange since Damian had never known Amena, but he did not say anything. Datil did not find anything strange in this, and she did not say anything either.

Damian began to paint with indescribable fury, the controlled fury of a fierce panther who wildly obeys the orders of the master who holds the chain and the whip. The panther would kill if it got loose.

It was strange but he began with the eyes. Very soon the green waters of those deep and risky seas began to shine and seethe. The flakes of gold began to burn. The eyes were perfect, but the look escaped him, the lance look, the dagger look, the killer look. How difficult it is to paint the invisible! Damian went crazy, became desperate. When this happened, he looked like his queenly mother singing a Valkyrie or dancing around her altar.

Unable to overcome this obstacle, for now, he went on to paint the face. Everything went well. The fine alabaster skin, as if lit up from within, with its subtle, almost invisible, tint of green. The exquisite nose, pointed, with a certain touch of aristocracy. The mouth was perfect, but he could not capture the smile. As with the look, he had to leave it incomplete. The elegant and arrogant chin gave him no problems. The black hair either. He found a way, who knows how, to give it the green flashes that vitalized it. A queen's hands. The rings of an empress. He dressed her in silk and black lace. He made her an oriental princess. A Jewess, Hungarian, Gypsy, Arabian, Russian? An actress or a goddess?

All of this took a long time. Damian worked as if possessed. He hardly slept. Sometimes he would fall into his Moroccan leather armchair, and in total exhaustion he would contemplate his work for hours as if hypnotized. Suddenly a fit of passion would grip him, an impulse, an inspiration, and he would jump up and paint a tiny touch, a dot, a flick, perhaps a sigh or a sob, that completely changed the appearance. In these moments it seemed that an invisible hand guided him.

The look and the smile perplexed him. Some looks and some smiles have something angelical or something diabolical about them. And who can handle them? The portrait was finished except for these two imponderables.

Damian was worn out. Bearded, thin and dirty. He fell asleep in the armchair because there was nothing more he could do. He dreamed he had gone out to pray at his mother's altar, that he was dressed in white, that Datil had prepared the altar for him and was now playing the drum for him. He saw himself go, step by step, through his mother's ancient ceremony. He felt the fire of her passion.

He awoke calmly. He yawned. Then quietly, he picked up the brush and did something to the portrait. Maybe it was a kiss, maybe it was a sigh or a sob. Suddenly the look came alive, full of light and shadow, life and death, love and hate. The smile caught fire with flashes of irony, malice and tenderness. The work of love was ended.

The family and Father Nasario came in the following day to see the portrait. They were shaken and curious. No one was prepared to see what he saw. That was Amena! What she once was and what now she continued to be. The supreme woman, the complete woman. With all of her life, all of her mystery. All that was missing was for her to sing, laugh and dance. Everyone spoke in whispers, gripped by a strange reverence, or respect, or superstition.

They all wondered how Damian, without ever having known her, could capture the volatile personality, the enigmatic reality, the deep mystery, the indomitable character of his mother. It was as if they were seeing her for the first time—as she really was. Father Nasario put it into words: "The eyes of the spirit see farther and much more than the eyes of the body."

Sometimes the eyes of a portrait seem to follow the viewer from one place to another. Amena's eyes did not. They were fixed on an unknown vision. With one exception. They followed Damian everywhere, deliberately, it seemed. Damian did not find this unusual; it seemed natural. Nobody else noticed. Except Datil. She noticed, but did not say anything.

Petronilo had entered "my pillow" with deep emotion. He stayed behind and contemplated Amena from a distance. It was as if she had come back to life. He fell into a spell. Silently, slowly, large tears appeared and flowed on their own and unnoticed. When at last he came to, he had the presence of mind to resist a powerful inclination to kneel at Amena's feet as if she were a saint. He left the room sobbing desperately.

"Damian, my son," said Father Nasario, "I'm going to ask a favor of you. You know how kind and generous your mother was to the people of the parish, especially to the poor. The people loved her very much, always. Let me hang her portrait in the church so that everyone will have the opportunity to see it."

"Certainly, Don Nasario, I would like that very much too. Take it right now."

The word soon got around that the portrait of Doña Amena was in the church. Amena had been famous for her charity, friendliness and courtesy. Everyone went by to see her. She won them over as she had before. The beautiful picture of the woman and the magnetism and passion of the artist impressed them all. There is some superstition in the religious feeling of simple people. The generosity of Amena was well known. The beauty of the painting spoke for itself. The picture was in the church. The time came when all of this came together into a single concept: Doña Amena was a saint, a topic of conversation first, an act of faith later. It came to be that it was not at all unusual to see a little old lady on her knees in front of St. Amena. Father Nasario began to hear, and the word got around, that the saint had produced this or that miracle. The good priest after thinking the matter over for some time concluded that if Amena brought the people some consolation, it was best to leave the pantry where it was.

Damian felt physically and spiritually empty when he finished the portrait. He decided to go to the mountains. He went on horseback and led a packhorse. He cooked, ate and slept in the open air. Took long hikes, fished, read in the shade and in the sun. Sometimes he would catch himself whistling or humming one of La Karanova's tunes. The clean air, the cool water, long walks, good eating and good sleeping soon restored the young painter. He returned home strong and spirited to find himself famous. Museums, galleries and others wanted to buy his paintings, wanted to commission other works.

Datil gave him a new letter from his mother. Through the years she had been delivering these letters to him at the appropriate moments of his life according to Amena's instructions. In this manner she had marked out the path that had brought him to this moment through all the vagaries of his life. He always was deeply touched when he read these letters, but this time he felt a strange excitement when he received the letter. He anticipated, who knows how, that there was something portentous in this one. His hands shook as he read:

> My beloved son,
>
> The time has come for you to go out into the world. It is now necessary for you to make your way, to find and follow your star, to fulfill your destiny and mine.
>
> I want you to go to Europe for an extended visit. Enclosed I leave you the names of dear friends and old hotels I have known. Tell them both that you are the son of La Karanova.

They will receive you warmly.

There is a famous opera singer in Europe now. Her name is Amina Karavelha. On the 15th of August she is going to sing one of Wagner's works at the Parque del Retiro in Madrid. I want you to attend that performance. Afterwards I want you to do Amina's portrait.

That portrait will make you famous in Europe. It will open doors for you. Go, then, and act as my son. Forward, courage! Fame, faith and fortune await you.

My love and protection will be with you night and day.

Your adoring mother,

Amena

Damian remained pensive, strangely serene, thinking about the new perspectives now opening for him. What he had just read seemed perfectly logical, normal and natural to him. He did not wonder, for example, how his mother could have known twenty-five years before that there was going to be a famous singer by the name of Amina Karavelha now and that she was going to give a performance on August 15th of this year. The coincidence in the names did not surprise him either. The fact that Datil had not said a word, since she had read the letter too, did not bother him. It seems that Damian knew more than he said, that he already knew how to decipher and read the designs and writings his mother had left him in "my pillow."

The preparations for the trip were made. Petronilo wasn't told about Amena's letter or the details of the adventure. Damian was going to Europe to study art, that was all.

Datil had participated in all the events, even the thoughts and feelings that made up Damian's history. Nevertheless, she who knew it all was jolted and felt very emotional when she saw the photograph in Damian's passport. The face and the expression of this Damian were the face and expression of another Damian of another time.

On the 15th of August Damian was wandering through the Parque del Retiro in Madrid. It was a lovely afternoon. There would be a full moon tonight. His thoughts fluttered like butterflies and did not pause on a single thing, on a single rose. He was carrying a bouquet of black roses. Tonight he was going to attend an opera of Wagner.

A full moon. The scent of jasmine in the air. The orchestra playing rhythms of war. The actors singing and gesticulating on the stage. Damian was inattentive, waiting. Suddenly the music stopped. La Karavelha appeared on the stage. Tall, arrogant, majestic. An explosion of applause. Damian found himself repeating over and over again the same words his father had said one day: "This one has to be the most beautiful woman in the whole world."

She began to sing. The orchestra played. It was a magic voice that one moment rose violently and descended tenderly the next. Amina brandished her lance and the voice threatened. She lowered it and the voice caressed. Sometimes it rose tremulously, with rebellious or submissive tremors, as high as the open windows of the attentive moon. It came down slow and easy to rest tenderly on the collective lap of her listeners. She ended her performance with a fierce shout, a battle cry, a radiant challenge that shook the earth and made the moon cry. And she was still, like a triumphant goddess of marble.

The audience absorbed, stupefied, hypnotized until now, exploded in waves upon waves of admiration and adoration. Damian was screaming like a madman, along with everyone else, "*Encore! Encore!*" Amina came out to meet the sea of adulation. How small, how exquisite, how delicate she appeared now. She received many bouquets of flowers. Among them there was one of black roses. Amina handed them all to the ushers, but she kept the black bouquet.

Damian had sent his calling card along with the flowers. On the back he had written:

> Lovely lady,
>
> I am a painter and would like to do your portrait. Allow me, please, to speak with you.
>
> Respectfully,
>
> Damian Karanova.

He himself did not know why he had signed his name that way. He had never done it before. It just came upon him. Perhaps it was because of the color of the flowers, or because of the language of the message, or maybe it was the name. And Amina, who never received a man in her dressing room, decided to let him come. She sent her secretary, Mandarina, to find him. She did not have far to go. He was waiting outside. Amina and Damian greeted each other in their native language.

"Lovely lady, I appreciate your kindness. I've come to render you homage and to offer you my services."

"Have a seat, sir. My instinct tells me that you carry a mystery with you. Tell me, who are you?"

"I am a not-so-humble painter from very far away."

"Where are you from?"

"New Mexico."

"Wasn't it there that the great Karanova died?"

"Yes, she died there. She is my mother." The present tense of the verb apparently was not noticed.

"Ah! That explains the black flowers, the language of my people, the name. You and I are related."

"I hope you like that. It pleases me very much."

"I want you to know that your mother is still a goddess in the world of the opera. Her artistic triumphs are the model and the ideal for all of us who have theatrical ambitions. I have all her records, and I'm not ashamed to admit that I try to emulate her."

"Amina, your triumph tonight has to be at the level of the best of La Karanova. I want you to know that in my country my mother is a legend too."

"Damian, I wish you would tell me about her. I've always adored her voice and her person."

"Delighted, whenever you wish."

"And, are you a good painter?"

"I think so. In New Mexico they think I am."

"Don't you have a sample?"

"No, but I can prove it to you."

"How?"

"Put on a dramatic gesture, and assume a *prima donna* posture, and I'll show you."

Damian rose and picked up a La Karavelha poster. He looked at it for a while with complete appreciation and obvious satisfaction. Then he turned it over. He pulled out a piece of black chalk and waited. A spark danced in his eyes, a smile played on his lips. Amina laughed, intrigued, and assumed a theatrical pose. One hand raised on high as if she were holding a star she had just plucked from the heavens. The other hand stretched out at her side, like a wing she flapped at random. Her left foot raised behind her, as if she had taken off and was flying through space.

Damian drew fast and purposely, his brow wrinkled, his lips pressed tight, his eyes nearly closed. Intensity and passion. Amina looked at him out of the corner of her eye and was impressed with what she saw. In a few moments he was through and presented the sketch to the object of his obsession.

"Damian, what you've done is unbelievable. It's me, that is the one I was then. But there is more. You've put into this sketch something you can't possibly know and shouldn't know."

"You've liked it, eh? Then, what I want to know is if you're going to let me paint you."

"Of course! You are a talented painter. You can paint secrets."

"If that is so, and since you've been so kind to me, I feel bold enough to ask you to have dinner with me at a small café of our country my mother recommended to me."

"The Korovil? I've also heard about it but haven't been there."

"Yes, that one. Shall we?"

"Let's."

Mandarina saw them leave with a strange and deep satisfaction. They were an ideal couple. She was the sun that illuminated and heated. He was the land that the sun fired and fertilized.

The food at the Korovil was a true celebration. Everything was heavenly. Good wines, tasty dishes, soft music. Harmony all around, good cheer at the table. Those two seemed to be made for each other. They understood and liked each other. The conversation was animated and uninterrupted. You could almost say that they had grown up together, that they shared the same memories. Over and over again he knew what she was going to say before she said it. She too. It seemed like they had very much to say to each other after a long and painful separation.

They agreed that he would show up at her suite the following morning ready to work. He did. When Mandarina opened the door there was Damian loaded down with an easel, rolls of canvas, brushes and a box of jars of oils. He looked like a real laborer of art and cut a figure that was more than a little ridiculous. When Amina saw him, she burst out laughing. Later, Mandarina did too. And then, without conviction, Damian laughed too. Amina's laughter hurt him a little, but he forgave her immediately.

He set himself up by the window that faced the park where the light was best. She posed at the other end of the room, far from the light. He knew what he was doing. He wanted the light of his portrait to emanate from Amina and not from the window. He wanted to create the light and the air that surrounded her.

Before they started, they had a cup of tea and chatted for a while. Suddenly:

"What do you want me to wear?"

"For what?"

"For the portrait, dummy."

"Nothing."

"You didn't tell me you were going to paint me in the nude."

"Forgive me, Amina, what I mean is that the clothes are painted last." The "dummy" and the "nothing" were buzzing in his head. He felt like a fool.

"You mean, you're going to paint me naked, and then you're going to dress me? That's cute!" Amina was enjoying the discomfort of the young man.

"No, dummy, I'm going to paint your face and head first. Then comes the body, immaculately and virtuously clothed. Do you understand?"

Now they were both "dummies." The equilibrium was reestablished. They both laughed heartily and went to work. To work and talk. It seemed that they talked only about La Karanova and her house in New Mexico. He never tired of hearing details about her life *ante-Damian*, A.D. They laughed, somewhat uneasily, when they realized that A.D. meant the opposite in English, after Damian.

Sometimes Amina became tired or bored of holding the same posture for long periods and Damian would scold her: "Don't move. Open your eyes. Your face fell off. Don't bite your lip. Smile." Sometimes she pouted. She would fire a "Grasshoppers to you!" That evidently was a very strong expression in her country. And she would leave. When she returned, she would find Damian working passionately. She would take her pose with an innocuous question: "Did your mother have many jewels?" And the beat went on.

Now and then she would practice her arias with Mandarina at the piano. When this happened, Damian achieved his finest successes. Perhaps singing was Amina's life. She poured into it all her passion and tenderness. As she sang the voice and the music entered the canvas, dressed in royal colors and the voluptuous aroma of black roses.

The friendship of the painter and the diva was genuine and intimate, as if they were old friends or beloved siblings. He wanted to carry the relationship farther. She did too. He fell in love with her from the very beginning. She fell in love later. They both ran into a mysterious wall between them that did not allow love to cross. He was not shy and did not lack assertiveness. Neither did she. Yet, neither one of them could take the first step, however much they wanted to. A certain respect, a fear or an awe held them back. They did not know why. An anxiety, an uneasiness that verged on anger grew up between them. Their impotence was a constant irritation. They shook it off and went on with their work and friendly conversation. Only to return to it.

Damian and Amina were busy as usual when Mandarina came in.

"Señora, Count Barnizkoff insists on seeing you."

"Send him away, I don't want to see him."

At this moment the said count burst into the living room. He was a dandy, elegantly dressed and combed and sporting a little line of a moustache that looked painted. He had the appearance of a spoiled brat too big and too fat for his age. He was raging or blubbering, one or the other.

"Karavelha, my love!"

"Karavelha, I am. Your love, no." Her manner and tone could not be more sarcastic.

"I need to talk to you."

"I do not feel any such need." Her irritation was growing.

"Why do you return all my letters, my flowers, my gifts?"

"Because you have touched them, and what you touch rots."

"I adore you, my love."

"I retain the pleasure of choosing my friends and my lovers. You're no good as a friend, much less as a lover. Get out!"

At that moment Barnizkoff tried to touch her, tried to put her arms around her. Amina rose like an avenging goddess and fired her homicidal look, the look of green fire and sparks of gold. "Out!" The piercing look and the atomic cry fulminated the count. Destroyed him. It was as if Amina had ripped off his bathrobe and had left him naked, with all his imperfections exposed. She did not leave him a single veil of dignity. Demolished, humiliated, stripped of his manhood, Barnizkoff fell back toward the door, hunched over, covering his impotent parts, as if indeed he had no pants. He disappeared into the nothing from which he had come.

Amina remained stiff like Diana-the-huntress for an instant, still pointing to the door with a royal finger.

Damian, who had contemplated the whole scene in fascination, jumped from his stool, prey to unchained emotion. Beside himself, he took her in his arms, shouting, "At last, at last, Amina, at last you let me see you! At last you let me know you!" Amina, taken by surprise, remained stiff for an instant. Then she put her arms around him tightly, sobbing, "Damian, Damian!" They kissed in holy communion. Thus began the love affair that was going to blind two hemispheres for a long time and which is still remembered with affection.

The following day Damian approached his portrait as calm and serene as he had been one day when he approached his mother's portrait. That time he had found the key to the secret in a dream of religious fire. This time he found it in a dream of enchanted love. He went to the portrait and did something to it. Perhaps it was a kiss, a whisper, a sob. Suddenly Amina came to life and was complete inside the frame of the painting.

He dressed her in a black evening gown his mother had worn at a gala performance in the White House where she had sung and triumphed. Damian had seen it in a photograph. The gown had gone out of style years ago, but as frequently happens, the style was in vogue once again. Maybe it was the dress, or perhaps it was a subconscious prejudice of the painter, the portrait of this woman had a striking resemblance with that of another woman now hanging in a church in New Mexico.

Because Amina was who she was, the portrait was hung in the best art gallery of Paris in a ceremony where all the artistic groups, the intellectuals, all the servants of art, appeared. The painting was a resounding success. Damian became an instant celebrity, known and praised everywhere.

From this day on he painted her every day. His paintings appeared in many museums and galleries. Although he received many requests for portraits, he turned them all down. It seemed that his mission in life was to glorify Amina. The fame he gave her was added to the fame she earned.

At a party a famous and vain movie star insisted that Damian do her portrait. He resisted and begged off, but she persisted. Finally, to get rid of her and in jest, he said to her, "Very well, I'll do your portrait. I'll do it in fifteen minutes, not one minute more. If you like it, you keep it and pay me ten thousand dollars. If you don't like it, I'll tear it up, and you don't owe me anything." Nothing happened.

A newspaperman heard this interchange and published it and suggested that the portrait be done on television. This created a wave of curiosity and publicity. The telephone would not stop ringing, the television stations and the press offering their services. The actress came to challenge him personally (for her this publicity was priceless). Damian accepted. A date was set.

Because it was a case of three celebrities—Amina, Damian and Virgie Joy—the expectation for the event grew and grew. The publicity was unbelievable. It reached a point where it was decided to broadcast the performance around the world by satellite, so great was the interest. Damian collected a fortune. Damian appeared at the studio with Amina at his side. Virgie Joy was already there. He was amazingly calm and sure of himself. The possibility of failure did not even enter his mind. The words of his mother's letter echoed in his brain: "The portrait of La Karavelha will make you famous in Europe."

The canvas and Joy faced the cameras and the audience. A large clock was in the background. A bell rang. Complete silence. Damian moved deliberately, his brush strokes fast but controlled. He drew the contours of the body and head first, then he filled in the empty space. Everything with precision, no hesitation. It could almost be said that he had brought the portrait already made, and that he was only copying it. When the minute hand was at the point of marking the period, Damian faced the public, raised his brush on high like a torch and bowed from the waist in a chivalric gesture. *Fait accompli.*

The camera zoomed in on the artistic image of the famous and vain actress. The audience burst into resonant applause. The critics were united in their flattery and praise. His mother had been right. The portrait of La Karavelha had brought Damian fame, faith and fortune.

So, it was spring. The honeymoon of the newlyweds was a dual tribute, one to the moon and one to the honey. It was a song and a dance to Love. Smiling, bold and naughty, they went through famous hotels, sunlit beaches, elite casinos, select museums, guarded gardens, 24-karat yachts and theaters singing and dancing to the tune and the beat of Love's flute. From the heights the gods observed the celebration with satisfaction and carpeted their way with rose petals. Damian and Amina gave the world something to celebrate. Television and the press recorded the miracle of this odyssey of love for the rejoicing of lovers everywhere.

Then they returned to their enchanted house in their land of enchantment. They arrived at sunset. Amina was overwhelmed and fascinated by the violence of the light, the height of the skies, the distance of the horizon, just as Amena had been before.

Datil and Petronilo were waiting outside, impatient and excited. As the car approached it seemed the light itself was trembling. The new Karanova and the same Datil faced each other, both of them vibrating with emotion.

"Señora!"

"Datil!" They embraced, their tears flowing. Petronilo could not speak. Finally, his tongue worked.

"Welcome, Amina, to your house that waits for you with deep affection."

"Petronilo, I wanted to meet you so much. I owe you so much."

There were many more expressions of affection. Happiness seemed to hover in the air and fill the estate. Suddenly Amina looked at Damian and said, "I want to see 'My pillow.' " He had never told her the name of his apartment, perhaps because it sounded childish. But her knowing it did not appear to surprise him.

As they came into the room, the setting sun had lit it with color and fire through the large windows. It looked like a magic place. Amina approached the flaming white wall in a state of hypnosis. She remained speechless before it for a long time. Then she ran the tips of her fingers over the traces of Amena's deliberately, slowly and affectionately, all the while looking at Damian with eyes of infinite tenderness.

Datil prepared a meal, rich in odor and flavor and in exquisite liquors of their country. The house warmed up, cheered up and smiled. It lived again. It dreamed again.

The conversation was exciting. The good faith was boundless. There was so much to say, so much to share. Petronilo felt a happiness and a pride beyond words. Datil was in heaven. The newcomers felt like two love birds who had seen everything, enjoyed supreme freedom together, and had now returned to occupy and enjoy their nuptial nest.

Petronilo wanted to hear Amina sing. With Datil at the piano, as she used to be for Amena, Amina sang as she never had before. Petronilo was bewitched, with tears of utter joy in his eyes.

Damian saw Amina go out and he did not follow her. He went up to the balcony of his room that faced the garden and the patios.

The night was flooded with moonlight, with green light. The air was thick with the fragrance of the black roses. Amina was standing in front of Amena's altar, silent and thoughtful. Damian waited for his wife, also silent and thoughtful.

Ed Vega

Ed Vega is a Puerto Rican fiction writer who bases many of his works on life in New York City's Spanish Harlem. Edgardo Vega Yunqué was born in Ponce, Puerto Rico, on May 20, 1936, where he lived with his family until they moved to the Bronx, New York, in 1949. He was raised in a devout Baptist home, his father having been a minister of that faith; today, Vega and his wife and children have adopted the Buddhist faith. As a child, books were very accessible at home, and he began both his education and writing at an early age in Spanish in Puerto Rico. After moving to New York and going through the public education system of the city, he served in the Air Force and studied at Santa Monica College in California under the G.I. Bill. In 1963 Vega almost graduated as a Phi Beta Kappa from New York University with a major in political science; he was short three hours of credit and did not actually graduate until 1969. He did not return to finish until that date because he had become disillusioned after personally experiencing racism at N.Y.U. After leaving there in 1963, he worked in a variety of social service programs and eventually became a full-time writer.

Vega is one of the most prolific Hispanic prose writers, although much of his work remains unpublished. In 1977, he began actively publishing short stories in Hispanic magazines, such as *Nuestro*, *Maize* and *Revista Chicano-Riqueña*. In 1985, he published his novel, *The Comeback*, a rollicking satire of ethnic autobiography and the identity crisis as personified by a half-Puerto Rican, half-Eskimo ice hockey player who becomes involved in an underground revolutionary movement for Puerto Rican independence. In 1987, he published a collection of interconnected short stories, *Mendoza's Dreams*, narrated by a warm-hearted observer of the human comedy, Alberto Mendoza. An additional common thread holding these barrio stories together is their charting of various Puerto Ricans on the road to success in the United States; thus once again we have a Puerto Rican interpretation of the American Dream. Vega's third book, *Casualty Report* (1991), is just the opposite; for the most part the collection of stories represented here chronicles the death of dreams, as characters faced with racism, poverty and crime succumb to despair in many forms: violence, alcohol and drug abuse, withdrawal and resignation. "Spanish Roulette" is from *Casualty Report*.

Spanish Roulette

Sixto Andrade snapped the gun open and shut several times and then spun the cylinder, intrigued by the kaleidoscopic pattern made by the empty chambers. He was fascinated by the blue-black color of the metal, but more so by the almost toy-like quality of the small weapon. As the last rays of sunlight began their retreat from the four-room tenement flat, Sixto once again snapped the cylinder open and began loading the gun. It pleased him that each brass and lead projectile fit easily into each one of the chambers and yet would not fall out. When he had finished inserting the last of the bullets, he again closed the cylinder and, enjoying the increased weight of the gun, pointed it at the ceiling and pulled back the hammer.

"What's the piece for, man?"

Sixto had become so absorbed in the gun that he did not hear Willie Collazo, with whom he shared the apartment, come in. His friend's question came at him suddenly, the words intruding into the world he had created since the previous weekend.

"Nothing," he said, lowering the weapon.

"What do you mean, 'nothing?' " said Willie. "You looked like you were ready to play Russian roulette when I came in, bro."

"No way, man," said Sixto, and as he had been shown by Tommy Ramos, he let the hammer fall back gently into place. "It's called Spanish roulette," he added, philosophically.

Willie's dark face broke into a wide grin and his eyes, just as if he were playing his congas, laughed before he did. "No kidding, man," he said. "You taking up a new line of work? I know things are rough but sticking up people and writing poetry don't go together."

Sixto put the gun on the table, tried to smile but couldn't, and recalled the last time he had read at the cafe on Sixth Street. Willie had played behind him, his hands making the drums sing a background to his words. "I gotta take care of some business, Willie," he said, solemnly, and, turning back to his friend, walked across the worn linoleum to the open window of the front room.

"Not like that, *panita*," Willie said as he followed him.

"Family stuff, bro."

"Who?"

"My sister," Sixto said without turning.

"Mandy?"

Sixto nodded, his small body taut with the anger he had felt when Mandy had finished telling him of the attack. He looked out over the street four flights below and fought an urge to jump. It was one solution but not *the* solution. Despairingly, he shook his head at the misery below: burned out buildings, torched by landlords because it was cheaper than fixing them; empty lots, overgrown with weeds and showing the ravages of life in the neighborhood. On the sidewalk, the discarded refrigerator still remained as a faceless sentinel standing guard over the lot, its door removed too late to save the little boy from Avenue B. He had been locked in it half the day while his mother, going crazy with worry, searched the streets so that by the time she saw the blue-faced child, she was too far gone to understand what it all meant.

He tried to cheer himself up by focusing his attention on the children playing in front of the open fire hydrant, but could not. The twilight rainbow within the stream of water, which they intermittently shot up in the air to make it cascade in a bright arc of white against the asphalt, was an illusion, *un engaño*, a poetic image of his childhood created solely to contrast his despair. He thought again of the crushed innocence on his sister's face and his blood felt like sand as it ran in his veins.

"You want to talk about it?" asked Willie.

"No, man," Sixto replied. "I don't."

Up the street, in front of the *bodega*, the old men were already playing dominoes and drinking beer. Sixto imagined them joking about each other's weaknesses, always, he thought ironically, with respect. They had no worries. Having lived a life of service to that which now beckoned him, they could afford to be light-hearted. It was as if he had been programmed early on for the task now facing him. He turned slowly, wiped an imaginary tear from his eyes and recalled his father's admonition about crying: "*Usted es un machito y los machos no lloran*, machos don't cry." How old had he been? Five or six, no more. He had fallen in the playground and cut his lip. His father's friends had laughed at the remark, but he couldn't stop crying and his father had shaken him. "*Le dije que usted no es una chancleta. ¡Apréndalo bien!*" "You are not a girl, understand that once and for all!"

Concerned with Sixto's mood, once again Willie tried drawing him out. "*Coño*, bro, she's only fifteen," he said. "*¿Qué pasó?*"

The gentleness and calm which Sixto so much admired had faded from Willie's face and now mirrored his own anguish. It was wrong to involve his friend but perhaps that was part of it. Willie was there to test his resolve. He had been placed there by fate to make sure the crime did not go unpunished. In the end, when it came to act, he'd have only his wits and manhood.

"It's nothing, bro," Sixto replied, walking back into the kitchen. "I told you, family business. Don't worry about it."

"Man, don't be like that."

There was no injury in Willie's voice and as if someone had suddenly punched him in the stomach to obtain a confession, the words burst out of Sixto.

"*Un tipo la mangó en el rufo*, man. Some dude grabbed her. You happy now?"

"Where?" Willie asked, knowing that uttering the words was meaningless. "In the projects?"

"Yeah, last week. She got let out of school early and he grabbed her in the elevator and brought her up to the roof."

"And you kept it all in since you came back from your Mom's Sunday night?"

"What was I supposed to do, man? Go around broadcasting that my sister got took off?"

"I'm sorry, Sixto. You know I don't mean it like that."

"I know, man. I know."

"Did she know the guy? *Un cocolo*, right? A black dude. They're the ones that go for that stuff."

"No, man. It wasn't no *cocolo*."

"But she knew him."

"Yeah, you know. From seeing him around the block. *Un bonitillo*, man. Pretty dude that deals coke and has a couple of women hustling for him. A dude named Lino."

"*¿Bien blanco?* Pale dude with Indian hair like yours?"

"Yeah, that's the guy."

"Drives around in a gold Camaro, right?"

"Yeah, I think so." Willie nodded several times and then shook his head.

"He's Shorty Pardo's cousin, right?" Sixto knew about the family connection but hadn't wanted to admit it until now.

"So?" he said, defiantly.

"Those people are crazy, bro," said Willie.

"I know."

"They've been dealing *tecata* up there in El Barrio since forever, man. Even the Italians stay clear of them, they're so crazy."

"That doesn't mean nothing to me," said Sixto, feeling his street manhood, the bravado which everyone develops growing up in the street, surfacing. Bad talk was the antidote to fear and he wasn't immune to it. "I know how crazy they are, but I'm gonna tell you something. I don't care who the dude is. I'm gonna burn him. Gonna set his heart on fire with that piece."

"Hey, go easy, *panita*," said Willie. "Be cool, bro. I know how you feel but that ain't gonna solve nothing. You're an artist, man. You know that? A poet. And a playwright. You're gonna light up Broadway one of these days." Willie was suddenly silent as he reflected on his words. He sat down on one of the kitchen chairs and lowered his head. After a few moments he looked up and said: "Forget what I said, man. I don't know what I'm talking about. I wouldn't know what to do if that happened to one of the women in my family. I probably would've done the dude in by now. I'm sorry I said anything. I just don't wanna see you messed up. And I'm not gonna tell you to go to the cops, either."

Sixto did not answer Willie. They both knew going to the police would serve no purpose. As soon as the old man found out, he'd beat her for not protecting herself. It would become a personal matter, as if it had been he who had submitted. He'd rant and rave about short skirts and lipstick and music and then compare everything to the way things were on the island and his precious hometown, his beloved Cacimar, like it was the center of the universe and the place where all the laws governing the human race had been created. But Sixto had nothing to worry about. He was different from his father. He was getting an education, had been enlightened to truth and beauty and knew about equality and justice. Hell, he was a new man, forged out of steel and concrete, not old banana leaves and coconuts. And yet, he wanted to strike back and was sick to his stomach because he wanted Lino Quintana in front of him, on his knees, begging for mercy. He'd smoke a couple of joints and float back uptown to the Pardo's turf and then blast away at all of them like he was the Lone Ranger.

He laughed sarcastically at himself and thought that in the end he'd probably back down, allow the matter to work itself out and let Mandy live with the scar for the rest of her life. And he'd tell himself that rape was a common thing, even in families, and that people went on living and working and making babies like a bunch of zombies, like somebody's puppets without ever realizing who was pulling the strings. It was all crazy. You were born and tagged with a name: Rodríguez, Mercado, Torres, Cartagena, Pantoja, Maldonado, Sandoval, Ballester, Nieves, Carmona. All of them, funny-ass Spanish names. And then you were told to speak English and be cool because it was important to try and get over by imitating the Anglo-Saxon crap, since that's where all the money and success were to be found. Nobody actually came out and said it, but it was written clearly in everything you saw, printed boldly between the lines of books, television, movies, advertising. And at the place where you got your love, your mother's milk, your rice and beans, you were told to speak Spanish and be respectful and defend your honor and that of the women around you.

"I'm gonna burn him, Willie," Sixto repeated. "Gonna burn him right in his *güevos*. Burn him right there in his balls so he can feel the pain before I blow him away and let God deal with him. He'll understand, man, because I don't." Sixto felt the dizzying anger blind him for a moment. "*Coño*, man, she was just fifteen," he pleaded, as if Willie could absolve him of his sin before it had been committed. "I have to do it, man. She was just a kid. *Una nena*, man. A little innocent girl who dug Latin music and danced only with her girlfriends at home and believed all the nonsense about purity and virginity, man. And now this son of a bitch went and did it to her. *Le hizo el daño*."

That's what women called it. The damage. And it was true. Damaged goods. He didn't want to believe it but that's how he felt. In all his educated, enlightened splendor, that's how he felt. Like she had been rendered untouchable, her femaleness soiled and smeared forever. Like no man would want to love her, knowing what had happened. The whole thing was so devastating that he couldn't imagine what it was like to be a woman. If they felt even a little of what he was experiencing, it was too much. And he, her own brother, already talking as if she were dead. That's how bad it was. Like she was a memory.

"I'm gonna kill him, Willie," said Sixto once more, pounding on the wall. "*¡Lo mato, coño! Lo mato, lo mato*," he repeated the death threat over and over in a frenzy. Willie stood up and reached for his arm but Sixto pulled roughly away. "It's cool, man," he said, and put his opened hands in front of him. "I'm all right. Everything's cool."

"Slow down," Willie pleaded. "Slow down."

"You're right, man. I gotta slow down." Sixto sat down but before long was up again. "Man, I couldn't sleep the last couple of nights. I kept seeing myself wearing the shame the rest of my life. I gave myself every excuse in the book. I even prayed, Willie. Me, a spic from the streets of the Big Apple, hip and slick, writing my *jíbaro* poetry; *saliéndome las palabras de las entrañas; inventando foquin mundos* like a god; like *foquin* Juracán pitching lightning bolts at the people to wake them from their stupor, man. Wake them up from their lethargy and their four-hundred-year-old sleep of self-induced tyranny, you know?"

"I understand, man."

"Willie, man, I wanted my words to thunder, to shake the earth *pa' que la gente le pida a Yuquiyú que los salve*."

"And it's gonna be that way, bro. You're the poet, man. The voice."

"And me praying. Praying, man. And not to Yuquiyú but to some distorted European idea. I'm messed up, bro. Really messed up. Writing all this jive poetry that's supposed to incite the people to take up arms against the oppressor and all the while my heart is dripping with feelings of love and brotherhood and peace like some programmed puppet, Willie."

"I hear you."

"I mean, I bought all that stuff, man. All that liberal American jive. I bought it. I marched against the war in Vietnam, against colonialism and capitalism, and for the Chicano brothers cracking their backs in the fields, marched till my feet were raw, and every time I saw lettuce or grapes, I saw poison. And man, it felt right, Willie."

"It was a righteous cause, man."

"And I marched for the independence of the island, of Puerto Rico, Willie: *de Portorro, de Borinquen, la buena, la sagrada, el terruño, madre de todos nosotros; bendita seas entre todas las mujeres y bendito sea el fruto de tu vientre pelú*. I marched for the land of our people and it felt right."

"It is right, man."

"You know, once and for all I had overcome all the anger of being a colonized person without a country and my culture being swallowed up, digested and thrown back up so you can't even recognize what it's all about. I had overcome all the craziness and could stand above it; I could look down on the brothers and sisters who took up arms in '50 and '54 when I wasn't even a fantasy in my pop's mind, man. I could stand above all of them, even the ones with their bombs now. I could pay tribute to them with words but still judge them crazy. And it was okay. It felt right to wear two faces, to go back and forth from poetic fury to social condescension or whatever you wanna call it. I thought I had it beat with the education and the poetry and opening up my heart like some long-haired, brown-skinned hippy. And now this. I'm a hypocrite, man."

Like the water from the open fire hydrant, the words had rushed out of him. And yet he couldn't say exactly what it was that troubled him about the attack on his sister, couldn't pinpoint what it was that made his face hot and his blood race angrily in his veins. Willie, silenced by his own impotence, sat looking at him. He knew he could neither urge him on nor discourage him and inevitably he would have to stand aside and let whatever was to happen run its course. His voice almost a whisper, he said, "It's okay, Sixto. I know how it feels. Just let the pain come out, man. Just let it out. Cry if you have to."

But the pain would never leave him. Spics weren't Greeks and the word katharsis had no meaning in private tragedy. Sixto's mind raced back into time, searching for an answer, knowing, even as it fled like a wounded animal seeking refuge from its tormentors, that it was an aimless search. It was like running a maze. Like the rats in the psychology films and the puzzles in the children's section of weekend newspapers. One followed a path with a pencil until he came to a dead end, then retraced his steps. Thousands of years passed before him in a matter of minutes.

The Tainos: a peaceful people, some history books said. No way, he thought. They fought the Spaniards, drowned them to test their immortality. And their *caciques* were as fierce and as brave as Crazy Horse or Geronimo. Proud chiefs they were. Jumacao, Daguao, Yaureibo, Caguax, Agueybaná, Mabodamaca, Aymamón, Urayoán, Orocobix, Guarionex all fought the Spaniards with all they had ... *guasábara* ... *guasábara* ... *guasábara* ... their battle cry echoing through the hills like an eerie phantom; they fought their horses and dogs; they fought their swords and guns and when there was no other recourse, rather than submitting, they climbed sheer cliffs and, holding their children to their breasts, leapt into the sea.

And the blacks: *los negros*, whose blood and heritage he carried. They didn't submit to slavery but escaped and returned to conduct raids against the oppressors, so that the whole *negrito lindo* business, so readily accepted as a term of endearment, was a joke, an appeasement on the part of the Spaniards. The *bombas* and *bembas* and *ginganbó* and their all night dances and *oraciones* to Changó: warrior men of the Jelofe, Mandingo, Mende, Yoruba, Dahomey, Ashanti, Ibo, Fante, Baule and Congo tribes, choosing battle over slavery.

And the Spaniards: certainly not a peaceful people. For centuries they fought each other and then branched out to cross the sea and slaughter hundreds of thousands of Indians, leaving an indelible mark on entire civilizations, raping and pillaging and gutting the earth of its riches, so that when it was all done and they laid in a drunken stupor four hundred years later, their pockets empty, they rose again to fight themselves in civil war.

And way back, way back before El Cid Campeador began to wage war: The Moors. *Los moros* ... *alhambra, alcázar, alcohol, almohada, alcalde, alboroto* ... NOISE ... CRIES OF WAR ... A thousand years the maze traveled and it led to a dead end with dark men atop fleet Arabian stallions, dark men, both in visage and intent, raising their scimitars against those dishonoring their house ... they had invented algebra and Arabic numbers and it all added up to war ... there was no other way ...

"I gotta kill him, bro," Sixto heard himself say. "I gotta. Otherwise I'm as good as dead."

One had to live with himself and that was the worst part of it; he had to live with the knowledge and that particular brand of cowardice that eroded the mind and destroyed one's soul. And it wasn't so much that his sister had been wronged. He'd seen that. The injury came from not retaliating. He was back at the beginning. Banana leaves and coconuts and machete duels at sundown. Just like his father and his *jíbaro* values. For even if the aggressor never talked, even if he never mentioned his act to another soul for whatever reason, there was still another person, another member of the tribe, who could single him out in a crowd and say to himself: "That one belongs to me and so does his sister."

Sixto tried to recall other times when his manhood had been challenged, but it seemed as if everything had happened long ago and hadn't been important: kid fights over mention of his mother, rights of ownership of an object, a place in the hierarchy of the block, a word said of his person, a lie, a bump by a stranger on a crowded subway train—nothing ever going beyond words or at worst, a sudden shoving match quickly broken up by friends.

But this was different. His brain was not functioning properly, he thought. He tried watching himself, tried to become an observer, the impartial judge of his actions. Through a small opening in his consciousness, he watched the raging battle. His heart called for the blood of the enemy and his brain urged him to use caution. There was no thought of danger, for in that region of struggle, survival meant not so much escaping with his life, but conquering fear and regaining his honor.

Sixto picked up the gun and studied it once more. He pushed the safety to make sure it was locked and placed the gun between the waistband of his pants and the flesh of his stomach. The cold metal sent slivers of ice running down his legs. It was a pleasant sensation, much as if a woman he had desired for some time had suddenly let him know, in an unguarded moment, that intimacy was possible between them. Avoiding Willie's eyes, he walked around the kitchen, pulled out his shirt and let it hang out over his pants. It was important that he learn to walk naturally and reduce his self-consciousness about the weapon. But it was his mind working tricks again. Nobody would notice. The idea was to act calmly. That's what everyone said: the thieves, the cheap stickup men who mugged old people and taxi drivers; the burglars who, like vultures, watched the movement of a family until certain that they were gone, swooped down and cleaned out the apartment, even in the middle of the day; the check specialists, who studied mailboxes as if they were bank vaults so they could break them open and steal welfare checks or fat letters from the island on the chance they might contain money orders or cash. They all said it. Even the young gang kids said it. Don't act suspiciously. Act as if you were going about your business.

Going to shoot someone was like going to work. That was it. He'd carry his books and nobody would suspect that he was carrying death. He laughed inwardly at the immense joke. He'd once seen a film in which Robert Mitchum, posing as a preacher, had pulled a derringer out of a Bible in the final scene. Why not. He'd hollow out his Western Civilization text and place the gun in it. It was his duty. The act was a way of surviving, of earning what was truly his. Whether a pay check or an education, it meant nothing without self-respect.

But the pieces of the puzzle did not fit and Sixto sat down dejectedly. He let his head fall into his hands and for a moment thought he would cry. Willie said nothing and Sixto waited, listening, the void of silence becoming larger and larger, expanding so that the sounds of the street, a passing car, the excitement of a child, the rushing water from the open hydrant, a mother's window warning retreated, became fainter and seemed to trim the outer edges of the nothingness within the silence. He could hear his own breathing and the beating of his heart and still he waited.

And then slowly, as if waking from a refreshing sleep, Sixto felt himself grow calmer and a pleasant coldness entered his body as heart and mind finally merged and became tuned to his mission. He smiled at the feeling and knew he had gone through the barrier of doubt and fear which had been erected to protect him from himself, to make sure he did not panic at the last moment. War had to be similar. He had heard the older men, the ones who had survived Vietnam, talk about it. Sonny Maldonado with his plastic foot, limping everywhere he went, quiet and unassuming, talked about going through a doorway and into a quiet room where one died a little and then came out again, one's mind alive but the rest of the body already dead to the upcoming pain.

It had finally happened, he thought. There was no anger or regret, no rationalizations concerning future actions. No more justifications or talk about honor and dignity. Instead, Sixto perceived the single objective coldly. There was neither danger nor urgency in carrying out the sentence and avenging the wrong. It seemed almost too simple. If it took years he knew the task would be accomplished. He would study the habits of his quarry, chart his every movement, and one day he'd strike. He would wait in a deserted hallway some late night, calmly walk out of the shadows, only his right index finger and his brain connected and say: "How you doing, Lino?" and his voice alone would convey the terrible message. Sixto smiled to himself and saw, as in a slow motion cinematic shot, his mind's ghost delicately squeeze the trigger repeatedly, the small animal muzzle of the gun following Lino Quintana's body as it fell slowly and hit the floor, the muscles of his victim's face twitching and life ebbing away forever. It happened all the time and no one was ever discovered.

Sixto laughed, almost too loudly. He took the gun out from under his shirt and placed it resolutely on the table. "I gotta think some more, man," he said. "That's crazy rushing into the thing. You wanna a beer, Willie?"

Willie was not convinced of his friend's newly found calm. Reluctantly, he accepted the beer. He watched Sixto and tried to measure the depth of his eyes. They had become strangely flat, the glint of trust in them absent. It was as if a thin, opaque veil had been sewn over the eyes to mask Sixto's emotions. He felt helpless but said nothing. He opened the beer and began mourning the loss. Sixto was right, he thought. It was Spanish roulette. Spics were born and the cylinder spun. When it stopped one was handed the gun and, without looking, had to bring it to one's head, squeeze the trigger and take his chances.

The belief was pumped into the bloodstream, carved into the flesh through generations of strife, so that being was the enactment of a ritual rather than the beginning of a new life. One never knew his own reactions until faced with Sixto's dilemma. And yet the loss would be too great, the upcoming grief too profound and the ensuing suffering eternal. The violence would be passed on to another generation to be displayed as an invisible coat of arms, much as Sixto's answer had come to him as a relic. His friend would never again look at the world with wonder, and poetry would cease to spring from his heart. If he did write, the words would be guarded, careful, full of excuses and apologies for living. Willie started to raise the beer in a toast but thought better of it and set the can on the table.

"Whatever you do, bro," he said, "be careful."

"Don't worry, man," Sixto replied. "I got the thing under control." He laughed once again and suddenly his eyes were ablaze with hatred. He picked up the gun, stuck it back into his pants and stood up. "No good, man," he said, seemingly to himself, and rushed out, slamming the door of the apartment behind him.

Beyond the sound of the door, Willie could hear the whirring cylinder as it began to slow down, each minute click measuring the time before his friend had to raise the weapon to his head and kill part of himself.

Victor Villaseñor

Victor Villaseñor is a novelist and screenwriter who has brought Chicano literature to the widest of audiences through his novel of immigration, *Macho!* (issued in 1973 by the world's largest paperback publisher, Bantam), through the epic saga of his own family in *Rain of Gold* (1991) and through the television screenplay of "The Ballad of Gregorio Cortez." Born on May 11, 1940, in Carlsbad, California, the son of Mexican immigrants, he was raised on a ranch in Oceanside and experienced great difficulty with the educational system, having started school as a Spanish-speaker and a dyslexic. He dropped out of high school and worked on the ranch and in the fields and as a construction worker. After attempting college at the University of San Diego for a brief period, he again dropped out and went to live in Mexico, where he discovered the world of books and learned to take pride in his identity and cultural heritage. From then on he read extensively and taught himself the art of writing fiction. During years of work in California as a construction worker, he completed nine novels and sixty-five short stories, all of which were rejected for publication, except for *Macho!*, which launched his professional writing career. His second publishing venture was the non-fiction narrative of the life and trial of a serial killer, *Jury: The People versus Juan Corona* (1977). Negative experiences with stereotyping and discrimination of Hispanics in the commercial publishing world led Villaseñor to publish his most important literary effort, *Rain of Gold* (1991), with a small, not-for-profit Hispanic press, Arte Público Press of Houston.

Macho! tells the tale of a young Mexican Indian's illegal entry into the United States to find work, along the classic lines of the novel of immigration; however, it departs from the model in that, upon return to his home town in central Mexico, the protagonist has been forever changed, unable to accept the traditional social code, especially as concerns *machismo*. *Rain of Gold*, on the other hand, is the non-fiction saga of various generations of Villaseñor's own family and how its members experienced the Mexican Revolution and eventually immigrated to establish themselves in California. The saga is narrated in a style full of spirituality and respect for myths and oral tradition, derived from Villaseñor's working-class background and from the years of interviews and research that he did in preparing the book. The popularity of *Rain of Gold* has brought to millions of Americans the family stories of the social, economic and political struggles that have resulted in Mexican immigration to the United States, where new stories of racism, discrimination and the triumph over some of these barriers continue to develop in the epic of Mexican-American life. The following selection is from *Rain of Gold* and is based upon an episode in the life of Juan Villaseñor, Victor's father.

From *Rain of Gold*

"Okay," said Epitacio as he and Juan came walking down the busy street of Douglas, Arizona, "I feel lucky! Let's have a drink and double our paychecks!"

Juan and Epitacio had been working at the Copper Queen Mining Company for over a month and they'd just been paid.

"All right, whatever you say," said Juan, feeling good about his brother-in-law who'd returned across the border to get them.

But Epitacio got drunk and lost both of their paychecks, then he refused to go home with Juan. The next day Epitacio didn't show up for work. Rumor had it that he'd taken off, gone back to Mexico.

Juan wasn't able to support his family by working only one shift at the Copper Queen, so he decided to change his name to Juan Cruz and get a second job on the night shift. After all, he was going on thirteen. He figured that he could hold down both shifts.

But, getting into line that night, one guy recognized Juan. His name was Tomás. He was seventeen years old and he had been in the poolhall the night Epitacio lost both of their paychecks.

Quickly, Juan winked at Tomás, signaling for him to keep still and not let on that he knew him. And it went easier than Juan had expected. Hell, the big, thick-necked *gringo* boss couldn't tell him apart from all the other Mexicans.

"Hey, Juan," said Tomás, once they were inside the smelter. Molten ore moved all about them in great kettles. "You want to make some extra money?"

"Sure," shouted Juan above the noise of the smelter. "Why the hell you think I'm working a second shift? Because I love the smell of wet armpits?"

"Well, then, meet me at midnight on our taco break," winked the handsome young man. "And I'll show you a fine trick."

"Sure thing!" yelled Juan. So they met at midnight and ate together and Tomás explained to Juan the plan. First, they'd put a sack of copper ore alongside the outside fence so they could steal it later; then the next day, they'd sell it in town to an American engineer.

"How much we gonna make?" asked Juan.

Tomás had to smile. He liked his young friend's greed. "Oh, maybe six dollars each," he said.

"Six dollars!" shouted Juan. He only made a dollar for an eight hour shift as it was. "That's a fortune!" But then he thought again and he became suspicious. "Wait," he said, "just how do you know about this *gringo* engineer, anyway?" Juan was only twelve, but he had forty years worth of experience.

"Buddy," said the tall, good-looking young man, rolling his eyes to the heavens with great style, "I got my means." And he laughed a good, full, manly laugh, and Juan believed him.

They did it, and it worked beautifully. The next day they sold the ore to the American engineer in town for six dollars each. But, the following night, as they came up alongside the fence to do the same thing again, the lights came on and they were surrounded by sixteen armed men. The American engineer that they'd sold the ore to had set them up. He also worked for the Copper Queen. They were immediately taken to town, tried, found guilty and taken to Tombstone, Arizona.

"But I'm only twelve years old!" screamed Juan. "And my family will starve without me!"

"Ssssshhh!" said Tomás. "You tell them that and they'll send you to a boys' place, and I won't be able to protect you! I got a plan. You just keep quiet and stick by me!"

So Juan stuck by his friend, saying he was eighteen, and that night in Tombstone, he saw what his friend's plan was. When the other prisoners saw them, and they came on them like wolves to rape the sheep, Tomás turned his ass up at them so they wouldn't beat him.

"Not me! You son-of-a-bitches!" bellowed Juan with all his might. "I'm from Los Altos de Jalisco! I'll castrate the first *puto cabrón* who touches me!"

That night, shooting broke out in front of the jailhouse, and a terrible explosion blew out the back wall. A Mexican on horseback yelled, "*Vámonos*, Aguilar!" Prisoners ran every which way as a dozen horsemen continued shooting. They had their brother on a horse, and they took off. Everyone else was left standing there, naked as plucked turkeys under the cold night sky.

Instantly Juan took off on foot after the horsemen through the *arroyo* behind the jail. He ran uphill all night. And daybreak found him at the foot of a great mountain. But in the distance, there came a dozen armed horsemen, cracking leather. He took off as fast as he could through the cactus. It was his birthday, August eighteenth, 1916. He was thirteen years old, but the only presents the *gringos* brought him were well-placed bullets singing by his ears. Finally, they caught him, beat him, tied him to a horse and dragged him back to town.

By the time his mother, two sisters, his nephew and two nieces finally found out what had happened to him, Juan was in the Arizona State Penitentiary at Florence, Arizona.

His mother cried and cried. Luisa screamed and cursed and banged her head. Emilia couldn't stop coughing, and his nephew and nieces wept hysterically.

Then, the rich Mexican from Sonora, who'd driven Juan's family to the penitentiary to visit him, asked to speak to Juan alone.

"Juan," said the tall and thin old man once they were alone, "your mother is a wonderful lady. She's nursed me back to health with herbs and massage. I love her dearly, and I regard you as my own son."

Juan almost laughed at the stooped-over old man. Why, the son-of-a-bitch was an even smoother talker than the big bastard who'd converted Tomás into a woman.

"You see, Juan, I have a very high-spirited son like you. And I love him and I'd do anything for him. But you see, *mi hijito* killed a Texas Ranger." The dignified old man began to cry, leaning on his gold-headed cane. "I've been told that it was an honest battle, but the *americanos* don't see it that way and they're going to execute him."

Juan's heart came to his eyes. "I sympathize with you, *señor*," he said.

"I'm glad to hear that," said the old man, "because, well, I have a proposition to make you. I'll give your mother, God bless her soul, two hundred dollars in American money if you confess to the crime my son committed."

Juan couldn't believe his ears. He felt like spitting in the old man's face. Hell, he only had six years to serve for stealing the six dollars worth of ore. But for murder, shit, man, son-of-a-gringo-bitch, he'd be executed or be in for life.

"Calm down," said the old man, "please, and listen to my whole proposition. After all, they already have you locked up, so how much more can happen to you?"

Juan calmed down and looked into the eyes of the old man who, it was said, owned more cattle in the State of Sonora than the rails had ties.

"Your mother, look at her," he continued, "see how desperate she is. This is a terrible time for us *mejicanos*." He went on and on, and Juan didn't curse him and send him packing—as the *gringos* said—but, instead, he listened and looked at his mother and sisters and nephew and nieces over there by the far wall. Finally, Juan pulled down into his gut with all the power of his balls, his *tanates*, and spoke.

"Make it five hundred in gold!"

And so the deal was made, and a new trial was set for the murderer of the famous, Mexican-killing Texas Ranger of Douglas, Arizona. Juan Salvador

Villaseñor—known as Juan Cruz—was found guilty and was sentenced to life imprisonment.

* * *

The big, fat Mexican cook from Guadalajara was the best man with a knife in the penitentiary at Florence, Arizona. He took Juan under his wing because they were both from Jalisco.

Two years before, the Mexican cook had won a lot of money in a poker game in Bisbee, Arizona. But then he'd been walking home when the three *gringos* that he had won the money from jumped him outside of town.

He was fat, so they'd made the very bad mistake of thinking that he was slow. Two died instantly, and the big Mexican had the third one down on the ground, ready to cut his throat, but the *gringo* kept crying for his life so much that the big Mexican finally decided to let him live on the promise that he'd admit to the authorities the following day that it had been a fair fight. But the next day, the third *gringo* went back on his word, saying that a dozen armed Mexicans had cut him and killed his two unarmed friends.

"So you see, Juan," said the fat cook, "I got life because I was soft in the head. If I'd killed him, no one would've fingered me."

The fat cook found out that Juan didn't know how to read, and he explained to Juan the power of the written word. "Look," he said, "the Mexican Revolution didn't start with Villa or Zapata, as so many people think. No, it started with the power of the words written by my friend, Ricardo Flores Magón. I learned from Flores Magón that if a man can't read and write, he's nothing but a little *puto* weakling!"

And so, there in the penitentiary, Juan's education began. He didn't want to be a *puto* weakling, so he worked hard at learning to read. His earthly body was locked up, but his mind was set free as a young eagle soaring through the heavens. The fat cook became his teacher, and Juan loved it. Juan ate better than he'd eaten in years, and life was wonderful except for the days when his mother came to visit him. Then Juan wanted out. He couldn't stand to see his mother's tears.

* * *

A year later, a new road camp was started outside of Safford, Arizona, near Turkey Flat, and prisoners got to volunteer. The big, fat cook warned Juan not to go because there'd be no guards with them at night and other prisoners would be sure to gang up on him and rape him like a female dog.

"Don't worry," said Juan, "I can take care of myself."

"But your reputation of having killed that Ranger won't protect you there," said the big cook. "Believe me, it's been my wing that's kept you from the fate that got your friend Tomás."

Tomás was now being bought and sold like a woman all over the prison to anyone who had the makings for half a dozen cigarettes. They'd knocked his teeth out and painted his ass for better service, it was said.

Juan looked at the big cook for a long time without speaking. "I'm going," he said. "It's my only chance to escape and stop my mother's tears."

"All right," said the big cook, "then good luck to you. And always remember, *un hombre aprevenido* is a man alive. A guarded man is a man who's wary, cautious, and lives life as if he's lived it many times before."

"I'll remember," said Juan, "*aprevenido*."

"Yes," said the big cook, and they shook hands, taking each other in a big *abrazo* like men do, and said farewell.

Five days later, Juan Salvador was in a Ford truck along with four other men chained by their feet to the bars of the iron cage. Two of the other prisoners were black-skinned, full-blooded Yaqui Indians with eyes as sharp as knives. Immediately, Juan liked them and he found out that they'd been put in prison for ten years for eating an army mule.

Getting to Turkey Flat, it turned out just as the big, fat cook had said it would. During the day they had armed guards on horseback all around them as they worked on the road over the mountain; but during the night, when they were locked up behind the barbed wire fence, there were no guards with them.

The things Juan learned in the first three nights were so awful—so completely inhuman—they would haunt him for the rest of his life. Here, men were worse than mad dogs. When he wouldn't let them rape him, they beat him with clubs; then they courted him with flowers as if he were a woman. When that didn't work, either, the big German pit boss and the black snake came at Juan in the night. But Juan was *aprevenido*, and he got the pit boss in the eyes with boiling coffee, but not before his big, black friend cut Juan's stomach open with a knife.

The last thing Juan remembered was the smell of his own intestines coming out of his stomach, between his fingers, as he desperately tried pushing the whole slippery mess back inside himself.

When Juan came to, he was in the tent hospital, and the big German and his friend were tied down to the beds next to him. They were screaming, foaming at the mouth, and straining against their ropes with all their might. The guards had castrated them, and blood covered their thighs. Juan pretended he was still unconscious and laid there quietly.

Later that same day, they brought in the two Yaqui Indians who'd been poisoned with canned food. For two weeks, Juan drifted in and out of death. The German raved and screamed. The big black died. The Indians never made a sound. Then one day, just at dusk, Juan heard the two Indians whispering, and they slipped away. Quickly, Juan got up and crawled after them.

"Turn to stone," one Indian said to him as they got out the door. He did as they told him, squatting down, and they were stones.

The guards walked right by, searching for them, but they didn't see them. Then the armed men saddled horses and took off after them. But they never moved. They just sat there, squatted to the earth like stone, moving a little and then a little more as they went down the mountainside and, finally, took to the creek.

For seven days and nights they walked and hid and ran. Juan never knew how they did it, but they'd turn into stone anytime anyone came near them.

Near Douglas, Arizona, Juan left the two Yaquis and went to church, waiting all day until his mother showed up for her daily prayers. They hugged and kissed, then she told him the news that his blind sister Emilia had died. They wept and prayed for Emilia to regain her sight in heaven. Then his mother got him a change of clothes and Juan took the name of his grandfather, Pío Castro. He immediately signed up with fifty other Mexicans to go north to work at the Copper Queen in Montana.

In Montana, Juan and his Mexican companions were put in with thousands of Greeks and Turks. The Greeks had never seen any Mexicans before and so, when they heard the other Mexicans call Juan "Chino" because of his curly hair, they thought he was Chinese, so they named him Sam Lee.

Sam Lee became Juan's official name. He lived among the Greeks and Turks for two years, working for the Copper Queen Mining Company in the winter, the railroad during the spring, and in the sugar beet fields during the harvest.

Then one day, a huge, brutally handsome Turk came to their camp. That night he stopped a fight between two armed men just by staring them down.

Immediately, Juan took a liking to this formidable-looking man of granite. He watched him set up a poker game that weekend and take everyone's money fair and square. The big man noticed Juan watching him and hired him to clean up the tables for him. They became fast friends. The big man's name was Duel. He told Juan that his mother had been Greek and his father a Turk.

"Here, inside the heart," he told Juan when they went out for dinner, "are the greatest battles a real man can fight. Blood to blood, a war is going on inside me that's ten thousand years old! The Greeks and Turks are mortal enemies! And I'm half and half, just like you with your Indian and European blood!"

Hungrily, he talked to Juan all night long, telling him of Greece and Turkey and the history of that part of the world. It was the first time in all his life that Juan had ever come close to a man who not only wasn't a Catholic, but readily admitted that he didn't believe in God.

Hearing this, Juan opened up his heart, too, and he sadly told the Greek-Turk how he, too, had left God at the Rio Grande.

"I knew it," said Duel, "the first moment I laid eyes on you. I said to myself, 'That boy, he's been to hell and back.' For no real man like us can believe in the puppet-God of the churches. The devil, yes, of course, but not God!"

And so that winter, Duel set up a gambling room in the basement of the best whorehouse in Butte which was owned by a famous English woman named Katherine. Duel made Juan his protege, teaching him the art of taking money from the greedy workmen who drank too much.

For the first time in his life, Juan saw cards as a solid business. He now realized that he and Epitacio had never had a chance in the world to double their paychecks back in Douglas. Why, he and Duel took money hand-over-fist every night, giving free liquor to the big losers and maybe even a girl. And the famous lady Katherine took her share, too. Over and over again, Duel explained to Juan that all of life was a gamble and so, "At gambling," he said, "a real man must be king!"

But there were problems. Especially with the local cowboys who didn't like foreigners taking their money. One night there was a bad knife fight. A big, powerful, raw-boned cowboy was going to cut up a girl that he blamed for losing all his money when, to everyone's surprise, Juan just stepped in, disarming the big cowboy with a number twenty-two cue stick and knocked him unconscious.

Katherine quickly gave the cowboy's two friends each a free girl and the tension broke. That night, after closing up, Katherine called Juan to her private room and thanked him for his quick action. The next day, she had her hair dresser cut Juan's wild-looking curly hair, then sent him to her private tailor.

Coming out of the tailor's shop wearing a new suit, Juan would never forget, as long as he lived, what happened when he saw his reflection in the window in downtown Butte, Montana. Why, he didn't even recognize himself, he looked so handsome and civilized.

That night back at the house, he was taken aside by Katherine once again, who presented him to the young girl whom he had saved. Her name was Lily, and she was beautiful. She was so grateful that he had saved her life that all night she purred to him like a kitten in love, teaching him things of the human body that he had never dreamed.

The next morning, he was taken in hand by the English woman again. They had tea together on fine china, and she spent the whole morning explaining to Juan the mysteries of life, love, women and good manners.

In the next year, Juan and Katherine became very close, and Juan came to respect her as the smartest and toughest woman he had ever known—except, of course, for his own mother—and she wasn't even Catholic.

But then Duel began to grow jealous of their friendship and one dark night, Duel got drunk and accused Juan and Katherine of cheating him out of some money. Juan denied it. But still, Duel drew his gun. The next thing Juan Salvador Villaseñor did was something he'd never stop regretting for the rest of his life. He had loved Duel, he really had, like his own father.

* * *

A few months later, Juan got a telegram from his sister Luisa in California, saying that if he wished to see his mother alive again, he'd better come home immediately.

The day that Juan left Montana by train, all the land was white. Only the tallest trees poked up through the blanket of snow.

Both Katherine and Lily stood at the depot, seeing him off. The year was 1922, and Juan Salvador was nineteen years old, but he looked more like twenty-five. He was well dressed, had a moustache, and the aura of a very cautious man, a man who'd lived many lifetimes.

"I'll be waiting!" called Lily.

"I'll be back!" said Juan.

Katherine only watched him go, following him carefully with her eyes.

Helena María Viramontes

Helena María Viramontes is known for her tightly crafted poetic vision of Hispanic women in American society. After serving as an editor of the pioneering cultural magazine, *Chismearte*, the coordinator of the Los Angeles Latino Writers association and the editor anthologies of other writers' works, she has found the time to publish her own stories in magazines and anthologies throughout the country. But her excellent reputation rests principally on her highly praised collection of stories, *The Moths and Other Stories* (1985). Viramontes was born and raised in East Los Angeles, California, which provides the setting for most of her stories. She is a graduate of the MFA program in Creative Writing of the University of California-Irvine.

The Moths and Other Stories portrays female characters of varying ages whose lives are limited by the patriarchy of Hispanic society and the imposition of religious values. Viramontes's stories treat such issues as abortion, aging, death, immigration and separation. Her images range from the beautifully lyric and evocative as in the story, "The Moths," to the violent and desperate, as in "The Cariboo Cafe." The grace and depth of these stories befits her humanistic and caring approach to the poor and downtrodden women depicted.

The Moths

I was fourteen years old when Abuelita requested my help. And it seemed only fair. Abuelita had pulled me through the rages of scarlet fever by placing, removing and replacing potato slices on the temples of my forehead; she had seen me through several whippings, an arm broken by a dare jump off Tío Enrique's toolshed, puberty, and my first lie. Really, I told Amá, it was only fair.

Not that I was her favorite granddaughter or anything special. I wasn't even pretty or nice like my older sisters and I just couldn't do the girl things they could do. My hands were too big to handle the fineries of crocheting or embroidery and I always pricked my fingers or knotted my colored threads time and time again while my sisters laughed and called me bull hands with their cute waterlike voices. So I began keeping a piece of jagged brick in my sock to bash my sisters or anyone who called me bull hands. Once, while we all sat in the bedroom, I hit Teresa on the forehead, right above her eyebrow and she ran to Amá with her mouth open, her hand over her eye while blood seeped between her fingers. I was used to the whippings by then.

I wasn't respectful either. I even went so far as to doubt the power of Abuelita's slices, the slices she said absorbed my fever. "You're still alive, aren't you?" Abuelita snapped back, her pasty gray eye beaming at me and burning holes in my suspicions. Regretful that I had let secret questions drop out of my mouth, I couldn't look into her eyes. My hands began to fan out, grow like a liar's nose until they hung by my side like low weights. Abuelita made a balm out of dried moth wings and Vicks and rubbed my hands, shaped them back to size and it was the strangest feeling. Like bones melting. Like sun shining through the darkness of your eyelids. I didn't mind helping Abuelita after that, so Amá would always send me over to her.

In the early afternoon, Amá would push her hair back, hand me my sweater and shoes, and tell me to go to Mama Luna's. This was to avoid another fight and another whipping, I knew. I would deliver one last direct shot on Marisela's arm and jump out of our house, the slam of the screen door burying her cries of anger, and I'd gladly go help Abuelita plant her wild lilies or jasmine or heliotrope or cilantro or hierbabuena in red Hills Brothers coffee cans. Abuelita would wait for me at the top step of her porch holding a hammer and nail and empty coffee cans. And, although we hardly spoke, hardly looked at each other as we worked over root transplants, I always felt her gray eye on me. It made me feel, in a strange sort of way, safe and guarded and not alone. Like God was supposed to make you feel.

On Abuelita's porch, I would puncture holes in the bottom of the coffee cans with a nail and a precise hit of a hammer. This completed, my job was to fill them with red clay mud from beneath her rose bushes, packing it softly, then making a perfect hole, four fingers round, to nest a sprouting avocado pit, or the spidery sweet potatoes that Abuelita rooted in mayonnaise jars with toothpicks and daily water, or prickly chayotes that produced vines that twisted and wound all over her porch pillars, crawling to the roof, up and over the roof, and down the other side, making her small brick house look like it was cradled within the vines that grew pear-shaped squashes ready for the pick, ready to be steamed with onions and cheese and butter. The roots would burst out of the rusted coffee cans and search for a place to connect. I would then feed the seedlings with water.

But this was a different kind of help, Amá said, because Abuelita was dying. Looking into her gray eye, then into her brown one, the doctor said it was just a matter of days. And so it seemed only fair that these hands she had melted and formed found use in rubbing her caving body with alcohol and marihuana, rubbing her arms and legs, turning her face to the window so that she could watch the Bird of Paradise blooming or smell the scent of clove in the air. I toweled her face frequently and held her hand for hours. Her gray wiry hair hung over the mattress. Since I could remember, she'd kept her long hair in braids. Her mouth was vacant and when she slept, her eyelids never closed all the way. Up close, you could see her gray eye beaming out the window, staring hard as if to remember everything. I never kissed her. I left the window open when I went to the market.

Across the street from Jay's Market there was a chapel. I never knew its denomination, but I went in just the same to search for candles. I sat down on one of the pews because there were none. After I cleaned my fingernails, I looked up at the high ceiling. I had forgotten the vastness of these places, the coolness of the marble pillars and the frozen statues with blank eyes. I was alone. I knew why I had never returned.

That was one of Apá's biggest complaints. He would pound his hands on the table, rocking the sugar dish or spilling a cup of coffee, and scream that if I didn't go to mass every Sunday to save my goddamn sinning soul, then I had no reason to go out of the house, period. Punto final. He would grab my arm and dig his nails into me to make sure I understood the importance of catechism. Did he make himself clear? Then he strategically directed his anger at Amá for her lousy ways of bringing up daughters, being disrespectful and unbelieving, and my older sisters would pull me aside and tell me if I didn't get to mass right this minute, they were all going to kick the holy shit out of me. Why am I so selfish? Can't you see what it's doing to Amá, you idiot? So I would wash my feet and stuff them in my black Easter shoes that shone with Vaseline, grab a missal and veil, and wave good-bye to Amá.

I would walk slowly down Lorena to First to Evergreen, counting the cracks on the cement. On Evergreen I would turn left and walk to Abuelita's. I liked her porch because it was shielded by the vines of the chayotes and I could get a good look at the people and car traffic on Evergreen without them knowing. I would jump up the porch steps, knock on the screen door as I wiped my feet and call Abuelita? Mi Abuelita? As I opened the door and stuck my head in, I would catch the gagging scent of toasting chile on the placa. When I entered the sala, she would greet me from the kitchen, wringing her hands in her apron. I'd sit at the corner of the table to keep from being in her way. The chiles made my eyes water. Am I crying? No, Mama Luna, I'm sure not crying. I don't like going to mass, but my eyes watered anyway, the tears dropping on the tablecloth like candle wax. Abuelita lifted the burnt chiles from the fire and sprinkled water on them until the skins began to separate. Placing them in front of me, she turned to check the menudo. I peeled the skins off and put the flimsy, limp-looking green and yellow chiles in the molcajete and began to crush and crush and twist and crush the heart out of the tomato, the clove of garlic, the stupid chiles that made me cry, crushed them until they turned into liquid under my bull hand. With a wooden spoon, I scraped hard to destroy the guilt, and my tears were gone. I put the bowl of chile next to a vase filled with freshly cut roses. Abuelita touched my hand and pointed to the bowl of menudo that steamed in front of me. I spooned some chile into the menudo and rolled a corn tortilla thin with the palms of my hands. As I ate, a fine Sunday breeze entered the kitchen and a rose petal calmly feathered down to the table.

I left the chapel without blessing myself and walked to Jay's. Most of the time Jay didn't have much of anything. The tomatoes were always soft and the cans of Campbell soups had rusted spots on them. There was dust on the tops of cereal boxes. I picked up what I needed: rubbing alcohol, five cans of chicken broth, a big bottle of Pine Sol. At first Jay got mad because I thought I had forgotten the money. But it was there all the time, in my back pocket.

When I returned from the market, I heard Amá crying in Abuelita's kitchen. She looked up at me with puffy eyes. I placed the bags of groceries on the table and began putting the cans of soup away. Amá sobbed quietly. I never kissed her. After a while, I patted her on the back for comfort. Finally: "¿Y mi Amá?" she asked in a whisper, then choked again and cried into her apron.

Abuelita fell off the bed twice yesterday, I said, knowing that I shouldn't have said it and wondering why I wanted to say it because it only made

Amá cry harder. I guess I became angry and just so tired of the quarrels and beatings and unanswered prayers and my hands just there hanging helplessly by my side. Amá looked at me again, confused, angry, and her eyes were filled with sorrow. I went outside and sat on the porch swing and watched the people pass. I sat there until she left. I dozed off repeating the words to myself like rosary prayers: when do you stop giving when do you start giving when do you ... and when my hands fell from my lap, I awoke to catch them. The sun was setting, an orange glow, and I knew Abuelita was hungry.

There comes a time when the sun is defiant. Just about the time when moods change, inevitable seasons of a day, transitions from one color to another, that hour or minute or second when the sun is finally defeated, finally sinks into the realization that it cannot with all its power to heal or burn, exist forever, there comes an illumination where the sun and earth meet, a final burst of burning red orange fury reminding us that although endings are inevitable, they are necessary for rebirths, and when that time came, just when I switched on the light in the kitchen to open Abuelita's can of soup, it was probably then that she died.

The room smelled of Pine Sol and vomit and Abuelita had defecated the remains of her cancerous stomach. She had turned to the window and tried to speak, but her mouth remained open and speechless. I heard you, Abuelita, I said, stroking her cheek, I heard you. I opened the windows of the house and let the soup simmer and overboil on the stove. I turned the stove off and poured the soup down the sink. From the cabinet I got a tin basin, filled it with lukewarm water and carried it carefully to the room. I went to the linen closet and took out some modest bleached white towels. With the sacredness of a priest preparing his vestments, I unfolded the towels one by one on my shoulders. I removed the sheets and blankets from her bed and peeled off her thick flannel nightgown. I toweled her puzzled face, stretching out the wrinkles, removing the coils of her neck, toweled her shoulders and breasts. Then I changed the water. I returned to towel the creases of her stretch-marked stomach, her sporadic vaginal hairs, and her sagging thighs. I removed the lint from between her toes and noticed a mapped birthmark on the fold of her buttock. The scars on her back which were as thin as the lifelines on the palms of her hands made me realize how little I really knew of Abuelita. I covered her with a thin blanket and went into the bathroom. I washed my hands, and turned on the tub faucets and watched the water pour into the tub with vitality and steam. When it was full, I turned off the water and undressed. Then, I went to get Abuelita.

She was not as heavy as I thought and when I carried her in my arms, her body fell into a V, and yet my legs were tired, shaky, and I felt as if the distance between the bedroom and bathroom was miles and years away. Amá, where are you?

I stepped into the bathtub one leg first, then the other. I bent my knees slowly to descend into the water slowly so I wouldn't scald her skin. There, there, Abuelita, I said, cradling her, smoothing her as we descended, I heard you. Her hair fell back and spread across the water like eagle's wings. The water in the tub overflowed and poured onto the tile of the floor. Then the moths came. Small, gray ones that came from her soul and out through her mouth fluttering to light, circling the single dull light bulb of the bathroom. Dying is lonely and I wanted to go to where the moths were, stay with her and plant chayotes whose vines would crawl up her fingers and into the clouds; I wanted to rest my head on her chest with her stroking my hair, telling me about the moths that lay within the soul and slowly eat the spirit up; I wanted to return to the waters of the womb with her so that we would never be alone again. I wanted. I wanted my Amá. I removed a few strands of hair from Abuelita's face and held her small light head within the hollow of my neck. The bathroom was filled with moths, and for the first time in a long time I cried, rocking us, crying for her, for me, for Amá, the sobs emerging from the depths of anguish, the misery of feeling half born, sobbing until finally the sobs rippled into circles and circles of sadness and relief. There, there, I said to Abuelita, rocking us gently, there, there.